"What of the Future of Calgary? Can it be doubted? NO! Calgary's future is assured. She will not only maintain but will improve her position commercially and industrially in years to come. Nothing but a catastrophe can even temporarily impede her progress. The "cow town" of YESTERDAY, the City of 55,000 TODAY, will be the big Metropolis of the Canadian West TOMORROW. Can you grasp the thought?"

from
Calgary The City Phenomenal
1912

COWTOWN
An Album of Early Calgary

TOM WARD

City of Calgary Electric System/
McClelland and Stewart West

Contents

Chapter 1 First Days

McCLELLAND & STEWART
WEST LTD.
No. 202, 509 - 8th Ave S.W.
Calgary, Alberta T2P 1G1

December 8, 1975

GIFT FROM: MR. J. D. DEVDEY,
7624 - 21A Street S.E.,
CALGARY, ALBERTA, CANADA.
T2C 0W2.

*Never will I forget the sight that met our eyes —
the confluence of the two winding rivers with their
wooded banks, the verdant valley, and beyond,
the wide expanse of green plain that stretched itself
in homage to the distant blue mountains. After
the barren March of 1874 through the barren lands
of the south, after the hard winter in Fort Macleod
and the wide, bare prairies of the early part of
this trip, that at last we had received our reward,
that this was the 'Promised Land'. A wonderful
country! A Garden of Eden! A place to live
forever! My home ever since. We descended the hill
to the river ford — near where Langevin Bridge
is today. As there were no boats or ferries, we
quickly improvised one. We tied our tarpaulins,
which were closely woven and fairly water proof,
underneath the wagon box, and with the aid of
some long poles rowed ourselves across the river in
safety. I was the first out.*

G.C. King from the Calgary Herald

Setting Up Fort

James F. Macleod as a youth at Kingston Military College *(above)*, and as NWMP officer *(below)* twenty years later.

On a beautiful day in the late summer of 1875, "F" Troop of the North-West Mounted Police, commanded by Inspector E. A. Brisebois, rode east across the prairie and halted on the top of the cut bank on the north side of the Bow River just east of present-day Centre Street. There they surveyed what was to be the location of their new post. Conveniently situated between Fort Edmonton and Fort Macleod, the site had seemed a logical place for a fort; and now, viewing it for the first time, the men were convinced their choice had been a happy one. One of the constables later recalled, "It was by far the most beautiful spot we had seen since coming west." Another was to write, "Our first sight of this lovely place was one never to be forgotten and one to which only a poet could do justice."

In founding the new fort, Inspector Brisebois and his sixty-five men were acting on the direct orders of Colonel Macleod. In the summer of 1875, the year following the famous March West of the North-West Mounted Police and the building of Fort Macleod, the first Police outpost in the far West, there were rumours of impending trouble on the North Saskatchewan River. Gabriel Dumont, a noted half-breed buffalo hunter, and later the fighting leader in the second Riel Rebellion, was said to be planning to set up an independent state. To be on hand in case of trouble, Assistant Commissioner Macleod headed north with a police detachment. At the Red Deer River he met Major-General Selby Smyth, the Commander of the Canadian Militia, who was on an inspection trip across Canada to inspect and report upon the Mounted Police. He had met Dumont near Batoche and found the rumours groundless. Colonel Macleod returned with General Smyth to Fort Macleod, but before leaving the Red Deer River he detached "F" Troop under Brisebois to build a post at the confluence of the Bow and Swift (Elbow) rivers. The fact that the detachment came from the Red Deer River and not from Fort Macleod explains why they arrived at the north side of the Bow River.

Brisebois established a post as directed, calling it "The Elbow". Living in dugouts and tents, he and his men managed as well as they could until the first buildings, six in number, were erected. The bull teams of I. G. Baker & Co., a trading outfit from Fort Benton Montana who were the chief suppliers to the NWMP, were not long in arriving on the scene laden with supplies and building materials.

Under the command of construction foreman D. W. Davis the company's men quickly erected the necessary buildings using dry pine logs cut six miles up the Elbow

I.G. Baker & Co. bull teams at Fort Benton, Montana, supply depot for the entire West in the 1870's.

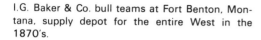

Above: The confluence of the rivers as it looked to Calgary's first citizens.

Below: "F" Troop at Fort Calgary turned out smartly for inspection, 1876.

I.G. Baker & Co. bull teams wait to be ferried across the river near Fort Macleod. A bull team averaged about ten miles a day. But they were the best transportation available in pre-railroad days, and vast trading empires relied on their slow but sturdy progress.

and floated down by boom to the site. They also put up a store and several houses for their own purposes.

Sub-Inspector Cecil Denny of "F" Troop left us some impressions of those first days:

A small tent near the mouth of the Elbow River, a white speck in the distance, attracted our attention . . . it was occupied by Father Doucet, a Catholic Priest not long out from France who had been sent south to study the Blackfoot speech. His only companion was an Indian boy, and he was delighted to see us . . . . We chose a site for the fort on a plateau of high ground at the forks of the two rivers. In trenches three feet deep we set upright twelve-foot pine logs side by side to form the stockade and the outer walls of the buildings. The men's quarters were on one side of the square, store room and shops opposite; on the north, stables for fifty horses, and on the south, officers' quarters and guardroom. The pole roofs were covered with clay. The whole formed a square of 150 or 200 feet with a gate at either end. The floors were bare earth which when continually moistened became as hard as brick. Large stone fireplaces were built in all rooms. This work was done by John Glenn who had taken up a ranch at Fish Creek.

Guard room at Fort Calgary.

Fort Calgary was a "stone-troop fort" until 1879, when it was reduced to a detachment post. Then in August 1882 the tiny outpost was upgraded to the status of District Headquarters, and "E" Troop, commanded by Superintendent McIllree, replaced "F" Troop. Personnel under his command included Inspectors Dowling and Prevost; Sergeant Major Lake; Quartermaster Sergeant Hamilton; Veterinarian Staff Sergeant Riddell; Sergeants Ward, Dann, Wilson and Fury; Corporals Grogan, Smart, Gordon, Greete, Wilde, McInnis and Cudlip; and seventy-three constables, as well as fifty-eight horses.

The fort at that time, described as neat and tidy, consisted of a one hundred and ten by twenty-five foot barracks block with an attached twenty-five by fifteen foot kitchen and dining hall; a fifty by twenty-five foot guardroom providing accommodation for twelve prisoners; stables; a blacksmith shop and a sixty by twenty-five foot hospital (the eight beds boasted hair mattresses) under the supervision of Surgeon Kennedy and Hospital Steward Alexander.

To accommodate the new establishment of one hundred men the following additions were added: a thirty-four by twenty-four foot officers' quarters; a fifty

Right: An early view of the fort. Note the Red River carts in the foreground. These light-weight carts were the traditional freighting vehicles of the muddy northern plains.

Fort McLeod, 31st December, 1876.

North-West Mounted Police: In account with J. G. Baker & Co., Dr.

To building barrack at Bow River........................... $2,476 00
" extra expense incurred by locating post by Captain
    Brisebois further from timber than agreement with
    Col. McLeod.. 1,000 00
                                                                    _____
                                                                    $3,476 00

My returns show only 8,520 feet closed in, which, according to agreement, at 25 cents per foot, reduced amounts to $2,130.00; balance disallowed. Messrs. Baker and I disagree about the extra expense of locating Fort more than one mile away from timber. I have made enquiries and do not think that any extra expense was incurred. They reserve the right to make good their claim for the balance.

(Signed)   JAMES F. McLEOD.

Left: After the fort was built Baker's upped the price, blaming Brisebois for the extra expense. *Below:* The log buildings constructed in 1875 were still being used by Baker & Co. eight years later, as this old photograph shows.

13

by twenty-five foot orderly room and sgt. major's quarters; a seventy-five by thirty foot quartermaster stores and a one hundred and ten by twenty-five foot barracks block. Provision was made for a recreation room, a washroom, a bathroom, a sergeant's mess and a new blacksmith and carpenter shop.

The Force was armed with Winchester repeating rifles and side arms. Two seven-pound muzzleloading bronze field guns brought to the Territories by Sir Garnet Wolseley in 1870 and turned over to the NWMP in 1878 were mounted in a conspicuous place. Mounted parades and inspection were held daily at ten hundred hours; full dress parades were held twice a week.

Right: Reconstructed photograph of the hospital at Fort Calgary.

Right: The care and welfare of horses was of primary importance to a mounted establishment such as the NWMP. This blacksmith shop, primitive as it may seem, was one of the key buildings of the fort.

14

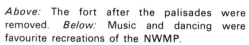

Above: The fort after the palisades were removed. *Below:* Music and dancing were favourite recreations of the NWMP.

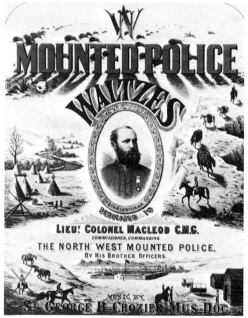

15

Fort Brisebois Indeed!

Captain Brisebois in 1876.

Despite the auspicious beginnings of the new outpost, problems quickly developed. Considerable grumbling and tension prevailed among the men, and the genuine danger of mutiny threatened. It quickly became obvious that Inspector Brisebois had lost control of the men. One of the foremost complaints that was expressed against the commanding officer was that he had, on his own authority, named the outpost after himself - Fort Brisebois. The senior officers were aware of the problem, and quickly took steps to correct it. In a letter written February 29, 1876, from Fort Macleod by Assistant Commissioner Irvine to Colonel Barton, the Deputy Minister of Justice in Ottawa, Irvine reports the building of the new post and the desirability that it should be given a different name. He goes on to say that while he and Colonel Macleod had been at the Bow River post a fortnight before, Inspector Brisebois, without consultation with Colonel Macleod or himself, had given an order that all public documents issuing from the post should be headed "Fort Brisebois". Irvine went on to say that he had cancelled the order at once, as in the first place Brisebois had no authority to issue such an order, and secondly, neither the members of the troop nor the other residents of the area wished that name. He then recommended the name Fort Calgary, which had been suggested by Colonel Macleod, and which, he said meant "clear running water" in Gaelic. Irvine thought this was very appropriate.

The letter was brought to the attention of the minister, the Honourable Edward Blake, who decreed that the Assistant Commissioner should not be interfered with in the matter of the new name. The presumptuous Brisebois, his bid for glory and immortality overruled, resigned soon after.

In view of the fact that there are printed accounts that the name was given by Colonel Macleod, and that he was at that time in command of Fort Calgary, it might be well to describe the respective positions of Macleod and Irvine. Colonel Macleod, who had already won distinction and the CMG for his services as Brigade Major of Wolseley's Force in 1870, was commissioned September 25, 1873, as Superintendent and Inspector in the newly formed North-West Mounted Police. By Order in Council of November 15, 1875, effective January 1, 1876, he was relieved of his police duties and appointed Stipendiary Magistrate, an office created by the North-West Territories Act of 1875. Appointed to succeed him as Assistant Commissioner was Colonel Acheson Gosforth Irvine, formerly the officer commanding the force of active militia left in Winnipeg

Fort Macleod
29: February 1876

Sir,

As we have now a Post or Fort at
Bow River it would be as well if it
was known by some name, I visited
the Post about a fortnight ago with
Colonel Macleod and when we were
there Inspector Brisebois (who is in
command of the station) issued an order
without consulting either Col: Macleod
or myself - stating that all public
documents sent from his Fort were to be
headed Fort Brisebois, I of course cancelled
the order at once, as in the first place Inspector
Brisebois had no authority to issue such
an order and in the second place the Fort
was not built by Inspector Brisebois'
troop & neither the troop or the people
about there with the place called
Brisebois

Colonel Macleod has suggested the
name of Calgary which I believe in Scotch
means clear running water, a very appropriate
name I think. Should the Minister be
pleased to approve of this name I
will issue an order to that effect -

I have the honour to be
Sir
Your Ob.t Servant

W.F. Irvine

A.so Com.r

Li.t Ch: Bernard C.M.G.
Dep.t Minister of Justice
Ottawa
Canada

after the suppression of the first Riel Rebellion. Thus at the time of the naming of Calgary, Colonel Irvine was Assistant Commissioner and in command of the North-West Mounted Police in western Canada. Colonel Macleod was for the time being out of the police force. On July 22, 1876, following the resignation of Colonel French, Colonel Macleod succeeded him as Commissioner, an office he held until October, 1880, when he resigned to again become Stipendiary Magistrate under the North-West Territories Act. Colonel Irvine remained as Assistant Commissioner under Macleod.

It has been generally accepted that Macleod named the fort after Calgary on the Isle of Mull, Scotland. Some claim, however, that it was called after another Calgary, in Skye, which was the Macleod family's ancestral home. The final explanation in all likelihood will never be known, but will remain an interesting puzzle for the enjoyment of historians. There is also some doubt about the real meaning of the word "Calgary". The meaning "clear running water" given by Colonel Irvine was, it may be assumed, given him by Colonel Macleod. Professor MacKinnon, Professor of Gaelic, Edinburgh University, has stated that in Gaelic that term would be spelled *calgaraidh*. He was unable to find a meaning for *calg*, but the term *araidh* meant "a place remote". There is no doubt, however, that the name was never "Calgarry" with the accent on the second syllable, as is sometimes suggested; it was always spelled and pronounced as we spell and pronounce it today - Calgary.

Sketches of Fort Calgary by NWMP Surgeon R. B. Nevitt.

Fort Calgary
Bow River

Who Was First?

Before the building of the Mounted Police post at the confluence of the Bow and Elbow rivers, there are only the vaguest indications that the immediate locality was ever used as a centre either for trade or military purposes. It has been said that it was the site of Fort La Jonquiere built in May 1751 by ten Frenchmen. They had been sent by de Niverville from The Pas to build a post on the Upper Saskatchewan River. "The order which I gave to Chevalier de Niverville," wrote Legardeur de Saint-Pierre in his journal, "to establish a fort 300 leagues above that of Paskeye was executed on May 29, 1751." The exploring party, he added, had penetrated "aux montagnes de roches" - to rocky mountains. On the strength of Saint-Pierre's reference, they were probably the first white men to sight the snowy peaks of the Canadian Rockies. Travelling three hundred leagues (a league is about two and a half miles) would place the explorers within sight of the Rockies on the south branch of the Saskatchewan, but not on the north.

There does seem to be a difference of opinion. Inspector E. A. Brisebois is supposed to have told Benjamin Sulte that when the Police arrived at the Bow River they found the ruins of an old post. G. C. King, former postmaster and mayor of Calgary, who was a member of the troop which built Fort Calgary, claimed the story was not true and that no such ruins had been found. Dr. J. B. Tyrrell, an authority on Western history, is of the opinion that the site of La Jonquiere might have been in the neighbourhood of the later Fort Carlton, as its builders could not have gone further from The Pas in the time given in the account of their journey. It is thus an improbable, but not entirely impossible, conjecture that there may have been a white settlement predating Fort Calgary.

Another interesting theory is that the junction of the Elbow and the Bow might have been a meeting place for even earlier explorers than the French — the Spanish and perhaps even the Russians. It is reputed that the Blackfoot Indians of the early eighteenth century had in their possession fragments of armour of a type common to the Spaniards of California. The Blackfoot claimed that they had traded for the armour with mounted strangers who had come to their territory for trading purposes.

The Indians also had a tale of men who had traded with their ancestors, men who had come over the mountains and met them at the confluence of the rivers. It is known that four hundred years ago the Russians traded with the inhabitants of Alaska. Thus it is not incon-

ceivable that the men of the Indian legend might have
been these same Russian traders looking for new areas
of commerce.

Apart from these elusive but fascinating items there
is little evidence to show that anyone exploited the
obvious advantages of the site as a centre of trade,
though it is quite possible that most of the early white
explorers were familiar with it or had at least come
upon it in their travels. Anthony Henday, for instance,
may have come very close to the environs of Calgary.
It is recorded in his diary that in October 1754
he crossed the Red Deer River north of the present city
of Drumheller. After three days walking, he was welcomed with hospitality at a Blackfoot camp of over
three hundred lodges. From this camp he was able to
see the Rocky Mountains.

Another explorer who visited the area was Peter
Fidler. According to the diary that he kept, Fidler
apparently spent the winter of 1792 in southern Alberta while in the employ of the Hudson's Bay Company, and camped on the banks of the Little Bow
River. And David Thompson, while exploring for the
Hudson's Bay Company, spent the winter of 1787-88
in a Peigan camp on the banks of the Bow River. As the
Peigan country at that time was along the foothills between the North Saskatchewan and Missouri rivers,
it is probable that the location of this camp was on the
south side of the Bow, somewhere between the Cap and
the point where the river makes a sharp turn to the
east — that is, a few miles below Calgary.

On November 17, 1800, David Thompson, then with
the North West Company, left Rocky Mountain House
on horseback with Duncan McGillivray, a fellow officer,
and four men; they travelled up the Clearwater River,
crossed the Red Deer River, and reached the Bow River,
according to his recorded survey, at latitude 51° 2' 56"
north and longitude 113° 59' east. This point is about
where the Bow crosses the eastern city limits.

From August 1832 till January 1834 the Hudson's
Bay Company maintained a post on the Bow River near
the mouth of Old Fort or Bowfort Creek. This post was
intended to replace Rocky Mountain House so that the
Company could compete at shorter range for the Peigan
Indian trade, and thus gain a competitive edge over
the American Fur Company at Fort Peigan and Fort
Mackenzie on the Missouri. This post was officially
named Peigan Post — its ruins are now known as Old
Bow Fort. As the establishment was not successful,
it was abandoned in January, 1834, and Rocky Mountain House reopened.

After the Old Bow Fort was abandoned there was no permanent trading centre anywhere near the site of present Calgary until Fred Kanouse built his whisky fort seven miles up the Elbow in 1871. He was backed by Johnny Jerome Healy, the main proprietor of Fort Whoop-Up, the centre of the whisky traffic along the Whoop-Up Trail that led over the border into Montana Territory. The American free-traders, often with Canadian associates, were exploiting the state of lawlessness existing when the Hudson's Bay Company finally surrendered its much-eroded suzerainty over the vast North-West. They were also mercilessly exploiting the Indians' craving for liquor.

The Kanouse post — it never had a formal name — is described by W. B. Fraser in his history of Calgary. "The post at the Elbow was a fair sized building — built strongly of logs with a yard on one side protected by a log palisade. Along the front was a passageway about seven or eight feet wide and this passage was the place where Indians came to trade. The passage was connected to the trading room by a trapdoor which could be let down quickly if any Indians tried to get inside, for the small garrison of six men had good reason to fear their customers . . . under the influence of the horrible excuse for liquor sold at the posts, they went wild. Frequently they turned on the traders . . . who led dangerous lives." This was the miniature fort defended against White Eagle's men in 1871. The post was abandoned in 1874 when the North-West Mounted Police brought the law to Whoop-Up country.

In the winter of 1874-75 John Bunn, the Hudson's Bay Company officer at Rocky Mountain House, sent Angus Fraser to open a small outpost on the Bow River above the mouth of the Ghost. After the building of the Police post at Calgary, Rocky Mountain House was abandoned, and that establishment moved to the Bow River just east of the Elbow. They thus became the first serious business rivals of I. G. Baker & Co. To distinguish this post from Fort Calgary, it was known as Fort Bow River. The post was occupied under that name until the Canadian Pacific Railway reached Calgary and the townsite moved west across the Elbow.

Whisky trader Fred Kanouse.

Right: Ruins of Old Bow Fort, near Morley, sometimes called Peigan Post. *Below:* This painting by W. Winder depicts Fort Calgary in 1876. In the foreground is the I.G. Baker & Co. store. At the right, across the Elbow, are the Hudson's Bay Company buildings.

Jerry Potts

While never a citizen of Calgary, Jerry Potts has been attributed with suggesting the confluence of the Bow and the Elbow as its location. A familiar figure to all the residents of southern Alberta, Potts has entered the lore of every town, the symbol of everything Westerners hold dear — individuality, resourcefulness, and taciturn horse sense.

Jerry Potts is inseparably linked with the famous March West of the NWMP. Stories are legion of the hardships experienced by the Police during the gruelling March, that all but prostrated both men and horses. Frustrated by the unfamiliar terrain and language, and weary and deathly ill from their trek, they had difficulty in even choosing a suitable campsite, let alone executing their objective of dealing with the whisky traders.

While the main force rested at Sweet Grass, French and Macleod, with sixteen men, went south to Fort Benton to purchase horses and supplies. Hearing about the skills of Jerry Potts they hired him for ninety dollars a month.

For the next twenty-two years this legendary man guided, aided, and advised the tenderfoot lawmen until they were thoroughly accustomed to life in the frontier West. His uncanny sense of direction, his vast knowledge of watering holes and camping places, and his great influence among the warlike natives were all virtues which made him indispensable to the cause of the red-coated Force. The colourful stories of his career — stories both factual and legendary — should raise him to the status of national hero.

Jerry Potts is the one standing at the right in this picture of NWMP scouts at Fort Macleod. Cecil Denny is at the left, in the middle row.

Jerry Potts was born in 1840, the first son of Andrew Potts, a clerk in the American Fur Trading Company at Fort Mackenzie on the Missouri River; and Namo-Pisi, or Crooked Back, of the Blood tribe. After the murder of his father, Potts was adopted by Alexander Harvey, one of the most notorious characters on the Missouri. For the next five years Harvey took care of the boy but at the same time exposed him to the seamier side of life on the frontier. To illustrate, on one occasion, while Harvey was sitting beside an injured native, he passed him a pipe to smoke and then shot his brains out. Other traders, incensed by this and other erratic actions, planned his murder. Taking the hint, Harvey abandoned young Potts and moved to parts unknown.

Potts was next adopted by Andrew Dawson, a Scot known as "The Last King on the Missouri". Under Dawson's guidance the young boy learned English, the business of trading in furs, other Indian languages, and the ways of both the Indian and the white man. In the late 1840's he rejoined his mother's people. When occasion demanded he visited his friends at the American trading post. On coming of age he adopted the carefree life of the early West, which included a notorious capacity for drinking whisky.

On October 24, 1870, a brother of the Blood chief Red Crow was killed by a party of Crees and Assiniboines. Jerry Potts, who was hunting out of Fort Whoop-Up at the time, was included in the Blackfoot war party that gathered in the counter-attack. Armed with repeating rifles, the party met the offenders in a coulee on the banks of the Old Man River near the present site of Lethbridge. In the ensuing battle a Cree fired point blank into Pott's face. As the musket roared he threw himself to the ground, shook his head, got up and continued the fight. Examination later revealed that apart from powder burns he was unhurt. This miraculous escape, plus the fact that he had never at any time been wounded in battle, convinced the Blackfoot that he had supernatural powers.

Jerry Potts was thirty-seven years of age when hired by the North-West Mounted Police in 1874. Moustached and gruff, dressed in the jacket, trousers, and cap of the white man and the leggings, moccasins, knife belt, and cat skin "medicine" of the Indian, he cut a curious figure.

"He won the confidence of all ranks the first day out," recalled Sam Steele, "and when morning came he rode boldly in front of the advance guard. It was noon when the party reached Milk River to find him there, sitting near a fat buffalo cow which he had killed and dressed for the use of the force. To those new to such life he appeared to know everything." It was then early October, and Colonel Macleod, realizing the urgent need for winter quarters, asked Jerry to lead them to a suitable site for a fort. Following an Indian trail westward, he guided the caravan to an island in the Old Man River. This first site of Fort Macleod had obvious advantages: natural water protection, poplar for buildings and fuel, and proximity to a well travelled route.

Potts's first years with the Mounted Police were certainly his most colourful, and in all probability, his most eventful. Apart from locating suitable sites for Police posts, his chores included calming worried Indians, weathering blizzards, routing the whisky traders, and interpreting for the Force.

Jerry Potts's first wife was a Crow woman named Mary, who bore him one son, Mitchell, in 1869. When Potts's work took him north, she rejoined her people. He remarried two sisters, Panther Woman and Spotted Killer, daughters of the South Peigan chief Sitting-in-

The most famous shot of Potts. Actually he preferred wearing plain clothes rather than the outfit in this picture.

the-Middle. After the death of his two wives, Potts married Isum-Its-tsee, which translated means Long Time Lying Down.

Indians were given names related to important events which affected their lives. Potts in the company of a younger cousin was once ambushed by three Crows. In the fight the cousin fell with a fatal bullet in the chest. Gesturing in sign language, the Crows said they were content with a single scalp, and told Potts he could go home. This was a trick, and in the ensuing fight Jerry revenged the death of his cousin. In this battle he obtained a gun made of blue steel. He named his youngest son "Blue Steel" in commemoration of the event.

Jerry Potts obtained his second good-luck charm while duck hunting with Constable Tom Clarke, a member of the Force. By accident Clarke fired in Potts's direction. The scout toppled over. Rushing to his side, Clarke was relieved to find Jerry sitting up. "I thought somebody hit me in the head and knocked my damn block off." Clarke investigated and found a single pellet lodged in the skin behind his ear. Potts, always superstitious, would not let the Police Surgeon Dr. John Kittson remove the lead shot, but carried it as another good-luck charm. At first an interesting subject of conversation, the story became a bore to the men at the barracks. During a party Potts became befuddled, and the host, John Clancy, asked to see the scar. Potts obligingly leaned forward, the policeman opened his penknife, and removed the shot before Potts realized what happened. Sobering up the next morning, Jerry realized what had taken place. He mourned the loss of his good-luck charm, and voiced his fears for the future. A few months later he died.

"Jerry Potts is dead," the Fort Macleod *Gazette* announced on July 14, 1896. "Through the whole North-West, in many parts of Eastern Canada, and in England itself, this announcement will excite sorrow, in many cases sympathy, and, in all, interest. His memory will long be green in the hearts of those who knew him best, and 'faithful and true' is the character he leaves behind him — the best monument of a valuable life."

Left: Jerry Potts beside ceremonial Teepee in 1892. *Below:* R. B. Nevitt's painting shows Jerry, third from left, with some of his cronies.

First Citizens

John Glenn

John Glenn, one of Calgary's first citizens, was here before the Police.

When the NWMP arrived in 1875 there were already two enterprising settlers in the vicinity — John Glenn, who had staked out a homestead near present-day Midnapore, and Sam Livingston, who was squatting on land since submerged by the Glenmore Reservoir. Glenn and Livingston had many things in common. Both were Irish. Both had emigrated to the USA, had prospected for gold in California and the Cariboo, and had explored the West and its opportunities to their own satisfaction before settling down to farm. Furthermore they were both resourceful and innovative in their approach to pioneering. Livingston was the first to introduce farm machinery in the area. Glenn devised the first irrigation project in the Territories.

Born in Galway, Ireland, John Glenn left that country at an early age to seek his fortune in England. He returned to Ireland with the intention of visiting his native heath, but within a few miles of home changed his mind, recrossed the Irish Sea to Liverpool, and booked passage to New York.

In the USA Glenn's various experiences included serving with the Confederate Army until the surrender of Vicksburg, prospecting for gold in California, and mining for four years in Lincoln Gulch, Montana. Hearing of the gold strike in the Cariboo, he followed the prospectors into that central British Columbia community. Finally tired out by this varied and arduous life, he decided to look for land on which to settle down and farm. His wanderings took him to Dunvegan in the Peace River country and then south to Kamloops.

The Reverend George Grant, later Principal of Queen's University, Kingston, was accompanying the Sandford Fleming expedition when he met up with Glenn on the trail between Kamloops and Fort Edmonton. Glenn, a solitary prospector with two loaded wagons, so impressed the Minister that on parting he was moved to say, "God save thee, John Glenn, and give thee thy reward." Catching up with another famous Alberta pioneer, "Kamoose" Taylor, Glenn made his way over the pass at Jasper to Fort Edmonton. In 1873, travelling south again, he found the land of his dreams just south of Calgary, on Fish Creek near the present site of the Lacombe Home. Glenn married Adelaide Belcourt, and after one or two more years of adventuring — mainly trading with the newly arrived NWMP at Fort Macleod — he settled down to farm his homestead. Through hard work Glenn proved up his land. By trial and error he produced record grain crops — oats, barley, and wheat — to feed his cattle. He set up his own irrigation system to water twenty-one acres of bottom land. The fertile soil responded by producing "bragging crops" of roots and garden product, to challenge the Palliser Report and the theory that the country was only good for raising cattle.

Glenn's acreage was a showplace. The "latch string was always out" for visitors, and anyone was welcome to spend the night at the home of the heavy-set, determined son of Ireland. Warm-hearted and good natured, he could always find time from his work to show would-be homesteaders available land and advise them of the best location for setting up a farm.

By virtue of the draw John Glenn had first choice of lots in the CPR subdivision of what is now downtown Calgary, and backed his faith in his chosen community by erecting some of the first buildings in the new town.

As a businessman John Glenn was famous for being strict and honourable in all his engagements. He lived and died a devout Catholic, although he was a man whose sense of charity was by no means restricted to his own faith. His name can be found on almost any subscription list of the time supporting any worthy cause that would contribute to the advancement of the community.

Affectionately referred to as "Old Glenn", he hung up his hoe as a comparatively young man fifty-two years of age; his death removed one of the truly great pioneers in the Calgary area.

Glenn's homestead on Fish Creek, where Alberta's first irrigation ditch was dug. This picture was taken by Samuel Shaw, another well known pioneer, in 1885.

Sam Livingston

Three of Sam's sons: Sam Jr., standing, and Robert and Joe, seated. Behind Joe is a man named Morton, who worked with Sam.

Sam Livingston was born in Ireland, year unknown, the son of an Anglican clergyman. He had little formal schooling, but what he lacked in education he made up in conversational skill, personality, and good humour. Add to this a tall, distinguished bearing and a fearless but friendly attitude, and you have Sam Livingston — a man to be reckoned with.

Sam's adventures in North America began during the 1849 California gold rush. He did not strike it rich, and so drifted north to the central British Columbia Cariboo. At this time his objectives in life were travel, adventure, and gold. This desire to travel resulted in his being the first white man to see many parts of western Canada, including the head waters of the mighty Peace River.

While fur trading in the north, he met and married the daughter of a Scottish employee of the Northwest Trading Company, and decided the settled life had its charms. Moving to Calgary in 1875, he staked a homestead on what is now the Glenmore Dam site, built a log cabin to accommodate his family, and directed his energies to farming. During the next few years he raised good crops, and developed a herd of three hundred cattle carrying the Quarter Circle Brand. On his own initiative he brought in mowing, raking, and threshing implements, the first to be used in the district. This enterprise was a great success. What have been described as "phenomenal" vegetables, milk (at five cents per quart), and meat were sold to the North-West Mounted Police. Sam, on the strength of this success, accompanied a western agriculture exhibit to the Toronto International Fair. Like John Glenn, he had demonstrated that Captain Palliser's "Report on the Triangle" was not the definitive evaluation of the area. In short, along with John Glenn, he helped give farming in southern Alberta a good name.

Sam Livingston was a success because he had the imagination and initiative required to take up pioneering, and the energy and determination to turn his dreams into reality. While harvesting his crop in 1897, he suffered a heart attack and died a few hours later in a Calgary hotel room. It is recorded that when the pioneer physician Dr. Rouleau saw Sam he remarked, "Well, Sam, I see you are on your knees at last," to which Livingston replied, "Yes, Doctor, for the last time."

Left: Sam Livingston *circa* 1890. *Below:* His house when it was submerged by the Glenmore Reservoir.

The example of such men as Glenn and Livingston probably convinced a good many prospective citizens of the possibilities of Fort Calgary. In fact many of the NWMP settled down in the environs of the fort when their tour of duty was over. Some made lasting contributions to the development of Calgary. To mention a few, there was Joseph Butlin, who operated one of the first sandstone quarries in the area; there was Tim Dunne, who built the first hotel in town, the Calgary House on the east side, and produced Calgary's first theatrical performance; and there was S. J. Clarke, who served on the first town council and ran the saloon they held their meetings in; and, of course, there was G. C. King.

Constable George Clift King, "F" Troop, North-West Mounted Police, was the first man in the troop to cross the river and set foot on the flats which later became the site of the city of Calgary. For many years he enjoyed the title "Calgary's First Citizen". He enlisted with the Force when he was twenty-four years of age, and came west with the first contingent in 1874. In later years he was to recall the March West as a great experience. "It was only the splendid organization behind it that was responsible for its completion," he said.

It was characteristic of King and probably of many others in the Force to minimize his own personal part in the great event. He also chose to play down the hardships he had endured. The shortage of rations, the inadequate clothing and equipment, the filthy alkali drinking water, the ravages of September snow storms, the shortcomings of the only fuel (buffalo chips) that would not burn when wet - these were all things to be endured for the sake of the great adventure.

In 1875 he found himself under the command of Inspector Brisebois, part of the contingent of men who were to establish Fort Calgary. He continued as a member of the Force until his enlistment period expired in 1877. He was then appointed Manager of the I. G. Baker & Co. store located on the site of the old General Hospital on Twelfth Avenue E.

About this time King met Louise Munroe, daughter of Felix Munroe, a fur trader. In winter, the fur traders moved from place to place bartering supplies for furs. Come spring they would load the furs onto their Red River carts, and with their families journey to Winnipeg where the furs would be traded for more supplies. The six weeks' trip was a great holiday. Game was plentiful; many a toothsome meal of fresh meat, fish, or wild fowl was cooked over an open fire. No-one was lonesome in this nomadic life. In the evening they gathered

G. C. King

32

Left: G. C. King, the first of the Mounted Police to set foot on the present site of Calgary. This lovely frame structure *(below)* was his residence in 1902. It was located in the Germanstown area, on what is now Sixth Street N.E., Riverside.

Right: Unpacking crates of dishes behind King's store.   *Below:* The store, one of the more splendid shops of the early town, if its richly stocked windows are any indication.

around the campfire to sing or tell stories, then turn in early and arise with the sun, ready for any adventure the day might bring. Felix Munroe was one of this hardy breed.

In 1877, two days out from Winnipeg in no man's land, Munroe died on the trail. The family brought his body to the nearest mission at Calgary for burial in the churchyard. His third daughter, Louise, then secured a position at the mission house as housekeeper to Father Doucet, Father Scollen, and Father Marchand. In addition to her duties of preparing meals and keeping the house clean, she looked after the garden, the chicken coop, and managed the mission store.

In those days a young, vivacious, good-looking girl had many admirers, but George King won her hand. They were married on November 16, 1879, by Father Scollen. By virtue of their being the first married couple in the settlement, they became Calgary's first host and hostess.

Their wedding reception — a celebration, supper, and dance — was attended by Sam Livingston, "Bob" Fletcher, Captain Denny, "Sandy" Gilmour, Jim Barwis, George Emerson, John Glenn, Tom Lynch, Angus Fraser, many of the nearby ranchers, and all the police boys who could get away. The supper, prepared by the bride, consisted of buffalo meat, pie, and cake. The rest of the night the guests danced the good old square dances.

Their first home was a lean-to off the store. They had three rooms — a kitchen, living room, and bedroom, heated by wood-box stoves — and they were very comfortable.

In 1883 King went into business for himself as a general merchant. His firm, G. C. King & Co., was one of the most extensive of its day. He sold a wide variety of goods — groceries, clothing, drugs, stationery, and tobacco.

In 1885 he accepted the position of Postmaster for the town of Calgary, a position he was to hold for more than thirty-six years. King also served as Calgary's second mayor, from 1886 to 1887, during which time he had the opportunity of welcoming Sir John A. and Lady Macdonald, passengers on the first transcontinental passenger train to reach the young frontier town. On January 1, 1934, as a reward for his faithful services in the development of Calgary and district, he was made a member of the Order of the British Empire by King George V.

Every province and every city has its own marked individuality. Calgary has traditions, historic landmarks, and pioneers — distinctly its own. In few places in the world can be found men with experiences such as those of George King. He knew the prairies when the broad stretches were the home of the Indian, the trader, and the wild animals they hunted. He knew the lovely upland of the Bow and Elbow in its virgin beauty and lived to see Calgary develop into a dominant western city.

Below: A full view of King's building. Located at Stephen Avenue and Osler Street (now Eighth Avenue and First Street S.E.), it housed the post office and was known as the Post Office Block.

When the newly formed NWMP set out on its great March West in 1874, Colonel James Walker was one of the officers in charge. Walker had been with the Force from its inception in 1873, and with his commanding officer, Colonel George French, had been responsible for outfitting and equipping the men for the arduous trek.

Walker, an Ontario man, had shown an early interest in the soldier's life. His education was a military one. At twenty he received a Captain's certificate from the Toronto Military School. By the time he enlisted with French he had organized a company of infantry in his home town, taken part in the defence against the Fenian Raids of 1870, and had attended the Royal Military College in Kingston, Ontario. He was a natural leader noted for his energy and perseverence — qualities that undoubtedly served him well during the unbelievable trials and hardships of the March West.

James Walker

Scrip Commissioners James Walker and J. A. Cote during a treaty payment tour, *circa* 1899.

Walker remained with the NWMP until 1881. By this time he could be said to have earned old-timer status, having served at Forts Pelly, Battleford, Walsh, and at Calgary. At any rate his knowledge and expertise in the ways of the West were good enough to impress the owners of the Cochrane Ranch Company, then operating under the name of the British American Horse Ranch Company. Upon his resignation from the Force, Walker was hired by Senator Cochrane to manage his ranch, which was one of the largest at that time, holding lease on one hundred thousand acres.

After two or three adventurous years on the range, Walker went into the lumber business. Purchasing a sawmill that the Cochrane Ranch had imported into the area he set up business under the name of Bow River Mills. When the CPR arrived in 1883 it was Walker who supplied the timber for their bridges and railroad ties. He also provided construction materials for most of the buildings in early Calgary. Photographs of the time and the following description of his mill in *Calgary, Alberta,* a promotion booklet about Calgary published in 1885 by Burns and Elliott, show that by 1885 he was capable of providing a fairly sophisticated product to his customers:

The mill is the most complete of the kind in the Northwest. Besides two gang-edgers, there is a planing-machine — the "Economist," manufactured by Frank & Co., Buffalo, N. Y. — a shingle and a lath cutter. The planing-machine is capable of doing all the finest and fanciest work, such as siding, ceiling, and other kinds of fancy lumber, and the way the power is utilized by using belts shows that there is no waste.

Last year Major Walker brought down the Bow River a million feet of lumber, and during the present spring he will add another million feet to his stock. The woods used are cypress, spruce, red and white, and red fir.

The booklet further credits Walker's establishment with providing employment for newly arrived citizens and with creating a sizeable turnover in capital:

The lumber-yard is an evidence of the mill's industry. Huge piles of boards, siding, shingles, laths, logs, and square timber are to be seen on all sides. There is a blacksmith's shop, and also a carpenter's shop, and a boarding-house for the mill hands. The foreman, Mr. John Patterson, has been in Major Walker's employ for two years, and the blacksmith has been with him since 1876.

Employment is given to at least fourteen men, and last year the major paid out in wages $31,500. This force will be considerably increased during the drive which will take place as soon as it thaws.

No private individual has done more to prove his faith in Calgary than Major Walker. His enterprise has given employment to a great many worthy persons, and he has been the means of bringing to the country from time to time at least fifty individuals, all of whom are doing well.

Like many early Calgarians, Walker invested in city property and real estate. His influence was most obvious in East Calgary, where he acquired a large ranch east of the Elbow, sub-divided it into lots, and erected a

Right: Walker and his cadets with some of their trophies. *Below:* Walker's sawmill, possibly Bow River Mills. Walker is at the extreme right with his son Selby.

large number of houses. His refusal to give in to the speculating methods rampant at the time and his insistence on selling these properties at reasonable prices was probably responsible for the rapid development of that area of the city.

The skills and experience that Walker had gained in his years with the NWMP never lay dormant. He assisted in supervising the treaty payments to the Indians, and acted as Commissioner in settling the various claims of the half-breeds in the area. His military enthusiasms found an outlet in the organizing and commanding of the 15th Light Horse Regiment and in founding Calgary's Cadet movement. Walker served on the school board and the hospital board, and was an active member of the Humane Society. As Burns and Elliott put it, James Walker was a man who was "thoroughly identified with the rise and progress, and especially the manufacturing industry, of Calgary."

Graveside salute by the 15th Canadian Light Horse at the Walker, Calgary.

40

f Colonel James

Sam Steele

Samuel Benfield Steele was born in Ontario in 1849 and received his first commission in a militia regiment at the age of seventeen. After serving as a private soldier in the Red River expedition of 1870 and in the campaign against the Fenian Raids, he took his discharge to join the North-West Mounted Police then being mobilized to bring law and order to the Prairies. By 1874 we find him Sergeant-Major of "A" Division which took the northern route to Fort Edmonton during the great March West. The trip of eight hundred and seventy-five miles over the old cart road was one to either make or break a man - and Steele proved like his name: hard, strong, and almost indestructible.

It took a good man to stand the rigours of service in the original Mounted Police for even five years; Sam Steele served for twenty-five. During that time he made life-long friends among the welter of mixed characters in the West - Indians, missionaries, Mormon settlers, ranchers, homesteaders, buffalo hunters, and the men in the Force. He served at all western detachments. In command of posts in the mountains and the Yukon, responsible for keeping law and order with prospectors and wild and lawless CPR construction workers, he gradually worked his way to the rank of Commissioner.

It is difficult to think of southern Alberta as a land of terror, but when it was the abode of the buffalo, warring Indians, and brutal whisky traders, it was considered dangerous ground. There were outlaws, gamblers, horse thieves, and cattle rustlers. There were, moreover, problems of diplomacy to deal with: the signing of the Treaties, the demands of Sitting Bull, the volatile Metis situation. Steele was well equipped to handle the dangerous aspects of his job. His diplomacy, however, was probably of the "might is right" variety if the following story is a typical example.

In the spring of 1884, the Mounted Police at Calgary received advanced warning of approaching trouble with the Indians and half-breeds. One of Louis Riel's half-breed agents tried to create discontent by telling the Blackfoot at High River that the white man should be driven out of the country and that they had full right to kill the settlers' cattle. The Metis was arrested and sentenced to imprisonment for thirty days.

On release, the recently punished half-breed again tried to stir up trouble. Two Police constables re-arrested the troublemaker near Gleichen. On the way back from Calgary, he slipped his handcuffs, jumped from the mail coach of the speeding train, and outran the constables. Colonel Steele and two constables visited Chief Crowfoot's lodge, to find the leading tribesmen

Above: Samuel Benfield Steele. *Opposite:* Some early NWMP views: a group of well-turned-out officers at Fort Calgary; Sam Heap on the banjo and some of his friends; and a wintry drill at the old fort.

having a pow-wow. The escaped Metis was sitting beside Crowfoot in the position of honour. The Indian chief was in an angry mood. Colonel Steele ordered the troublemaker to accompany him. Chief Crowfoot rose and made a vehement speech in defiance of the Police. The Colonel said he would have no nonsense, and Crowfoot sprang towards him in a hostile manner. Colonel Steele spoke sternly and when he moved forward to meet the chief, Crowfoot stood back. Colonel Steele, with one hand on his revolver, seized the half-breed by the collar and whirled him out of the teepee into the midst of the hostile Indians surrounding the Lodge. Steele then lectured Crowfoot on his duty as chief of a great tribe and warned him that when the Police came for a man they would get him dead or alive. That the prisoner was returned to Calgary without incident is probably more to Crowfoot's self containment than to Steele's diplomatic abilities.

In 1919, after years of distinguished service with the army in Saskatchewan, in South Africa, and in England, Steele died in London, England. In Alberta, Steele is remembered as Sam Steele, the soldier of the plains. The tall, red-coated policeman was a familiar figure on the prairie trails, and in a police force that prided itself on the quality of its men, he represented the very best. He was disciplined, soldierly, and tireless in a service which transformed the wild and wooly west into a land of peace and security.

On parade at Shaganappi Point, 1901. The occasion: a visit of the Duke and Duchess of Cornwall.

STOUT HEARTED MEN

Chapter 2   Steel Arrives

As the west bound train of the Canadian Pacific Railway approaches the first crossing of the Bow River, the view from the car window becomes full of interest. The valley converges as the old town site is reached. The walls of the "cut bank" to the north exclude the view in that direction. To the south, rounded dome-shaped hills stretch far away, interrupting the view of the mountains. To the west the valley is seen extending until it blends with the foot hills or is lost in the shadows of those great granite cones towards which straining eyes are directed. The immediate view is rich and picturesque, while beyond to the west it becomes majestic to sublimity.

From Calgary, Alberta, *published by Burns and Elliott in 1885*

The Front Train

Calgary 1883 Compliments of [signature]

The "front train" — the train "that never went back" — steamed cautiously across the Bow River over newly laid rails into the twentieth siding on the east bank of the Elbow. The date was August 11, 1883. Jim O'Hagan, engineer, with fireman John "Scotty" Ormiston, was at the controls of old engine number 87 that pulled the construction train with its accoutrement of boarding cars and flatcars. Behind came engine number 136, with Leslie McLaughlan and William Pullar in charge, pulling ten empty cars to a rattling halt at the assortment of tents and shacks that constituted the young Calgary. Admiring citizens, some of whom had never seen a train before, and others who had not been on one for years, witnessed the arrival from the hillsides.

Fifty-six years later, sixteen men, survivors of the original party of approximately one hundred who laid the lines of steel to the foothills of the Rockies, met for their annual reunion at the Old-Timers' log shack on the Exhibition Grounds. The fireman on old engine 87, "Scotty" Ormiston, recalled the arrival:

It was a hot day. That whole summer was hot and dry. Water was scarce and bad and there was a lot of typhoid among the men. All there was to downtown Calgary was a couple of trading stores and the Mounted Police barracks. There may have been some Indian encampments, I don't remember. On the east side of the Elbow there was quite a collection of tents and shacks. From east of the Elbow crossing there was a clear view across the valley to the bluffs of West Calgary. There was nothing to see, just bare open country.

Another old CPR employee, James Faulkner, recalled that the men had been drinking nothing but slough water for a couple of days and they were terribly thirsty. "We ran down to the bank of the Bow in a crowd. We must have spent nearly an hour there, just drinking."

On that August day, Calgary became "the summit", the name used to designate headquarters established at the end of track. Construction of the railway ceased, while a bridge was built over the Elbow River, and a minor labour incident ensued. Langdon and Shepard, having completed their contract with William Van Horne to construct the track as far as Calgary, paid off the labourers. Many of them, deciding they were through, jumped on to the empty flatcars heading back east. The loss of so many workers would have been a calamity —

there were many miles of railroad to be built before the summer's work was completed. The NWMP were called out, and an officer ordered the men off the flatcars. The men didn't move. The officer then ordered his constables to ready their rifles, warning the labourers that he would count to three before giving the order to fire. Most decamped on the count "One"; at "Two", only three were left, and at "Three" there was a clean sweep. Rehired, the gangs spent a few days building sidings in Calgary before the push westward.

A temporary construction camp was set up beside the twentieth siding on land now occupied by the Dominion Bridge Company. Sub-contractors under the direction of the North American Construction Company, then continued to drive the railway west through the more difficult foothills terrain to the mountains.

Construction headquarters were moved to an area bounded by present-day Centre Street on the east, Sixth Street on the west, and from the tracks north to Eighth Avenue. A large warehouse and store were built for camp supplies, provisions, clothing, blankets, buffalo robes — in fact, everything that might be needed. A large portion of the area was used as a material yard.

In the Calgary section of *When the Steel Went Through,* P. Turner Bone recalls:

When the CPR arrived in Calgary there was nothing on the west side of the Elbow but the fort *(far left)*, and the buildings of I.G. Baker & Co. seen in this early postcard view *(left)*. The citizens had opted for the east side and were putting up their shacks and tents accordingly *(below)*. However, one could never be too sure what the CPR intended to do, so mostly they were putting up tents.

53

The laying out of the siding to serve the material yard was my first work after moving from the Macleod Trail. The ground was low lying and was a rich hay meadow. The grass was so long that the stakes with which I started to lay out these sidings could not be seen. The stock of material in the yard was practically all imported: timbers from the States; steel rails from the Krupp Works in Germany. Some of these rails are still in use on the siding which serves the Robin Hood Mills and probably also on other sidings in that vicinity. They may be recognized by the words "KRUPP, CPR STEEL" which are moulded on them in relief.

The offices of the Chief Engineer, Moses Burpee, were located alongside the new warehouse. His staff included Turner Bone, office assistant Jack Griffith, a Mr. Walters, a cook, a teamster, and a general chore-boy and messenger about fourteen years of age named George. He didn't need a surname - everyone knew who George was. Years later George was more widely known as George Webster, Mayor of Calgary. James Lougheed had also taken up his quarters at Burpee's camp.

The first lady through-passengers over the CPR from Winnipeg arrived in Calgary on Saturday August 25, 1883. Mrs. Anderson, wife of the Crown Timber Agent at Edmonton; Miss Elizabeth Anderson; Miss Jennie Anderson; and Miss Mary Wilson from Picton, Ontario, were accompanied by Tom Johnston, Harold Cowan, and T. Anderson of Winnipeg. After taking in the sights, purchasing western outfits, and being entertained by the Hudson's Bay Company Chief Factor and Mrs. Hardisty, the "merry party" left the following Monday by stage coach for Fort Edmonton.

With the arrival of the CPR, Calgary's population more than doubled in one day. A tent city mushroomed overnight on the townsite east of the Elbow River. Construction workers and settlers converged on the I.G. Baker store and the Hudson's Bay Company trading post to purchase supplies, food stuffs, and clothing. Reinforcements were brought into the Police barracks. Calgary was in the midst of its first boom. The North-West Mounted Police had arrived at the junction of the Elbow and the Bow in the summer of 1875 to establish a fort; eight years later, the arrival of the "whiteman's fire wagon" signalled the "second founding" of Calgary. The greatest concern of the residents of the flimsy little tent town those first tumultous days was the location of the future city. As the NWMP owned the grazing rights of the lands west of the Elbow it was naturally assumed

that the east side of the river was the most likely spot. Speculation was high, and many people invested lavishly in east-side lots. However, the CPR as usual had the last word in the matter. James Lougheed has left us his account of the locating of Calgary:

Calgary may be said to date from the summer of 1883 when the railroad came here. There naturally arose a great deal of interest as to whether the official CPR townsite would be on section 14 east of the Elbow River or on section 15 west of the Elbow River. Section 14 was the only available land on which town settlers could locate, section 15 having been reserved by Order-in-Council as grazing land for the Mounted Police horses. It was said that the Canadian Pacific offered to establish their townsite on section 14 if the owners thereof, Colonel Irvine and Colonel John Stewart, would consent to the pooling of the proceeds of sale. This they would not consent to, thinking that the railway would anyway be compelled to select section 14 as the townsite. Then the railway, being entitled to the odd-numbered sections under its land grant, demanded the cancellation of the Order-in-Council of section 15. This in due course was done, much to the disappointment of the owners of section 14. A survey was made at once and steps taken to put the lots in section 15 on the market.

The CPR's first bridge across the Elbow was carried away in 1884 by Felix MacHugh's runaway log drive. The above view taken in the late 1880's shows their second bridge and an early traffic bridge.

Rather a novel plan of selecting the lots by purchasers was adopted. This was owing to the uncertainty as to where the centre of town would be. Some considered it would be near the Police barracks, others that it would closely hug the railway tracks, the consequence being a state of uncertainty which was rather interesting. Intending purchasers were required to send in their names to the CPR agent; and a date, I think in December 1883, was fixed for the sale of the lots. My recollection is that the sale took place in the Idyl Hall east of the Elbow. A number of tickets numbered consecutively corresponding to the number of the intended purchasers whose names had been recorded were placed in a hat, and each of the intending purchasers drew a ticket and the order of his choice depended on the number marked on the ticket.

John Glenn of Fish Creek drew ticket number one and consequently had first choice of lots. He selected the northeast corner of Eighth Avenue and Second Street W. and likewise the northwest corner of Ninth Avenue and Centre Street: two corners which may be said to rank amongst the most valuable today of city corners. At this time it was not generally known where the railroad station would be located, consequently the speculative character of the choice which purchasers made.

The first through train from Montreal arrived Dominion Day 1886. Citizens celebrating the First of July in the Roller Rink adjourned to greet the train with a huge bonfire and a fireworks display; the Italian String Band on the train returned with the Calgarians to the rink to play for the dance which lasted till sunrise.

The train officially opening the transcontinental service on the CPR arrived in Calgary shortly after noon on July 23, 1886. All Calgary assembled at the station to greet Sir John A. Macdonald, Prime Minister of Canada, and his wife, Lady Macdonald, with cheers and music. Judge Rouleau, Dr. Henderson, and Amos Rowe, representing the Town, officially welcomed the Prime Minister and his party.

Colonel James Walker took his son Selby, then a small wide-eyed boy, to witness the historic event. Years later he recalled the Mounted Police Guard of Honour: "as the engine came puffing and panting to the platform to stop with screeching brakes and its bell ringing, the Mounties' horses reared and plunged, creating a disturbance until they were brought in line

Thomas Edworthy stands proudly in the foreground in this picture of his farm in the Shaganappi district. It had a lovely location overlooking the Bow River. It also overlooked the CPR tracks, which can be seen running parallel to the river.

by their scarlet-coated riders." He remembered his amusement at railway officials' "stove pipe" hats, very funny compared to westerners' wide-brimmed, soft-crowned fedoras. Only Mounties wore stetsons and a man with a "Christie stiff" was invariably a section boss. "The beards on the CPR officals were pretty tremendous affairs. These Easterners were old men," he recalled. "One never saw an elderly man in the West in those days - look at any pictures and you will see that all the citizens were young and hardy. They had to be husky, I suppose."

At three o'clock the party was driven to the Geddes and Brown Ranch in the Shaganappi District overlooking the Bow to inspect the North-West Mounted Police, following which an illuminated address was presented to Sir John by Dr. Henderson in Boynton Hall.

To the Right Honourable
Sir John A. Macdonald
Prime Minister of Canada

Right Honourable Sir:
The Citizens of the Town of Calgary are assembled here tonight to give to you as Prime Minister of Canada a hearty welcome to our beautiful town, and to assure you of the honour in which they hold one who has so long and faithfully laboured in the public service.

You have now arrived at the Western limit of the territories, to the advancement and future prosperity of which you have devoted your best energies of mind and body and by a road, which has been truly designated, imperial, no less on account of the stupendity of the work than of its value to the vast empire of which we proudly form a part, and Sir, in reference to the CPR the people of Calgary have special cause to remember your name, and to its construction the residents of this now flourishing district owe the existence of their beautiful town.

We heartily join with you in feelings of gratitude to Divine Providence that your life has been spared to witness the final completion of that gigantic enterprise, along which commerce will, and even now has begun to make its way with ever increasing strides.

We offer you no excuse in calling your attention to the importance of the Town of Calgary, your first visit to which we now celebrate. Its rapid growth, together with the natural advantages it possesses, warrant the belief that e'er long it will become the commercial metropolis of the Territories.

Opposite: Selby Walker and some of his fedora-crowned friends at his father's mill. Colonel James Walker is in the left foreground.

We would be remiss in our duty were we to fail to acknowledge the obligations due to your estimable wife, Lady Macdonald, under whose care, directed by a special providence, the onerous duties of your public life have been lessened and lightened and your health and vigour thereby preserved to the service of your country to a marked degree, and we extend a right-warm welcome to that esteemed lady.

We cordially desire, Right Honourable Sir, that the visit you are now making may restore to you your strength and vigour and that both yourself and Lady Macdonald may carry back with you to your home at Ottawa a kindly remembrance of this Town and its people.

Signed
A. Henderson
Chairman Citizens' Committee.

In reply Sir John thanked the citizens for the address, saying it was a great pleasure to be among them. Surprised by the beauty of the location, he predicted Calgary would become a great metropolitan city. He humourously expressed the fear that when the advantages of Calgary became known to the other Ministers there would be danger of them running here and deserting their posts in Ottawa. In conclusion the Prime Minister stated he was more than refreshed by his trip and more than pleased with what he had seen.

From Boynton Hall the official party went to the site of the new Presbyterian Church at the corner of McIntyre and McTavish (Seventh Avenue and Centre Street) where Lady Macdonald laid the cornerstone. At Dr. Henderson's home Colonel Walker presented Sir John with another illuminated address expressing thanks and appreciation from the Conservative Party and an expression of loyalty from the NWMP. The celebration concluded with a dance in the Roller Rink.

Calgary's first station *(far right)* was simply a box car shunted in on a construction train when the tracks crossed the Elbow in 1883. By 1884 a spanking red station with white trim had been erected *(lower right)*. The railway was the focal point of the town. Here a collection of railway men and assorted kibitzers pose to be snapped by engine number 147, an old wood-burner. *Right:* Two Indians and a Mountie wait for a train. *Below:* The station during Calgary's sandstone era.

1st PASSENGER TRAIN REACHED CALGARY AUG, 1883.

C.P. RAILWAY STATION
CALGARY, 1884
ERNEST BROWN 813A
COPYRIGHT.

WOOD BURNING
ENGINE, NO! 144

Waiting for the Train

George Murdoch arrived in Calgary by team and wagon three months before the CPR and he was impressed. A saddle-maker by trade, he had left his family in New Brunswick and had been travelling by train across the West looking for a likely place to settle. Nowhere suited him particularly, and so he pushed on beyond the end of steel, arriving in Calgary on May 13, 1883. He records that arrival for us in his diary — a diary he kept faithfully for years. The graphic picture it paints of his life and of the life of early Calgary is intensely interesting. The following is an abridged version of his journal up to the arrival of the CPR.

Sunday, May 13th - Rain and snow. Eat cold grub in wagon and started at 7 a.m. Sighted Calgary at 10:30 a.m. Got stuck on banks of Crow Creek and had to get chain and yank out from the bank. Reached Calgary at 11:30 a.m. and camped opposite the fort. Cooked scones in wagon and kept fire all day on account of rain. Lots of dead cows all along the banks of the river Bow, rotting & stinking. In the evening went back two miles and called on Thomas and McLean's Outfit.

Monday, May 14th - Forded the river to the fort side and rigged up wagon box and borrowed tent for a temporary habitation. Major Dowling called on me, a fine old gentleman, knows Uncle well. Bought a loaf of bread at the Fort, 25 cts. Baked scone, prospects good, have to repair harness in tent. Very awkward as my head touches the roof. Calgary bottom is the finest natural town site I ever saw.

Tuesday May 15th - had two jobs of repairing, charge like the mischief, as a dollar is handled here like 25 cts. at home. Sold all my spurs at $2.00 each pair. Baked Beans & Scone. Mack off all day. Bought axe handle, 75 cts. Bed at 9:30. Clear as day.

Wednesday, May 16th - Clear, fine day. Light at 4 a.m. Bought five loaves of bread for $1.00. Got 350 feet of boards a lot of scantling at Major Walker's Mill. Put up shack 12 ft. square. Repairing. Wrote and posted letters to wife, Hilyard and Field. The view of the Rockies is beautiful tonight. They seemed about ten miles off. They are 45.

Thursday, May 17th - Put up benches and shelves. Ready for work and got at it in earnest. Mack away harrowing all day for Crosby. Major Dowling gave me some sacks and I tacked them on the walls to keep out the wind. The Sarcee Indians kicked up a shindy and

Left: George Murdoch had this picture of his log house taken on September 3rd or 4th, 1883, to send home to his family. He had begun construction on it in July of that year, a month before the train arrived. George is the man with the skillet. The others are McArthur (with the axe) and Grue (with the gun); both were staying with Murdoch at the time. *Below left:* A group of Calgarians in 1883. *Right:* The train at Medicine Hat.

the police are off to arrest the culprits. Bought meat 50 cts.

Friday, May 18th - Cloudy and blowing. Police came back without any prisoners as the squaws made it so hot for them that they had to let them go, so a force was sent off to do the work and when they got there they found that they had quit their reserve. Fears are entertained of a rising. I put up my name on the window and it is the first sign in Calgary. Indians back on the Reserve and one of the Culprits in the guard room. Bought five loaves of bread $1.00. Meat -1.00. Just two hours shot and very tough. Mack got back.

Sunday, May 20th - Up at 8:30 a.m. Went fishing on Bow River, caught a trout about one lb. Broke hook and quit. Made meat pot pie and cleaned and salted trout. Saw two horse races in the evening, one a bareback, one with four Indians and whites.

Monday, May 21st - Up at 6 a.m. Cooked Trout and breakfasted. Changed underclothes and shirt. Blowing like the mischief. I fear for my shanty. I shored it up as well as I could. Bought meat 50 cts. Bretzels $1.00. Evening wind fell. Mush $1.00.

Friday, May 25th - Clear and fine. Sent letters to Uncle via end of track by Mr. Carr a freighter. Horse race today. Bought bread and biscuits $2, Butter $1. Bought tongue and started boiling. Saw a ball in the evening. All on the floor were cowboys and halfbreed women. Danced Red River Reel and Eight-hand Reel. As good a show as I ever saw. The Belle was Capt. Denny's woman a half breed who is a niece of Sir Stafford Northcote.

Saturday, May 26th - Clear fine and warm. Gave one dollar for the barber who had his arm broken at the race. Kept tongue boiling all a.m. Bought milk tickets $1. Attended races saw one five mile, two police, one Blackfoot, a Sarcee and a Stoney. The Blackfoot won and I won on the Blackfoot.

Sunday, May 27th - Raining heavy. Mush for breakfast. Rev. Mr. Turner asked us to lead the singing at his preaching. Mack and I went and Mack took the fiddle, and we got along swimmingly.

Wednesday, May 30th - Clear fine. Mack got 3 quarts beans to plant for me at my place. Mack went down to his place. I gave McLean $90 and order for Field, also pouch and letters to post in Winnipeg. Bought:

Above: Trout from the Bow River, 1884. *Opposite above:* CPR construction team on the prairies, 1883. *Below:* At Medicine Hat, 1883.

saucepan and turner .... 75 cts.
2 lbs. crackers .... 50 cts.
1 can Salmon .... 50 cts.
1/2 lb. butter for pan .... 25 cts.
Comforter 5.00

Made Slap Jacks for tea. Read paper loaned me by Frith - a treat.

Friday, June 1st - Painted canvas sign - "Harness Maker"

Tuesday, June 5th - Cloudy & blowing a steady gale. I was dreaming about home almost all last night. How I long to see my wife, mother and little ones. My heart craves for them all today more than usual. Made corn mush for tea and eat hearty. Bought lard, cheese and oysters.

Thursday, June 14th - Clear and hot. Thermometer 84 in shack. Two outfits of graders arrived here yesterday waiting for work. I met the Rev. Mr. Robertson who arrived here two days ago. Fine day - no wind thunder at 10 p.m. with wind. Burpee arrived today.

Monday, June 18th - Evening attended business meeting of Presbyterian church in Hudson Bay Store. Old Roselle promised me a lot after I left the meeting on my way home when I met him.

Thursday, June 21st - Cloud and rainy all day - Ther - 60. Fire on all day, boiled tongue, evening took a walk. The first scrapers arrive in Calgary today.

Fort Calgary, July 7 1883.

Dear Father,

I have only time to send you a few lines as the mail is about leaving. I send a page from the Can. Illustrated News & in the lower left hand corner you will see a picture of the Fort here. Railroad news is all I have to write about. It is now 100 miles away & advancing at the rate of 3 miles a day. so, you see that it will reach here in less than a month. Write soon & let me know what is going on in Boston.

Frank.

Friday, June 22nd - Cloudy, cold, lightning at night. Graders coming on thick. Gov. Dewdney and suite arrived today. Trial of two Indians one got one month for stealing the other six months for stabbing a settler named Morse.

Saturday, June 23rd - Clear, fine, Ther. 85. Hard at work all day altering pack saddles for N.A. Railway C.C. Graders arriving in crowds.

Wednesday, June 27th - Clear and fine. Ther. 92. Up at 5 a.m. Cooked breakfast. Got notice to serve on jury. Bought two yards mosquito netting. At night blowing hard.

Thursday - June 28th - Very warm, Thermometer 96. Attended court and escaped the draft. It was a strange sight, the Military, Civilians and Indians in paint looking in at the windows. All were acquitted as they had been confined six months waiting trial. The mosquitoes are very bad. McLean got back from Winnipeg. My goods are with his.

Tues., July 3rd - clear fine. Ther. 75. Took dinner and supper at Restaurant. Got goods open. Gave Dixon voucher for $115 on acct. also sent by him to Field $39.37 balance on note. Got the papers made and signed for 3 acres of land from Mr. Roselle. Papers in Dowlings hands.

Wednesday, July 4th - Made bargain for logs delivered at my shack for $1.60 I am terribly crowded.

Friday - July 6th - Clear and fine. Ther. 80. Turned out double harness. Arranged with man to sink post holes on an acre on my Roselle place.

Saturday, July 7th - Warm. Thermometer 90. Received letters from P. J. Dealy, Wife, Sullivan and Field, Col. De Winton got his knee boots. Paid Roselle on account $4.00. Roselle hauled three loads of posts to my place. Gathered and pressed flowers to send in letters home.

Monday, July 9th - Cloudy. Had a shower last night. Made contract for building log house. Woods all on fire at Shaganappi.

July 10th - So much smoke that I cannot see a quarter of a mile across the bottom. Graders at the Elbow. J. Rivet started my shack. Roselle Hauling logs. Evening at Breed dance.

Wednesday July 11th - Clear, fine. Thermometer 90 Very busy all day. House getting along very well. Agent

Opposite: The approach of the train was of vital concern to everyone in the little tent town of 1883. Frank Crosby of I.G. Baker & Co. was no exception. In this letter to his father in July of that year, the advance of the train towards Calgary gets lengthy treatment. Crosby estimated that at that time the train was within a month of reaching the town.

of O'Brien & Co Clothiers, Winnipeg arrived today. First drummer in Calgary.

July 14 Clear fine. Thermometer 78. Seven fellows tried for gambling and fined from $7 to $50.

Monday, July 16th - Cloudy with showers. Thermometer 65. House ready for roof Bull train of 78 oxen arrived for Bakers — Also wagon train of 26 horses for King.

Thursday July 19th - Thermometer 60. Blowing a gale all day. Grading machine rigged ready for work on the bottom. Mule train arrived this a.m. Six wagons and 24 mules. Made wheat pancakes in the evening.

Saturday July 21 - Clear and fine. Thermometer 80. White prostis arrived today the first in the place.

Tuesday, July 24th Clear Warm Thermometer 85. Shingling shack Graders at work here. Roselle hauled 3 bundles of shingles.

Sunday, July 29 - Slept in shack last night for first time.

Wednesday, August 1st - Water man started to leave water today; 25 cents per week. Rained all night, still raining and cool Rain came in through canvas roof.

Sunday August 5th - Terrible drunken crowd around today. Bed at 9 p.m.

Monday August 6 - Smoky warm Ther 90. Paid Brynton $10 on the Hanlon Ross job. Shabot paid me $4 Tibideau $2. Saw Breed Dance at Clarke & Co's New hall. I must stop spending.

Wednesday August 8th Clear and warm. Ther 80 Strange trial today. I am summoned on the jury, a non-suit. Spike drivers at the Elbow. Got letter from Wife and Willie and papers from Uncle. Heavy rain in afternoon. Wrote to Wife and Willie.

Thursday August 9 - Cloudy Blowing Ther 60 Piles drove on east side of the Elbow. Evening raining heavy. Rigged up press in house.

August 10 - Rained all night still raining and cool. Rain came in through canvas roof. Bridge finished across the Bow, railroad at it.

Saturday August 11 - The train crossed the Bow and constructed and ran to the Elbow. The Telegraph was along with them. Got my goods from D & P and took them over to the shack.

Sunday August 12 - Building bridge over Elbow all day. A big bustle all day so many railway men around from the construction train. Horse and foot racing all day.

Monday August 13 - L & Co. finished contract on C.P.R. today. The men struck work and the Company would not give them passes. Appealed to the police. No go. Then boarded car. Police put them off — place crowded.

Tuesday August 14th - Cool then warmer. Senator Scott is around here viewing things. Sent Telegram to Uncle (Rail and Telegraph both here) "I'm well, how's all."

Calgary's first residents had less than luxurious living conditions. This tent home of Mr. and Mrs. J. Edwin McKibbin, 1883, was located at the present corner of Twelfth Avenue and First Street S.W. Mr. McKibbin and his brother were destined to lay the first concrete sidewalks in the town.

Apart from one or two hardy individualists like John Glenn and Sam Livingston, who were adventurers in general and could live happily on their resources in any locality, the immigrants to the West in the days before the railroad fell into specific and predictable categories: police, missionaries, fur traders, and, later on, cattle ranchers. With the coming of the railroad, however, the country was thrown wide open to anyone with the price of a ticket. Thousands took advantage of the opportunity. The year 1883 saw a whole new group of adventurers setting their sights on Calgary. Many were to follow the lure of cheap land and a new start. Others — professionals, tradesmen, and labourers — saw the possibilities of selling their services to the rapidly increasing population. It was a wild assortment of people that inhabited the tent town of Calgary and its surroundings. The conditions were rough but the climate was eminently optimistic. A saddler could become a mayor, a carpenter could become a lord and a millionaire — and did.

In 1882 the Shaws of Kent, England lived in a big house filled with fine furniture, staffed with servants, and surrounded by a large ornamental garden. Samuel Shaw, a successful chemist, was an avid reader of accounts of life in Western Canada — unlimited land, healthy climate, and predictions of a great future. Like many other Britishers, the Shaws succumbed to the lure of new territory. They put their comfortable and secure life behind them forever to become settlers in Canada.

Unlike most would-be pioneers, however, they anticipated every necessity and made every provision to ensure success. Having accumulated every possible item they might need in the new land, they sailed for Canada. They then journeyed by train to the end of steel - Swift Current, Saskatchewan. Camping on unfamiliar prairie they prepared to trek to their intended home in the Peace River country.

By now they constituted a minor expedition. They had five span of oxen, a prairie-schooner wagon, food, medicine, clothing for two years, cows, sheep, chickens, grain, and farm machinery. In addition their chattels included one ready-to-assemble British factory fortunately left at Winnipeg to be forwarded by CPR freight. Thirty tons of machinery destined to become Alberta's first woollen mill — what else would a son of the Industrial Revolution consider a necessity!

The spring of 1883 saw this bold, inexperienced, but nevertheless determined family set out across the plains. Unfortunately Samuel Shaw's research, thorough as it might have been, had not prepared him for the caprices of western climate. En route they encountered every sort of weather imaginable. Then, arriving in Calgary, they received dire warnings about the extreme weather conditions in the Peace River area. In the previous winter cattle had frozen to death, and the countryside was littered with their bleaching bones.

This discouraging information called for a quick change of plan. They decided against going north, turned their unwieldy caravan south towards Fish Creek, and settled in the Midnapore area. The decision was a propitious one for the Shaws: the future was theirs.

They set to work. They broke land, seeded it, and built a log house complete with sod roof. In turn they were homesteaders, ranchers, storekeepers, postmasters, and manufacturers of woollen goods. They fostered the civilizing interests of the church and school in the district, and became leaders in all the social gatherings of their community. Their neighbors learned to rely on Samuel and Helen Shaw and their children as an in-

Sam Shaw

Above left: Samuel Shaw in the 1880's. *Above right:* Shaw's woollen mill as it looked in 1910. *Left:* Four of the Shaw's nine children outside their first home. Part of Sam's preparation for the pioneer life was to have each of his children instructed in a different skill. One daughter was sent to an industrial school to learn weaving. Another was taught cobbling, and to the end of her days was able to mend shoes. *Overleaf above:* Mrs. Samuel Shaw. *Below:* The building with the folded awnings is the Midnapore Woollen Mills, Shaw's outlet for their woollen products in Calgary.

dustrious and adaptable family.

It is interesting that the western climate that had so influenced the course of his life was to become an absorbing hobby for Sam Shaw. In those early years he kept extensive meteorological records, including daily temperature readings, which he supplied to the Calgary press.

To the end the Shaws remained faithful to their British background and associated traditions. Mrs. Shaw is remembered in southern Alberta as a tiny figure clad in cape and bonnet, reminiscent of Queen Victoria. In her later years she was active in the Southern Alberta Old-Timers' Association. One of the features of this organization's annual meetings was the quaint figure of Helen Shaw sitting at a spinning wheel while her friends sang "The Old Spinning Wheel in the Corner".

Sam Shaw died in 1919, at the age of seventy-six. Helen lived to be ninety-four. They rest in St. Paul's Churchyard, Midnapore.

A pioneer who recognized the possibilities offered by "the thriving village" at the junction of the Bow and Elbow rivers, John Stewart came west to Fort Macleod in 1881 with a group of capitalists looking for a profitable investment opportunity. Stewart took a fancy to the country and decided to stay. He formed the Stewart Ranch Company and secured a fifty thousand acre lease bounded on the north by the middle fork of the Old Man River and on the south by Pincher Creek. Four thousand bushels of oats were harvested in 1882 from the shellout of the previous year's crop, and by 1886 twenty-five hundred cattle and three hundred horses were running on the ranch.

In 1883 Stewart purchased the land owned by Captain Cecil Denny in Section Fourteen south of the Bow and east of the Elbow for ten thousand dollars. In the September 7th, 1883, edition of the Calgary *Herald, Mining and Ranche Review and General Advertiser*, it was announced that "Captain Stewart arrived from Medicine Hat on Monday evening. He expects to survey into town lots his property in this place."

When the CPR finally surveyed Section Fifteen and put the lots up for sale through one of their subsidiaries, the North West Land Company, Stewart, through his Denny Land Estate Company, offered his land for sale as well. Residents had a choice of locating east or west of the Elbow, and competition between the two companies became spirited. The following is the Denny Estate advertisement that appeared on January 2nd, 1884:

John Stewart in his pre-Calgary days.

LAND SALE! Calgary city lots now on the market. The permanent location of the City EAST OF THE ELBOW! The Denny Estate. THE PEOPLE'S CHOICE! Over 200 lots already secured by our own citizens. Prices within easy reach of all classes! Salesroom opposite the Calgary House. Opens January 2nd where map can be seen and will continue until 15th instant. Terms Cash, Title perfect. (Signed) J. K. Oswald, Land Agent.

To promote sales, Stewart donated "a beautifully situated block of land for College or School purposes." At no cost, lots were made available to the Roman Catholic, the Anglican, the Methodist, and the Presbyterian Churches. Stewart retained the services of an architect, Mr. Moberly, to assist owners in the orderly development of the property. Stewart also planned to lay out a park and build a summer hotel on St. George's Island, and Colonel Macleod, H. Bleeker, G. C. King, Dr. Henderson, Major Dowling, Captain Hughes, I. Brady, J.

Oswald, and Captain Stewart purchased "villa" lots and built residences along the "Esplanade", which was the avenue extending from the Elbow River east along the Bow River. Stewart also agreed to provide security to the contractors for the balance of funds required to finance construction of a bridge over the Elbow at Ninth Avenue E. until such time as the City was in a position to liquidate the debt.

Three weeks after Stewart's original announcement, the following optimistic advertisement appearing in the *Herald* tells the story of the proposed early development of Section Fourteen east of the Elbow:

DENNY ESTATE! THE CENTRE OF CALGARY CITY! All surrounding sections now under subdivision. Proposed railroad to Edmonton to enter Calgary by Nose Creek Valley, junction with CPR *on Colonel Walker's claim.* PUBLIC GRANTS! *Calgary Market with Hall and Stores, Head Office Ranchers' Bank, capital — $1,000,000.00, City Hall Square with five acres for public buildings, passenger and freight grounds, schools and college reserve, a bridge will be built across the Bow River on the line of King Street connecting the trails from Macleod and Edmonton and leading to the Island Park.* LIBERAL TERMS TO ALL. SALES STEADILY PROGRESSING - J. STEWART, AGENT. *(Signed) J. K. Oswald, Land Agent.*

Although the CPR's choice of Section Fifteen was to become the business centre of the town, Stewart didn't lose a thing in his East Calgary promotions. At the time of the appearance of the above advertisement, land-hungry citizens had already invested sixty thousand dollars in Denny Estates.

Besides, Captain Stewart had other interests. He purchased a mine on Castle Mountain. He was awarded the mail contract between Fort Macleod and Calgary. And he was president of the Dramatic and Musical Club, whose productions were to provide a substantial if not remunerative outlet for his considerable dramatic talents.

Left: Captain and Mrs. John Stewart.   *Below:* Stewart's home in Calgary's east side. Overlooking the Bow River, it has lately been restored to its former elegance, and stands as proof that Stewart's plans for the development of Calgary might have been remarkably pleasing.

Felix Alexander McHugh was born in Ottawa on July 8th, 1851, the son of Felix McHugh, a native of Sligo, Ireland, who emigrated to Ottawa in 1840; and Rosena McHugh, the daughter of John Findley, a successful farmer who had cut the first tree that was felled on the Experimental Farm near Ottawa. In 1883 Felix McHugh, looking for a wider scope for his energies, answered the call to "Go West." With a complete set of farming implements, wagons, and mowing machines, and his prize-winning Clydesdale horses — one team of mares had cost 650 dollars, an incredible price in those days — he travelled by rail to Chicago and then to Emerson on the Manitoba border; from there he travelled by CPR to the end of steel at Swift Current. From Swift Current he drove to Calgary ahead of the railroad and crossed the Bow River on the first prairie boat built in Calgary.

In May 1883 McHugh located a homestead in Section Twenty-One (the present-day Hillhurst District) which at that time was not subdivided. He built a shack and stables, and broke and fenced twenty acres of land. Government Engineer La Roux, who subdivided the land, gave McHugh a certificate for his homestead, in which was stated the improvements he had made. However, his application for entry was rejected, on the grounds that the odd sections were reserved for the Canadian Pacific Railway. McHugh retained the services of a lawyer to handle the case, but the lawyer claimed to have lost the certificate. McHugh lost the decision in court, was compelled to relinquish his claim, and forced to relocate on an acre of land purchased from the Medicine Hat Land Company — an agency for the CPR.

Later the same year McHugh obtained a contract to supply the NWMP with cordwood and corral fencing. Arrangements were made to cut the logs on a lease twenty miles up the Elbow and float them down the river. The drive was not started until the latter part of October, and on reaching the Elbow Park district the logs were frozen in. Never a man to be thwarted, McHugh filled his contract with the Government by chopping the logs out of the ice and delivering them the two and one-half miles to the Fort by wagon. Out of this drive he reserved the best logs and arranged to have them sawn into lumber at Colonel Walker's mill. When the CPR put the land in Section fifteen up for sale, McHugh purchased two twenty-five-foot lots on the northwest corner of what is now Eighth Avenue and First Street E. for 175 dollars each; and using the lumber, erected the first building on

Felix McHugh

Above: Mr. and Mrs. Felix Alexander McHugh, 1884.

Above: The CPR bridge in 1884, after the June washout. Those are undoubtedly McHugh's logs in the foreground waiting to be salvaged by eager beachcombers. *Right:* The McHughs' home at 112 Seventh Avenue S.W.; the photo was taken in 1920.

the new townsite. The date was February, 1884. The first Council convened in Alberta by the Government of the North-West Territories was held in this building. Later two lawyers built Calgary's first jail at the back of the lots.

In 1884 McHugh, with thirty men and seven teams of horses, set up a lumber camp on his lease twenty miles up the Elbow. In June of that year, which was memorable for very high water and flooding, he brought down a boom of logs which carried away the CPR bridge and the traffic bridge across the Elbow near what is now Ninth Avenue E. To add insult to injury the boom ropes broke and the flood waters of the Bow carried the logs downstream to be salvaged and turned to good purpose by local settlers.

The McHugh family about 1903. The child in front is Florence McHugh, who became a noted stage actress in the twenties.

In the fall of 1885, to stock his lease of Government grazing land located just outside the Blackfoot Reserve near Queenstown, McHugh brought the first carload of cattle to be shipped over the all-Canadian CPR route. The next year he brought in a train load of horses and cattle. At one time over 1,600 horses carried his "H2&T" brand. Because of an overdraft of forty thousand dollars, the Union Bank of Canada seized his entire herd, and disposed of the stock by forced sale. McHugh instituted suit against the Union Bank for 75,000 dollars damages. In his statement he claimed to have paid 10,000 dollars on the 40,000 dollars and was only waiting for a favourable market when he would have sold and paid off the loan. The horses at the time of seizure were under quarantine by the Government; notwithstanding that fact, they were driven to Calgary in the shortest possible time and many died from the effects.

In addition to the lease, McHugh owned six thousand acres along the Bow River, which he stocked with six hundred head of horses and one thousand head of cattle. He also owned a 350-acre farm three miles from the centre of Ottawa.

As a contractor, McHugh built part of the CPR road-bed through the Crowsnest Pass, and his crews, equipment and horses also worked for the Canadian Northern Railroad. He completed contracts for the Southern Alberta Irrigation Company and the Southern Alberta Canal. When the local improvement district refused to sell bonds he was forced to discontinue work, at great loss, on the Springbank Canal.

McHugh was married in April 1883 to Miss Florence Elizabeth O'Dorothy, the daughter of one of the prominent citizens of Gloucester Township in the County of Russell, Ontario. They became the parents of eleven children, four of whom died in childhood. Nine were born in Calgary. Of the five sons, Walter grew up to manage the ranch, Alex supervised the construction company, and Oswald, Harold and John, after attending Ottawa University, went into business. A daughter, Florence, attended the convent school in Calgary and went on to a brilliant career on the British stage.

Troubled with a complication of diseases which started with rheumatism, McHugh was admitted to the Holy Cross Hospital where, at the age of sixty-one, he passed away. His estate was valued at $750,000.

The story of Felix McHugh would be incomplete without mentioning his brother John J. McHugh, and his nephew Frank "Bull" McHugh.

John J. McHugh came from Ottawa to Winnipeg in 1877, and boated up the Saskatchewan River to Fort Edmonton, where he worked as a teacher on a Government farm set up to instruct the Indians in agriculture. During this time he arranged for a first cousin, James W. O'Donnell, to come west and take up a homestead near St. Albert. In 1881 he returned to Ottawa and brought back a number of Easterners, including his brother Thomas. After serving for three years as Assistant Inspector of Indian Reservations, he was made first Land Agent in Assinaboia. In 1899 John joined Felix in the ranching business. Their brother Thomas was favourably known as the proprietor of the Palace Hotel at Gleichen which was then considered one of the finest and most modern buildings in the northwest.

"Bull" McHugh achieved a dubious sort of fame for having turned down an opportunity to purchase the Elbow Park district for five thousand dollars. Forty-five

WHEELER SWING. McHUGHS CAMP. C.N.R.

Above: McHugh teams east of Chestermere grading for CNR construction. *Overleaf:* The McHughs' Horse Ranch.

years later in 1950 he recalled the incident without any noticeable regret, "We were just using it for grazing and had a corral there and we weren't paying anything for it. I was just a boy so I let it pass." Within two years the property was purchased for five thousand dollars cash and resold for forty thousand dollars.

Shortly after the turn of the century, Frank went into the teamster business. His teams hauled the sand and gravel for many of the city's buildings, including the old Post Office and the City Hall, for many of the streets; and for the construction of the CPR roadbeds. He supervised the excavation of the basements under the Isis Theatre, the Underwood Block, and Knox Presbyterian Church; and the levelling of the hill in Rideau for "Lindsay's Folly", a castle-like home which was never finished. He poured the first concrete used for foundation purposes in Calgary, at Ninth Avenue and Fourth Street S.W., in 1905.

Frank could recall working in Kimberly when the town consisted of fifteen inhabitants — the miners at Sullivan Mine who were living at the mine site. "The logging camps in the area paid by cheque, cashable on the first of May, so money was hard to come by in those winters."

In 1909 he hauled gravel for the first Calgary Power Dam at Horseshoe Falls and four years later for the Seebe Dam. In 1912 "Bull" McHugh had fifty teams of horses of his own and fifty-seven hired teams working for him.

Weighing over two hundred pounds, "The Bull" played defence for several Calgary hockey teams. A contemporary newspaper account tells of a game he played in street clothes; hockey pants large enough to fit "Bull" McHugh were not available. He played inside wing for the old Calgary Tigers of the 1907-12 era, and also played polo in the United States. "Sport in those days was strictly amateur," he recalled. "Early Calgary athletic teams used their initiative and relied on the support of a lot of people. I remember in 1907 when we went to Macleod to play a championship game. We just got on the train; we had no tickets and no money to buy them. We just sat in the smoker and hopefully waited for the conductor. He came along. We explained what the situation was and he just laughed and wished us luck. The same thing coming home. Everybody was friendly and willing to help in those days."

James Lougheed

Lougheed for a time had taken up abode with me in my tent. One day he went to Medicine Hat to attend court, and it so happened that when he was there a strike of locomotive engineers took place. This put a stop for the time being, to the running of trains between Winnipeg and Calgary. So Lougheed could not get back to Calgary by train. News however reached Calgary that he and some others were pumping their way back on a hand-car. The night following this report I was awakened from a sound sleep by Lougheed as he came crawling into our tent. Between many moanings and groanings he gave me his account of the trip. He and his party had managed to get as far as Shepard with the hand-car but a sleet storm they encountered there had made the track so slippery with the sleet freezing to the rails that they could not get the car to go any further. They therefore abandoned it and walked the rest of the way some ten miles to Calgary. It was several days before he was able to straighten out the bend in his back which he had got through pumping the hand-car. From *When the Steel Went Through,* by P. Turner Bone.

Born in Brampton, Ontario, on September 1, 1854, James Alexander Lougheed was the son of a contractor-builder, and as a youth worked as a carpenter for his father. The trade, however, did not hold his attention for long, and at the request of his mother, an ardent church worker, he accepted a position as assistant librarian at Trinity Church, Toronto. It was in this position that he first became interested in literature. In later years he was recognized as an authority on the lives and works of the great writers. On matriculating from high school in 1875, he attended Osgoode Hall, and on graduation practised law in Toronto.

At the age of twenty-five Lougheed came west with his brother Sam. After stopping in Winnipeg he moved on to Medicine Hat, and in 1883 decided to practise law in the new settlement at the junction of the Bow and Elbow rivers.

In the Medicine Hat chapter of *When the Steel Went Through,* P. Turner Bone writes: "We bunked in a car-shaped building and had our meals in a similar shaped one with Curran and his staff. Besides the staff there was a former member of it who made one of our party too. He had been in charge of supplies for engineers' camps but had given up that position, and, having studied law, had opened up an office in Medicine Hat. Force of habit or maybe some other reason made him still patronize the company's boarding house. His name was James Lougheed, for a long time afterwards a prominent lawyer in Calgary and a Senator and later known as Sir James Lougheed." Arriving in Calgary on a CPR train that was carrying a number of company officials, he hung out his shingle. The young man who had heeded a friend's advice "Jimmy, you've got a good head on those shoulders. Why don't you take up law?" quickly learned the rough processes of law as practised in a frontier community.

Reminiscing on his experiences, Calgary's first lawyer had this to say:

The enforcement of law and order in the early days of Calgary reflected the highest credit upon the Mounted Police, who were the exclusive dispensers of justice. They combined in themselves all the offices of judge, of sheriff, of bailiff, and of jailor, and did it well. At the time of the arrival of the CPR, the nearest judge we had to Calgary was Colonel Macleod, Stipendiary Magistrate, living at Pincher Creek. Up to that time a court had not been held in Calgary. The Police Commandant was a Justice of the Peace and from his conviction there was no appeal. He administered what might be termed a "System of Natural Jurisprudence". That is to say he sized up the situation, whatever it might be and applied his common sense, and the machinery of the Mounted Police he commanded, to the solution of the difficulty. Almost invariably he dealt out a justice that would equal the wisdom of Solomon. Such a thing as 'the law's delay' was then unknown. Natural justice was administered and notwithstanding the elaborate machinery which today makes up our system of jurisprudence, I think it is not an exaggeration to say that the Mounted Police of that day met the situation with as much satisfaction to their public as the judiciary of today give satisfaction to the public of the present time. All such systems are the product of the times in which they are administered and thus reflect the happy faculty of human nature to adjust itself to the requirements of their day.

This enforcement of law was in strict contrast to the conditions of more or less lawlessness which prevailed upon the other side of the line. Calgary at that time was favoured by many outlanders from the United States who found it more convenient to cross the border than to remain on their own side of the line. Horse and cattle stealing was then in its prime; hence the Mounted Police had no small task in maintaining that observance of law which has characterized that body since its inception.

Above: Sketch of James Lougheed by John Innis.

To illustrate the extent to which this was carried I recall a case in which a Mr. Oxerat of Montana drove a band of about 400 horses to Calgary, with a view to selling them to settlers. He passed the Customs at Macleod but upon reaching Calgary, the Customs Officer here, learning of the value placed upon the horses at Macleod, insisted upon the amount being an under-valuation, and seized them pending payment of the increased customs. He placed them in charge of a well-known cowboy, who formerly had his home in Montana, who was to have them close-herded within easy reach of the town; but a day or so later the 400 head, together with the cowboy, in whose charge they were, had absolutely disappeared. They were evidently driven into a pass in the mountains and so concealed that no trace of them could afterwards be found.

This placed the Customs Officer at Calgary in a very awkward position. Oxerat demanded his horses. They were not forthcoming. Hence the Crown should have been liable for the value. The resourceful expedient occurred to the Customs Officer, by way of escaping his responsibility, that he would charge Oxerat with stealing his own horses, which he did. He was accordingly arrested and put in the guard room until bail of $4,000 cash was forthcoming. Shortly after this Oxerat left Calgary and settled in Maple Creek. As an American Subject of Washington he made a demand upon the Canadian Government for compensation. Whether the Canadian Government paid the money or not I cannot say.

Another chief duty of the police in those days was that of enforcing the prohibition law, which then obtained in all its sanctity. Under the old Northwest Territories Act the importation of liquor was prohibited on account of the Indians, but a permit was issuable by the Lieutenant-Governor for sick or domestic purposes. Needless to say that the permit system, worked 24 hours a day, fell far short of meeting the public demand. The consequences were that the whisky trader and the bootlegger were much in evidence and kept alive the activities of the police. There was scarcely any expedient that was not resorted to for the smuggling in of liquor.

It came in under all guises. Firkins of butter with a layer of cheesecloth and butter covering the top of the firkin and a tin of liquor underneath was a favourite mode of shipment. On one occasion a carload of iron safes came in with the combinations of course turned on, devoid of fittings in the interior, and filled with whisky.

Opposite: The Clarence Block under construction in 1892.

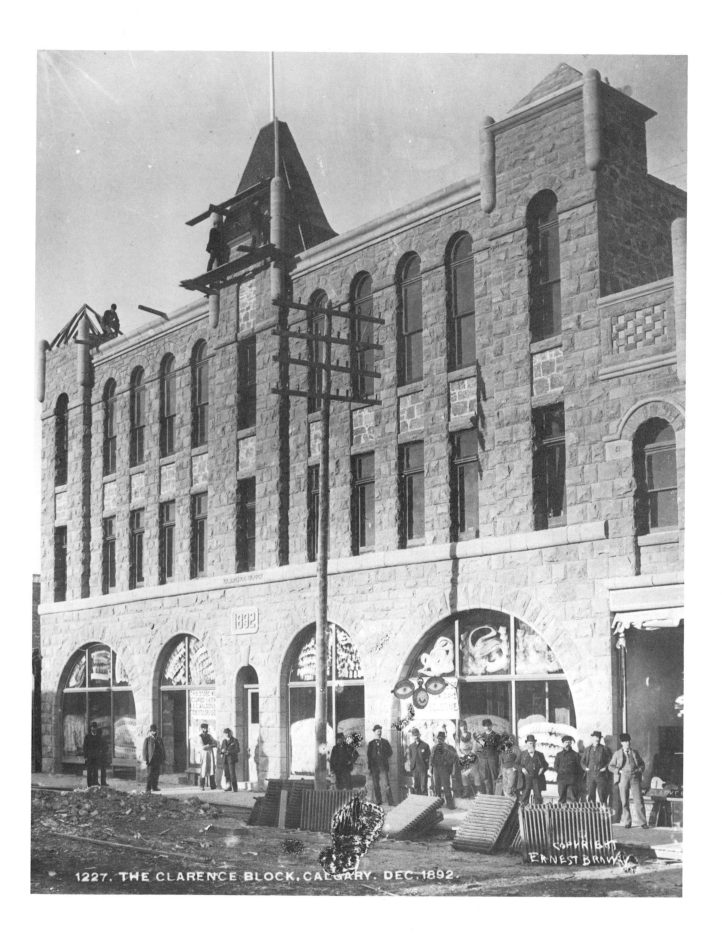

1227. THE CLARENCE BLOCK, CALGARY, DEC. 1892.

COPYRIGHT
ERNEST BROWN

8th AVE, CALGARY, CAN.

Opposite: The Norman Block *circa* 1911 and the Clarence Block in its present-day form.

too was t
close to
mansion
(the site
houses a
fine old
stand an
However
changes
the large
the mans
Donors C
to the ol

The first
where it
abandone
had not b
for some
considere
peculiar t

Throu
strated hi
the busin
he under
Calgary s
and at hi
eight maj
Calgary. H
his contrik

It was needless to say that the value of the contents readily paid for the entire shipment of safes. What appeared to be nicely bound morocco books of favourite authors, not even excluding the Bible, with a concealed flask between the covers which opened on touching a certain point of contact, was a resourceful method of evading the law. I knew of a flour and feed merchant who brought in a carload of bagged oats with a keg of whisky carefully concealed in each bag. These are only a few of the expedients which were resorted to in the early days to defeat prohibition.

In September 1884, James Lougheed married Belle Clarke Hardisty, eldest daughter of William Hardisty, Chief Factor of the Hudson's Bay Company. They prospered in the new town. Lougheed's practice grew. He formed a partnership with R. B. Bennett under the name of Lougheed, Bennett, McLaws, and Company. When that company was dissolved, he headed the law firm of Lougheed, McLaws, Sinclair, and Redman.

James Lougheed expressed his faith in the city of his adoption by buying real estate — all the land he could finance. Other property owners, frightened by the economic depression of the mid-1890's began to unload. Lougheed continued to buy and build, especially in the downtown area. The Lougheed Building, the Grand Theatre (at the time one of the finest in Canada), the Clarence, Norman, Edgar, and Douglas blocks (named after his four sons) — all were monuments to his foresight. At one time Lougheed was paying almost half of all the taxes in the city.

His distinction as a lawyer and his progressive attitude led to his appointment in 1889 to a seat in the Senate of the Dominion of Canada. He believed the Senate had a real and vital part to play in the life of the country. "Democracy is fine but it has its weaknesses," he commented. The Calgary Senator saw the Upper House as a "bulwark against the clamour and caprice of the Mob." For thirty-six years he sat in the Senate, and for the last nineteen years he was Conservative leader. When Robert Borden came to power in 1911, Senator Lougheed was brought into the Cabinet as Minister without Portfolio. In 1917, he was knighted, the first and last Alberta resident to be so distinguished.

A special news dispatch datelined February 21, 1918, reads as follows:

An Order-in-Council has been passed creating a new portfolio of the government to be known as the

Chapter 3   Frontier Politics

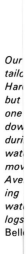

Our
tailo
Hard
but
one
dow
duri
wate
mov
Ave
ing
wate
logs
Bell

I consider that this town with the resources at our disposal has done wonders during the last twelve months. No person that has not seen it would believe it that a council of five men had framed By-laws, many of them very lengthy, which necessarily took up a great deal of time and consideration; sunk nine wells and put good pumps in each, and I say without hesitation that these wells are complete in every particular; procured for the town nine lots; and erected a hall that is a credit to the place, on them; and surmounted and overcome the most difficult things, such as removing mountains and making the rough places smooth on Stephen and Atlantic Avenues. Surely it must have taken great faith in the people of Calgary to do all this but the fact is apparent all the same.

From George Murdoch's Notes and Journals, *circa 1886.*

Calgary 1883

In spite of strong lobbying on the part of eastside interests to keep the business section where it was, the CPR had no difficulty in auctioning off its westside lots.

February and March of 1884 found most of the denizens of Calgary's tent city dragging their various establishments across the frozen Elbow to the west side. William Bannerman was one of the first to go with his flour and feed store. As he was postmaster, his decision was influential in persuading others. Bain Brothers moved their huge livery stable and also lent a hand to twenty or so other firms that wanted to move.

By March of '85 there were 248 buildings, most of them strung along the two main streets of the town, Stephen Avenue (now Eighth Avenue) and Atlantic Avenue (Ninth Avenue). The town had been incorporated, having over a thousand citizens, and boasted a newly elected council. George Murdoch was mayor. As yet there were no sidewalks or telephone poles, but the residents were confident enough in the future of Calgary to publish an elaborate promotional booklet containing optimistic descriptions of the town and a directory of its businessmen. This was *Calgary, Alberta: Her Industries and Resources* by Burns and Elliott. Many of the businesses portrayed in snapshots of the period carried bold and confident advertisements in this publication. The little wooden village, humble as it was, was here to stay.

96

GRAND CENTRAL HOTEL,

(Opposite C.P.R. Freight Warehouse),

ATLANTIC AVENUE,

CALGARY, ALBERTA.

———

THIS WELL-KNOWN HOSTLERY HAS RECENTLY BEEN

REFITTED THROUGHOUT

AND GREATLY IMPROVED.

—

First-Class Accommodation

FURNISHED.

—

THE BAR IS SUPPLIED WITH THE BEST

Beers, Porters & Fancy Drinks

——AND WITH THE——

CHOICEST BRANDS OF CIGARS.

—

Livery and Stable

IN CONNECTION WITH THE HOTEL

—

HUGH S. McLEOD, Proprietor.

BAIN BROS.,
Sale, Feed and Livery Stables
ADJOINING GRAND CENTRAL HOTEL,
CALGARY, ALBERTA.

———

☞ ALL KINDS OF RIGS FURNISHED. ☜

Traders and Explorers furnished with outfits at MODERATE RATES.

Calgary in 1886.

Murdoch's Town

Minutes of the First Council Meeting

Boynton Hall, December 4, 1884.

The first meeting of the Council of The Corporation of the Municipality of the Town of Calgary as called by Mr. Elliott, Returning Officer, assembled at ten o'clock A.M. when the following elected members presented their certificates and Oaths of Office to the aforesaid Returning Officer, viz:- George Murdoch, Mayor and Councillors S. J. Clarke, N. J. Lindsay, M.D., and J. H. Millward.

The Council now called to order by the Mayor - Present Councillors Clarke, Lindsay and Millward.

Moved by Councillor Millward, seconded by Dr. Lindsay that the Council adjourn until eight o'clock P.M. to meet at the Hall in rear of Beaudoin and Clarke's Saloon. Carried.

Eight o'clock P.M.

The Council met pursuant to adjournment. The Returning Officer, being present, stated that he had received Mr. Hogg's papers and they were correct.

Moved by Dr. Lindsay, seconded by Mr. Hogg that we now receive applications for the Clerkship. Carried.

Moved by Mr. Hogg, seconded by Dr. Lindsay, that Thomas T. A. Boyes be appointed Town Clerk. Carried.

Moved by Dr. Lindsay, seconded by Mr. Hogg, that this Council act as a committee of the whole to draft By-laws for the governing of the said Council, together with such other By-law or By-Laws as may be, for the time, thought necessary. Carried.

Moved by Mr. Millward, seconded by Mr. Hogg, that Councillors Lindsay, Hogg and Clarke be a Committee to make arrangements for a Hall or place of meeting for the Council, and report. Carried.

Moved by Mr. Millward, seconded by Mr. Hogg, that this Council meet once a week, and further, that we meet on Friday evening at eight o'clock p.m. Carried.

Moved by Mr. Hogg, seconded by Mr. Clarke, that Councillor Millward be a committee of one to design a Corporate Seal for this Municipality, and report. Carried.

Above and *Opposite:* Councillor's advertisements. *Below:* Calgary's First Council, 1884. *From Left to Right, Standing:* S. J. Hogg, Councillor; J. Campbell, Assessor; H. Bleeker, Solicitor; Dr. Lindsay, Councillor; J. H. Millward, Councillor; S. J. Clarke, Councillor; J. S. Ingram, Chief of Police; J. S. Douglas, Collector; I. S. Freeze, School Trustee; *Sitting:* George Murdoch, Mayor; C. Sparrow, Treasurer; T. T. A. Boys, Clerk.

The First Mayor

George Murdoch was elected Calgary's first mayor in December 1884. His first year of office was a stormy one, as was only to be expected in a town of such mixed and individualistic personalities. Everyone wanted a say in the running of things and was ready to actively back his own opinion. Murdoch boldly faced the melee, stated the duties of his office as he saw them: "Preside, preserve order, enforce the rules," and mixed in.

His notes and memoranda give brief and tantalizing hints of the juicy battles he engaged in, and also reveal an engagingly humorous view of himself. The following are random selections:

Some said the Masons were running the town, others that the Mayor was from sad experience. I have to acknowledge the latter charge.

One said the Mayor runs the town, others that I wink at whiskie business. Plenty to do without taking on myself to turn Policeman.

When we dug the wells some found fault as they did not want them on account of water men.

Byers served papers ordering us to stop grading street in front of his place. The more one tries to benefit the more opposition you meet.

Our hall is nearly completed and it is a credit not a shack as Mr. ------------------ stated in his letter of protest.

Great tales by some who said that one councillor had promised them his support and then went back on them after the election.

Sept. 22   Meeting of Rate payers at Town Hall who ratified our action in the [Fire] Engine. I went for Grant on his chronic opposition.

Sept. 23rd   Grant threatened to horsewhip me.

When railroad arrived our town was as a newly discovered inhabited island on a landless oasis, on a desolate desert, all towns along the line having been made by the railroad with this exception. Other towns pay their Mayor.

Then I was branded as a bad man by the same outfit a libertine and so forth because I was seen talking to half-breeds and Indians both male and female. Why, I always have been on good terms with both, and why should I cease speaking to either just because some busybodies, who have not good sense enough to remember they are not in an Eastern village, choose to set their tongues wagging. Why, I make a business of being on more friendly terms with the natives than usual, and they should have done the same.

School trustees elected by a slant. A hard time in the Council; half my time spent in keeping my colleagues in humour.

Fined Prettis twenty dollars for kicking up a fuss in lockup Saturday night. Also six boys for throwing dice for money. Those who have been chronic gamblers have found no time to attend to any citizen meeting.

The article in the leader shows how little some people understand our people. They would find, were they in my position, that Alberta men are an independant and non-subserviant lot who feel that they are all equal.

Among other things Murdoch also served for a time as Justice of the Peace. His summary of that office shows the fondness and concern he felt for his chosen town:

While on the bench I have endeavoured to act impartially, and justly, but at the same time using as much lenience as I could possibly do, as I believe that Human feeling can be exercised even on the bench.

I have endeavoured (as in duty bound) to enforce the By-laws of the Municipality by fines or imprisonments, but the fines have been imposed moderately, and imprisonment has not occurred, except transient today. In cases that have come before me of contravention of the liquor act I have acted in the only possible way I could do, as a Fixture in this town; and, having the welfare of the place at heart, I have not imposed the heaviest fines on residents of this place, as that would be suicidal: the proceeds of the fine having to be sent out of the place, we would therefore be deprived of Just so much working capital. In cases of outsiders coming in to sell the stuff here and pack the proceeds off, I acted much more severely and gave them a full benefit.

As regards vagrants and idle characters I have tried to clear the place of them as soon as my attention was drawn to them, and I hold that, although a frontier town, we have nothing to be ashamed of.

Opposite and above: George Murdoch. *Overleaf:* The North-West Council, 1886, the governing body of the Territories.

LIEUT-GOV DEWDNEY AND MEMBERS OF NORTH WEST COUNC

Two Councils

For more than three months (December 23rd, 1885 to April 3rd, 1886) to all intents and purposes Calgary had two Councils, one duly elected by the citizens in accordance with procedures set out in the Ordinances of the North-West Territories, with George Murdoch mayor, and S.J. Clarke, J.H. Millward, N.J. Lindsay, M.D. and S.J. Hogg as aldermen; and the other with James Reilly as Mayor, and J. Bannerman, T. Soules, G. Grant, and A. Davidson the aldermen (these were citizens who had been defeated in the civic election). The second body was declared the legal Council by Stipendiary Magistrate Jeremiah Travis.

Let us review the chain of events leading up to the existence of the two Councils. James Lougheed gives a delightful and urbane account of Calgary's first election scandal:

In 1884 legislation was passed constituting what was known as a high Court of Justice for the Territories. That introduced a procedure much more pretentious than formerly obtained. Colonel Macleod who previously was only Stipendiary Magistrate in Alberta, presided over the Court at Fort Macleod while Jeremiah Travis, of New Brunswick, was appointed Stipendiary Magistrate for the Calgary District. At this time Calgary's ambitions demanded a municipal council. There were two factions in the town at the time both possessing a good deal of activity, which manifested itself in the municipal election which then took place. George Murdoch headed the mayorality ticket for the one faction while James Reilly headed the other. The Murdoch ticket was elected and proceeded to administer the municipal government of the town. The Reilly ticket took exception to the many irregularities in the election and filed a petition contesting the right of the Murdoch ticket to assume office. The case was tried before Stipendiary Magistrate Travis: he voided the election of the Murdoch Council and declared elected the Reilly Council. The Murdoch Council refused to be thus summarily wiped out and proceeded, notwithstanding the judgement of the court, to discharge the duties of a Council. The Reilly Council at once entered upon office and proceeded to also govern the town. Calgary was thus in the analogous position of having two municipal councils administering its affairs, viz the Murdoch Council and the Reilly Council. The municipal machinery as to police, assessment, and all other branches of municipal duty was duplicated; both councils were contracting financial

Hugh St. Quentin Cayley *(above)*, and James Reilly *(below)* as sketched by John Innis, cartoonist for the Calgary *Herald.*

obligations and imposing their will on the community. Thus dual municipal machinery was for a time in full operation.

Finally the executive of the North-West Territories saw the necessity for intervening and legislation was introduced at the following session of the legislature to straighten out the tangle. A new election was held and Calgary settled down to one Council and from that time to the present the city has been fully impressed with the fact that one Council is quite sufficient for all purposes.

Calgary having thus started to grow up cast off its swaddling clothes and the old-timer of 1883 and 1884 felt that he had given sufficient impetus to its growth to throw upon the tenderfoot, who afterwards would come in, a share of the responsibility of making Calgary the cosmopolitan city which it is today.

For the first ten years, the North-West Mounted Police were responsible for law enforcement in Calgary. In this they were aided by a number of Justices of the Peace: Colonel Herchimer, Major Dowling, Captain Antrous, Major Walker, Thomas Burns, George Murdoch, Richard Hardisty, T. A. Maclean, and Joseph H. Millward. As the town grew it became evident that the Police and the Justices of the Peace did not have the authority to deal with the increasing number of crimes committed in the pioneer settlement. In his diary, Mayor George Murdoch says "Plenty to do without taking on myself to turn policeman." Representation was made to the Federal Government requesting the appointment of a Stipendiary Magistrate. On July 29th, 1885, City Fathers were advised that Jeremiah Travis, a native of New Brunswick, a stranger to life in the Territories and unfamiliar with "western justice", had been appointed to the position on the bench. Travis was furthermore a strict teetotaler and from his arrival in Calgary on September 3rd, 1885 enforced the liquor laws of the Territories with a rigidity and determination that dismayed the easy-going Calgarians.

Hugh St. Quentin Cayley, the editor of the Calgary *Herald,* and a lawyer by profession, wrote a number of editorials to express contempt for the appointment. Travis dismissed Cayley from his position as Clerk of the District Court; charged him with contempt; and ruled that he must apologize, publish his apology in his newspaper, present the Court with twenty-five copies, and pay one hundred dollars court costs "before Tuesday morning." Cayley, believing in his duty to the community, his right to resist injustices, and the freedom of the press, did not apologize. The Magistrate then fined Cayley five hundred dollars or, in default, a jail term of three months plus a fine of two hundred dollars. On the appointed day, January 5th, 1886, Calgarians formed a procession headed by a brass band and, stopping at the saloons en route, escorted the editor to the guard room (there was no jail) in the Police barracks.

In the meantime, Travis had already encountered another prominent Calgary citizen. Alderman S. J. Clarke was sentenced to jail for six months for interfering with the NWMP in pursuit of their duty. Clarke (according to *Calgary, Alberta)*, was the "proprietor of the Castle Mountain Billiard Hall — one of the most popular resorts in the Town . . . . (with) two Brunswick-Balk billiard tables and a bar with the best temperance drinks in the North-West and the choicest cigars and tobaccos." The account continues, "Mr. Clarke is esteemed among oldtimers. He was six years with the NWMP, having been stationed at Fort Walsh, Fort Macleod, and Calgary. He is one of the most devoted friends of the town and he has proved his confidence by actual works." Clarke was elected councillor in 1884. According to a record kept at the time, two men entered Clarke's saloon to conduct "a search". The alderman asked to see their search warrant, and when one was not produced, ordered them out, allegedly having used force to back up his order. The ejected men returned with the Police and arrested him for "resisting". When Clarke appeared before Judge Travis, Mayor Murdoch gave evidence of good character. Nevertheless he was sentenced to six months, hard labour.

All hell broke loose. Citizens held a protest meeting; speaker after speaker denounced the conviction and the severity of the sentence. Ed Bleeker, the Town Lawyer, who had publicly expressed his opinions, was warned that he too might be sent to jail. At a second indignation meeting, held in Boynton Hall, it was agreed to raise two hundred dollars to send a deputation to Ottawa to plead for Clarke's release. By this time even the most conservative of Calgary's citizens were ready to agree with an observation that appeared in an Eastern magazine: "The Magistrate may be within his rights, but it looks as if there is not room enough in one town for him and the people of Calgary."

The Town Council passed a Resolution, for the purpose of record,

Above: Councillor S. J. Clarke, 1884. *Below:* Constable S. J. Clarke in plainsman costume, 1876.

That this Council views with regret the decision of Stipendiary Magistrate Travis insofar as he has passed a very severe and arbitrary sentence on one of our citizens who is a member of this Council Board. Our reason for knowing as we do that he acted on principle as Councillor of this municipality and considered it his duty to take a stand, so as to make a test case of the matter, and have a final decision as to whether or not Mounted Police have the right to force their way into private houses and business places of citizens in this town, without a search warrant or even their badge of office, which is their uniform. It is therefore resolved that in the opinion of this Council the sentence passed is very unjust, considering the fact the assault was simply a technical one and purely to test the law.

A sum of five hundred dollars was subscribed, and a delegation headed by Mayor Murdoch left for Ottawa on December 5th, 1885, to protest this judicial autocracy.

On returning to Calgary on December 20th, the Mayor was met with more trouble. "Things in great muddle in civic affairs," he wrote in his diary. James Reilly a partner in the Royal Hotel and the man whom he had defeated in that month's election, laid an information stating that the Court of Revision had withdrawn the authority of the Mayor, and Council had in fact added names of non-property-owners to the voters' list; the petition therefore prayed that George Murdoch should be declared ineligible to take his seat as Mayor and James Reilly should be declared elected by certificate of the court.

In his desire to "run the town", Magistrate Travis, after hearing the evidence (Murdoch was not in town when the voters' list was compiled), ruled to amend the returning officer's statement, declared "James Reilly duly elected as Mayor; and Soules, Bannerman, Grant and Davidson as Councillors," imposed a fine of two hundred dollars on the Mayor, and one hundred dollars on each of the aldermen and disqualified all five from holding public office for five years. If the bill of costs was not paid in a stipulated time (ten days), executions and attachments were threatened to enforce payment.

Mayor Murdoch defaulted and a levy of distress was made on the goods in his harness shop by the Sheriff, J. G. Fitzgerald. When the authorities realized the trifling amount of their claim against Murdoch's estate, the auction sale was stopped. The Calgary *Herald* on February 6th, 1886, announced: "The Auction Sale of

Opposite: Randolph Bruce's caricature of Judge Jeremiah Travis, Calgary's first stipendiary magistrate. As far as the town was concerned he was the next best thing to a "hanging judge". In spite of his unpropitious beginning, he was to remain in Calgary, and live happily ever after, in the town he ruled so sternly.

Judge Davis

Mr. Murdoch's goods by the Sheriff to pay the fine Mr. Murdoch refuses to pay, has been postponed for two weeks."

From Murdoch's point of view the situation was most discouraging. One of his aldermen, S. J. Clarke was in jail; his best friend Hugh Cayley, the editor, was in jail; Town Council had been unseated by Magistrate Travis; and the merchandise in his harness shop had been seized by the sheriff for non-payment of a two-hundred-dollar fine.

Calgarians held mass meetings in protest. At a meeting held in Boynton Hall "jammed from end to end by angry citizens" it was announced that the Minister of Justice had ordered Hugh Cayley's release from jail with remission of fines. There were three cheers for the Minister, three cheers for George Murdoch, and three cheers for Hugh St. Quentin Cayley. The assembled crowd instructed the chairman to send the following telegram to the Minister: "At a mass meeting held at Calgary tonight it was unanimously resolved to tender you the thanks of the citizens and residents of Calgary for the prompt release of Mr. Cayley and the recognition thereby on the part of the Government of the liberties for which the people in this distant part of the world are struggling."

According to another version of the order for Cayley's release, the North-West Mounted Police received a telegram from Sir John A. Macdonald, Prime Minister of Canada, which read, "Let the little beggar go!"

The most urgent problem, however, was to decide which Mayor and Council constituted the legitimate government of Calgary. A firm of solicitors, F.H. Chrysler, was consulted, and in arbitration pronounced in favour of the council "elected by the people", with George Murdoch the mayor, as the only persons entitled to act as a council for the year 1886. Exasperated by that opinion, one of the members of the Reilly-appointed council purloined the Town Seal and documents. The Reilly faction tried to convene a meeting on February 6th, 1886. Town Clerk Boys refused to cooperate.

Reilly did not give up in his efforts to administer the town, however. In the city documents file there are two completely different copies of "By-law Number Ten". The first, dated February 7, 1885, and signed by Mayor Murdoch, reads as follows:

Item number eight of the minutes of the first meeting of the town council held on December 4th, 1884, at the hall in the rear of Beaudoin and Clarke's Saloon, reads as follows: "Moved by Mr. Hogg, seconded by Mr. Clarke, that Councillor Millward be a Committee of One to design a corporate seal for the Municipality and report." The motion was carried and duly signed. At the next council meeting a week later, "Councillor Millward, Committee of One appointed to prepare an appropriate design of a Seal for the Corporation, submitted several designs . . . . and design No. 2 (was) adopted as a design for the Seal of the Corporation of the Municipality of the Town of Calgary." The result is reproduced on the opposite page.

A By-Law to create the office of Treasurer for the Municipality of the Town of Calgary and prescribing the duties of such office.

The Mayor and Councillors of the Muncipality of the Town of Calgary in Council assembled, enact as follows:

1.   There shall be appointed a Treasurer for the Municipality of the Town of Calgary, a Treasurer who shall discharge the duties of his office as laid down in Section 115 and Section 123, both inclusive, of Ordinance Number 4 of 1884 - and as laid down in Section 80 of By-Law Number I of this Municipality.
2.   The Treasurer shall give as security for the faithful performance of his duties, the Guarantee, Bond, Covenant or Policy of Guarantee of any Incorporated or Joint Stock Company of the Dominion of Canada empowered to grant the same, for the integrity and faithful accounting of public affairs, as the Mayor and Council shall approve, in such sum as the Mayor and Council shall by resolution from time to time fix upon, before entering upon the duties of his office.
3.   There shall be paid to the said Treasurer for discharging the duties aforesaid, such percentage upon the amount of money that will pass through his hands in any one year, as the Mayor and Council shall decide upon after the completion of the revised Assessment Roll.

This By-Law shall come into force and effect immediately after the passing thereof.

Done and Passed in Council at the Town of Calgary, this Seventh day of February, in the year of our Lord One Thousand Eight Hundred and Eighty-Five.

(Signed Geo. Murdoch, Mayor)
Thos. T. A. Boys, Town Clerk

Affixed to the by-law was the Town Seal, "The Corporation of the Municipality Town of Calgary Incorporated November 1884" that featured an Indian with a lance in his left hand riding a charging pony.

Reilly, evidently, saw fit to reappoint this by-law and affix it with his own seal. His version specifically appoints C. Sparrow as treasurer, who was already treasurer for the Murdoch Council. It is possible that Reilly hoped that by doing this he would gain access to the civic books and town funds. The second By-law Number Ten, dated March 24, 1886, reads as follows:

A By-Law to appoint a Treasurer for the Municipality of the Town of Calgary.

Whereas it is necessary to appoint a Treasurer for the Municipality of the Town of Calgary,

Therefore the Mayor and Council of the Municipality of the Town of Calgary in Council assembled enact as follows:

I.   That C. Sparrow be appointed Treasurer for the said Municipality.

II.   The duties of the Treasurer shall be those prescribed by ordinance or by By-Law of this Municipality.

III.   This By-Law shall come into effect immediately after the passing of this By-Law.

Done and passed Council this Twenty-fourth day of March, in the year of our Lord One Thousand Eight Hundred and Eighty-Six in the Municipality of the Town of Calgary.

(Signed)   James Reilly, Mayor
G. E. Grogan (?) Clerk

The rather ramshackle building above is reputed to be Calgary's first city hall. The first council actually met in a variety of places — Boynton Hall, Clarke's saloon, wherever they could find the space. *Opposite:* Beaudwin and Clarke's saloon, the Castle Mountain Billiard Hall, the year after it was moved over from the east side. It was located at Stephen Avenue and Drinkwater Street, and was replaced a few years later by the Queen's Hotel. *Right:* Reilly's variation on the town seal. It has been suggested that the symbol employed in this seal gave Calgary its name of "Cow Town".

Affixed to *this* version of the by-law was the Town Seal, "Municipal Corporation, Town of Calgary, Alberta, 1886" that featured a placid range cow.

That Sparrow was not about to join forces with Reilly despite the "second" By-law Number Ten is suggested by the following satirical article on "The Limekiln Club" that appeared in the *Herald* at that time. (By word of explanation of the term "Limekiln Club", Reilly and his Council were holding fort in a hen coop. Calgary of 1886 probably had little to offer in the way of meeting places — Mayor Murdoch was attempting to administer civic business from Clarke's saloon.)

The Limekiln Club has appointed Mr. Player Auditor
for Calgary, and that gentleman has been having a
parrot-and-monkey time of it with the Town Treasurer.
The other day he appeared before Mr. Sparrow with a
Seal which had apparently been made by drawing a
line around an ink bottle on a white sheet of paper and
putting a hen to roost in the enclosure. Armed with this,
Mr. Player demanded the Civic Books. "This," said Mr.
Sparrow, gazing at the seal curiously, "is not the Seal
I have been accustomed to. I cannot give up the Books
to you, as you have not entered into heavy bonds for
their safekeeping as I have. More than that," he
continued, rubbing his chin, "the Limekiln Club seems
to have abolished me and all the other By-Laws and in
that case I suppose you would not now consider me the
Steward of the Corporation, so I do not know what you
are giving orders to me for. I think," pursued the Town
Treasurer, gazing again at the Seal, "that this Seal is a
forgery; can you give me the name of the forger,
because I think he ought to be arrested in the interests

of morality. After all, the Limekiln Club don't appear to be very smart. Now if they had appointed another Town Treasurer, under bonds, there might have been some show in asking me to hand him the Books, but as it is - well, well, boys will be boys! Good Morning!"

We understand Mr. Player is going to send in a large bill to the Limekiln Club for paying sixteen wild goose visits to Mr. Sparrow according to the instructions of the Club.

The situation was in deadlock. The stalemate continued for some time and very little town business was executed.

The following note, handwritten and signed by Town Clerk Thomas T. A. Boys, appears in the Municipality of Calgary Council Minute Book Number One, dated April 3rd, 1886: "During the late legal troubles in which the Mayor and Council of the Corporation of the Town of Calgary, who were duly elected for the year 1886, have been involved, no legal quorum has been able to meet for the transaction of business since the 23rd day of December, 1885 until the 3rd day of April, 1886."

At last Judge Taylor of Winnipeg was appointed to examine the differences of opinion between the citizens of Calgary and Judge Travis; his findings resulted in the release of Alderman Clarke from jail and the replacement of the Stipendiary Magistrate by Judge Rouleau of Battleford.

Then the Council of the Territories authorized a special civic election to end the deadlock. A new slate of candidates was submitted to the electorate. Exhorted by the slogan "The Resurrection of the Missing Seal and Municipal Documents", the taxpayers thronged to the polls to exercise their franchise. They elected a new mayor and a new slate of aldermen. G. C. King, the first policeman to set foot on Calgary soil, the manager of the I. G. Baker store, the town auditor and later the Postmaster, defeated John Lineham for the office of mayor, with a vote of 195 to 172. When the election was over, the missing documents were discovered. From that day to this the citizens of Calgary have taken an active interest in the government of their community.

And what of Travis? H. Frank Lawrence in *Early Days in the Chinook Belt* had this to say:

Our first Judge in Calgary was Judge Travis, in appearance and manner an early Victorian whom Thackeray would have enjoyed to make the most of. But what was of more importance, he brought with

Opposite: This improbable structure was Calgary's first official city hall. Erected in **1885**, it was shared by the police department, the fire brigade, and by a number of schoolchildren who attended classes upstairs. The lockup was downstairs at the back. This shot taken in 1900 shows the police department smartly if curiously arranged in front. It wasn't until the new sandstone city hall opened in 1911 that Calgary at last had a corporate building worthy of its city status.

him two charming daughters at a time when ladies were scarce indeed. Barter, an old-time rancher and a fine example of life with the appearance of an Irish gentleman, was a lucky winner but the pace was killing amongst so many eligible suitors. Gibb married the other; he forsook cattle for commerce and in those days judging by what we paid, profits in trade must have been enormous. Travis continued to live in Calgary administering his "considerable estate".

As for James Reilly, his Royal Hotel prospered; he continued to lend his talents to the development of his adopted community; he played an active part in persuading the CPR to build the stockyards — and he was elected mayor in 1891.

The editor of the Calgary *Herald*, Hugh St. Quentin Cayley, was one of two elected to represent Calgary on the Council of the North-West Territories. He was later elevated to the bench to become Judge H. S. Cayley of the Court of the Province of British Columbia.

The 1885 city hall was a dismal and uninviting place, not at all conducive to inspired government. When the first firehall was built *(Below)* in 1887, the town council was so impressed with its fittings and amenities they immediately moved in. Objecting to this the fire brigade resigned en masse and it was some time before tempers cooled and everyone was reinstated. *Right:* Workers take a break in their construction of the new city hall.

"Cappy" Smart, Calgary's famous smoke-eater, recalled this early municipal election for the Calgary Herald:

A Frontier Election

Even in its earliest days, Calgary took its political campaigns seriously. It mattered not whether the town dog catcher or a member of parliament was to be elected, the whole town threw its heart and soul into the proceedings; so when the municipal elections of 1887 were announced Calgary prepared to enjoy the campaign to the full. On December 27, 1887, the townspeople were called upon to nominate candidates for mayor and council. Six councillors, in addition to the mayor, were to be elected. E. P. Davis was named returning officer, and the town fire hall was selected as the returning officer's headquarters. Nominations were called for the hour of ten o'clock in the morning, and closed at noon.

Shortly after the office opened for nominations, it was soon seen that there would be no dearth of candidates. George Murdoch, who was Calgary's first mayor, was nominated. Mayor G. C. King was also nominated, as was Councillor A. E. Shelton. Nominations were closed with these three contestants in the field. A regular flock of citizens were nominated for the six councillor seats as follows: Sandy Allan, dry goods merchant; Jack McCallum, contractor; Charlie Watson, accountant; Howard Douglas, cartage and hauling; W. F. Orr, gentleman; Joe Maw, implement dealer; James Reilly, hotel owner; George Duncan, harness maker; Joseph Bannister, flour and feed merchant; Jim Martin, hardware; Thomas Ede, lawyer, Frank Dick, lumber merchant; Michael O'Keefe, contractor; Dr. N. J. Lafferty, physician and surgeon; Dr. J. D. Lafferty, physician and banker; I. S. Freeze, merchant; Henry Collins, dry goods; and James C. Linton, stationer.

Following receipt of nominations, a public meeting was called for two o'clock in the afternoon, and Calgarians closed up their places of business to attend to the more important business of electioneering. There wouldn't be another election for a year, and they wanted to make the most of it. The hall was soon packed to capacity, and the speeches started. It was a somewhat uproarious gathering, to say the least. The hecklers got oiled up before the meeting, and when some of them started to show signs of hoarseness they dropped back to the nearest saloon to oil up afresh, and back they would come again, ready for more fun. Some of the

115

remarks directed against some of the candidates
became so pointed and personal that several of them
hurriedly withdrew from the contest. The mayoralty
candidates stuck, however, and when Councillor Shelton
declared himself in favor of a license system in the
town, and lower taxation, he was loudly applauded.
Former Mayor Murdoch appealed on his former record
of service, and Mayor G. C. King contented himself
with asking for re-election on the grounds that he had
served the city faithfully for two years. The first
Tuesday in January was named as election day, and
from early morning until late at night Calgarians
trooped to the polls. There was no proportional
representation system of voting in those days. The
candidates that secured the greatest number of crosses
were elected, and when all the returns had been
counted it was found that Councillor Shelton had been
elected mayor, and the six councillors had been named
as follows: H. Collins, J. McCallum, W. F. Orr, Alex
Allan, J. C. Linton, and Howard Douglas. The election
was celebrated in real frontier style, and after the
festivities had died down the new council got down to
business. The first meeting was held on January 24,
1888, and at this meeting it was decided to call for
nominations for the position of town clerk, assessor,
tax collector, town solicitor, and chief of police. In these
days, the town officials were fired and re-appointed
annually.

Right: The completed City Hall in the daytime *(below)* and at night *(above)* during the Stampede week of 1912. *Above right:* The construction crew of Calgary's new city hall about 1908. Construction work on this building started in 1907. When it was finally completed it had cost a total of $300,000.

Chapter 4   The News

Seated at a small desk in the one and only room of the establishment, which was also the typesetting room, the press room and the washroom, and with exchange papers heaped around me, I surveyed the world from China to Peru. The main interest of that world was horse and cattle raising. The lords of the earth were ranch managers and the heroes were the cowboys. We were told, and we had the will to believe, that southern Alberta could not grow wheat: it must be forever the home of cattle and horses. The stock brands advertised in the Macleod Gazette fascinated the eyes of Armour, Braden, *and myself, such columns of them. We in Calgary were too far north. We could only obtain a dozen stock ads. The happy editor of the* Gazette *could sit back in his chair and rake in wealth from stock ads alone.*

Hugh St. Quentin Cayley, editor of the Calgary Herald, *1884-86.*

The First with the News

It was August 20, 1883, a cold rainy uncharitable sort of day in Calgary. Six days previously, the CPR had straddled the Elbow, shunted the first train across to the west side, and deposited a portable station, little more than a glorified boxcar, in the general environs of what is now Ninth Avenue and Second Street E. And somewhere near that station, according to George Murdoch's diary, two enterprising young men, undaunted by the rain and the cold, were erecting the tent that was to be the birthplace of Calgary's first newspaper. The men were Andrew H. Armour of Barrie, Ontario and Thomas B. Braden, a former school teacher from Peterborough.

The tent having been pitched to their satisfaction, Armour and Braden got down to business. Later they would reinforce the foundations of their flimsy establishment with mud and boards and erect a frame entranceway to diminish the draughts, but now their primary concern was to get out the news.

Their printing plant, which had arrived on the first freight train from the East to reach Calgary, was set up. Help was enlisted from the NWMP when it was found that two of its members had had previous typesetting experience. Constable John Taylor, who had learned typesetting in his father's business in Hamilton, and Constable Tom Clarke from Meaford, who had been in the newspaper business for some years in Ontario, helped bring out the first edition of the Calgary *Herald*, or as it was then so grandly called, the Calgary *Herald Mining and Ranche Advocate and General Advertiser*.

On August 31, just eleven days after setting up shop, Armour and Braden published issue number one. Its proportions were modest enough, four pages in all, but its aims were grand and its prospects no less so (or so the editors ardently hoped). The following is from the first editorial:

The duty, then, and pleasure of the Herald *will be, categorically speaking this:*

The collation of all news items of local interest.

The encouragement and support of all legitimate manufacturing and commercial enterprises.

The publication of all agricultural, ranching, and mining particulars.

The encouragement of all measures, religious and moral, intended for the welfare of the community.

The exposure of all species of vice and immorality that come to our knowledge.

Opposite: The NWMP constable in this picture is Thomas Clarke, who helped typeset the first edition of the Calgary *Herald*. He is flanked by Andrew M. Armour on the left, and Thomas B. Braden. They are standing with an unidentified friend in front of the *Herald's* first office.

Left: The Calgary House was advertised on the back page of the first *Herald (overleaf).* It also was treated to a favourable writeup on page one. Built during CPR construction by Constable Tim Dunne of the NWMP it did not survive the townsite's move to the west side. It closed down soon after.

THE CALGARY HERALD.

MINING AND RANCHE ADVOCATE AND GENERAL ADVERTISER.

VOLUME 1.　　　　CALGARY, ALBERTA, FRIDAY, AUGUST 31, 1883　　　　NUMBER 1

LOCAL NEWS.

NEW STOCK.—I. G. Baker & Co. have just received 180 wood and coal stoves, which will be sold cheap.

POLICE HOSPITAL.—The hospital contains at present four patients, three civilians and one policeman.

C. P. CONSTRUCTION.—Tracklaying is being vigorously proceeded with by the C. P. R., about 10 miles west of Calgary.

FIRST ARRIVALS.—The first train of freight for Calgary, carried the plant of the CALGARY HERALD, and some goods for Winder & Co.

IN LIMBO.—The guard-room has but one occupant, an Indian named Cut Lip, who is serving his time for stabbing a white man last winter.

TROOP PHOTOGRAPHED.—Immediately after full dress parade, on Tuesday morning, the troop stationed here was photographed by Mr. Bingham.

ANTHRACITE COAL.—We have been shown some fine specimens of what has been pronounced "anthracite coal," lately brought from the mountains.

BIG DRIVE OF LOGS.—The Bow River Mills are now receiving a drive of about 8000 logs, and are sawing night and day to supply the wants of their customers.

PROSPECTORS.—Some of the prospectors have returned from the mountains, bringing fine specimens with them, and glowing accounts of what they have seen.

THE NAVVIES.—We have to congratulate Mr. C. W. Peterson, of the firm of Peterson & Peterson, Barristers of this place, on his success in securing peace over the C. P. R., for several hundred of Langdon, Shepherd & Co's men. It seems that when engaging, the men were promised passes back on the completion of the contract, but when the work was completed, and pay day came, these were refused and the men were lying here idle, without any shelter day or night for some time, and but for the clever management of the case by the above named gentlemen, might have caused serious embarrassment. Not the least pleasing feature of the affair, was the handsome fee received by Mr. Peterson.

TREATY MONEY.—The treaty money is to be paid to the Stony Indians, at Morley, to-morrow. The Sarcees receive theirs on the 10th and the Blackfeet on the 25th prox.

PRESBYTERIAN MISSION.—A meeting was recently held in the Hudson Bay store, for the appointment of Managers in connection with the above Mission, when the following gentlemen were appointed : Major Walker, Dr. Henderson, and Mr. Joseph McPherson. The management have adopted the envelope system for their weekly offering.

REGISTRAR DISTRICTS.—We understand that Alberta has been divided into two registration districts. One office will be established at Calgary, the other at Edmonton.

TRAIN SERVICE.—A passenger train now leaves Calgary, daily for the east, at 10.30 a.m., and one leaves Medicine Hat for Calgary, every morning at 3 a.m., arriving here about 3 p.m.

EXCURSION.—The Brandon Town Officials purpose visiting Calgary, in a few days. Mr. Egan has placed a sleeper at their disposal. Could not something be done towards giving them a public reception ?

FIRST ENGINE.—On the arrival of the first engine into Calgary, the hill sides were crowded with admiring spectators, many of whom had never seen one before, and others who had not been near a railway for eight or ten years.

ROYAL HOTEL.—Mr. Moulton has just closed his popular hotel for the season, owing to the fact that he could obtain no suitable building site, at present. We believe it is his intention to return to Calgary and erect a large hotel, when the town is surveyed. The outfit was sold at auction on Tuesday last, and owing to the successful manner in which Mr. T. S. Burns wielded the hammer, fancy figures were obtained.

GEOLOGICAL SURVEY.—Mr. J. H. Panton, geologist, of the Manitoba Historical and Scientific Society, spent a day in and about Calgary, and reports a very interesting field of study for men of his profession. He has promised to prepare a paper on his researches in this locality for THE HERALD, which we have no doubt will be hailed with interest by our readers. We hope also to be favored with a paper by the Botanist of the Society.

CALGARY HOUSE.—We have had the pleasure of inspecting the new hotel just completed by Dunne & Wright and find it a perfect model of taste and neatness. It contains a large comfortable parlour, and a number of bed-rooms, all handsomely carpeted and furnished in the best of style. The dining-room has accommodation for about 40 guests, and the reading room is well supplied with the latest papers. Messrs. Dunne & Wright are well and favorably known to the public, and we have no doubt they will receive the large share of public patronage, which they so justly merit.

SABBATH SERVICES.—Divine service is held at the Catholic Chapel every Sunday at 10.30 a.m. and 4.30 p.m.

PRESBYTERIAN SERVICE.—The service in connection with the Presbyterian Mission will be held in a tent near the Calgary House on Sunday next at 7 p.m.

CATHOLIC INDUSTRIAL SCHOOL.—Rev. Father La Combe is waiting for the specifications and forms of tenders from Lieut.-Governor Dewdney for the Indian Industrial School at High River. As soon as they arrive parties wishing to tender will be supplied with blank forms.

HUDSON BAY FORT.—The H. B. Fort, at Calgary, has lately been raised to the chief post of the district, from which the supplies for 5 posts in the Edmonton district, 6 in the Peace River district, and 1 in the Athabasca district will be forwarded.

THIEVES.—A number of petty thefts have lately been committed in the vicinity, but the smallest thing we have heard of, was the cutting and stealing of the ropes from the foot bridge across the Elbow. This is a matter of some importance, as strangers coming into town are very liable to get a cold bath gratuitously. We hope the ropes will soon be replaced.

METHODISTICAL.—We are pleased to see that the energetic Methodist missionary of this place, Rev. Mr. Turner, is always equal to the occasion. The hospital of the Mounted Police not being longer available, Mr. Turner has secured a tent, and made it comfortable, and will hold service therein next Sunday at 3 p.m. The tent is situated just east of the Hudson Bay store. There is some talk of securing an organ, and forming a choir.

HOUSE RAIDED.—Information was laid a few evenings since, at Police quarters, that a number of men were engaged in gambling in a certain house on the bank of the Elbow, accordingly Major Dowling, with a detachment of men, proceeded to the place in question and after entering, found eight or nine persons with cards and checks on the table, he arrested the parties and placed them in the guard-room. The next morning they were up for trial before Supt. McIlree, but as no direct evidence was forthcoming, they were discharged. Mr. Bleecker of Edmonton defended the prisoners.

A MURDEROUS ASSAULT.—On Sunday afternoon, about 3 o'clock, a telegram was received at the Police Barracks that a fracas had occurred at the end of the track, by which a man named Torrance had committed a murderous assault on another of the gang, knocking him down and kicking him about the head and face. Afterwards drawing a revolver, he "stood off" some men who interfered, and starting down the track, succeeded in gaining a dense bush. A detachment was sent up to keep guard, and see that he did not escape from the thicket, the night being too dark to search for him then. Sergt. Major Lake, with his men, proceeded at day-break next morning to scour the bush thoroughly, but unfortunately the man had effected his escape and has not since been heard of. The wounded man is progressing favourably.

the recipient, from the citizens of that town, of a gold-headed cane, and a well filled purse, and from the Masonic body, a Past Master's Jewel of gold, accompanied in each case by a very flattering address. The papers give Mr. Swan much credit for the zeal he has always displayed in advancing the best interests of the town, mentioning among other matters that he had a hand in running off the first paper printed by steam in that place—the Confederate. We may say that Mr. Swan arrived here in good health and just in time to render valuable assistance in setting up the first printing press in Calgary. From our personal knowledge of Mr. Swan, we think he is quite an acquisition to Calgary, and have no doubt he will put forth the same efforts to build up this place that he displayed in Mount Forest.

Mr E. H. Talbot, proprietor, and Mr. H. R. Hobart, editor, of the Railway Age, accompanied by their wives, and Miss Nellie Herrick, Secretary. Mr. John A. Frazer, R.C.A., Artist, paid Calgary a visit last week in their magnificent palatial car, they would require to lay in a stock of everything they required in the way of food, as nothing whatever could be grown in this cold climate, but imagine their surprise on receiving from the garden of the Mounted Police a liberal supply of fine vegetables. They intended remaining only for a day, but the beauty of the spot and the salubrity of the air induced them to prolong their visit from Wednesday till Saturday. Mr. Frazer visited the mountains and made sketches from which he intends to paint a picture to be exhibited at the Chicago Art Exhibition. The rest of the party remained in town, engaged in fishing and visiting the places of interest. Mr. Talbot informed us he purposes returning for the opening of the C.P.R. through British Columbia, when he expects to see Calgary a thriving city.

RAILWAY SMASH UP.

On Sunday evening about 8.30, Engine No. 80, C. P. R., left Calgary for the east drawing Mr. Ross's car, and a caboose, running about 20 miles per hour. On arriving at the 18th siding, through some one having meddled with the switch, they were turned off the main line, and run into a train of construction material. When the engineer found that they had been switched off, he whistled down brakes, but before the brakes could be reached by the brakemen, they struck heavily against the construction train, injuring more or less every one on board. A telegram was despatched to Calgary for medical aid, a car for the wounded, and a train to clear up the wreck.

The services of Dr. Lindsay were secured and accompanied by a Herald reporter, the train drew out for the scene of the catastrophe. On arriving it was found that Mr. Ross had received a contusion on the side of the head and a small cut over the eye. Brakeman E. Green had been crushed about the hips and was suffering severely. Another brakeman had a severe cut in the face, and the engineer and fireman some bruises about the face and head. After the wounds were dressed the patients were brought to Calgary and placed in the C. P. R. hospital.

We are pleased to learn that none of the injuries have proved at all serious—with the exception of the two brakemen, all the parties being able to be around the next day, and they will be out in a short time. The engine and a number of flats were thrown off the track and considerably damaged, and will have to be sent to Winnipeg for repairs. We cannot understand how any on board escaped.

Fergus Falls has an Enoch Arden case. His name is Arnott, and after a long absence from home he returned, to find his wife re-married. The wife chose to remain with husband No. 2, and Arnott was left out in the cold.

The Canadian artillery men have scored another success at Shoeburyness. The record of last year's team in the shifting ordnance competition was a great surprise, and this year's team has sustained the reputation gained then.

CALGARY.

...ove named town which, at ...resent time is creating so ...uch interest throughout the whole ...orth West, Ontario and England is ...tuated on a beautiful stretch of ...ottom land about six miles in length ...nd from one to three miles wi... ...nclosed on the north side by the Bo... River in a semi-circular form, and on the south by a range of hills from 100 to 150 feet in height.

It is divided into two parts by the Elbow River, which at its confluence with the Bow forms a number of beautiful islands well wooded, and admirably suitable for a park.

Both rivers are pure, clean and cold with pebbly beds and beaches, dotted with innumerable tree, and capable of supplying a waterpower for an unlimited number of mills and factories, while on the northside of the Bow another range of hills rises to about 200 feet from the bed of the river; and away to the west and southwest rise the Rockies in majestic grandeur, covered with everlasting snow, plainly visible to the naked eye, as though they were only a few miles distant.

The future of Calgary seems very bright indeed, viewed from several standpoints, any one of which is sufficient to confer on the happy possessor a position unexcelled in the North-West Territory

THE COMMERCIAL OUTLOOK.

Calgary has long been acknowledged as the great central point of the extensive fertile strip along the Rockies, extending from the Blackfoot reserve on the east, to the Mountains on the west, a distance of 200 miles, and an extent from north to south of scarcely less distance, but it will now assume a place of much more importance and become the greatest distributing point west of Winnipeg. As the base of operations for the C.P.R. for the next two or three years from which the supplies will be forwarded — as the point from which all merchandise for Edmonton on the North, 200 miles distant with all intervening points, (and through them the Peace River and Slave Lake districts.) to McLeod 100 miles on the south will be shipped, the immense supplies required for the miners' camps already filling the Mountains these together with the Indian supplies, and the goods required to meet the wants of the numerous settlers flocking to our district, will make it as we said before the greatest commercial centre west of Winnipeg.

THE MINING PROSPECTS.

Already the mines of the Rockies near the C. P. R. crossing are interesting the greatest and most experienced prospectors and capitalists of Canada and the United States, while several mining experts and engineers representing English Companies are at the present engaged in the mountains. The formation, we understand is identical with those of the richest mines of Montana, and every day rich leads are being discovered. Gold, silver and copper abounds, and the time is not far distant, when the eyes of the whole mining world will be directed to the mines of the North-West.

THE LUMBERING INTERESTS.

Residents of Ontario, whose towns have been built by the lumber trade, will be pleased to hear that in the Mountains, close to the railroad, large areas of fine timber exist. The supplies for the lumber camps can be brought in by rail. The logs when cut will be floated down the Bow River, the stream being so swift that a raft of logs descends from Morleyville to Calgary, a distance of 50 miles, in less than 10 hours. Major Walker has two very valuable timber limits, and has a large force of men operating in the woods and floating his logs here, where he has a large mill in operation. There are also large operators from Minneapolis, owning nine limits of 50 square miles each, at present in the mount-

...aim inspecting their claims, and who are prepared to begin work at once if the limits accord with their expectations, therefore we expect to be able ere long to announce to our readers, the commencement of some large mills on the Bow River.

THE FARMING INTERESTS.

There has been a good deal of speculation indulged in of late, as to whether this country produces all the necessary elements for a successful farming country. Tourists have been continually inquiring from us "what will the country produce? Do not summer frosts kill everything sown?" and all such questions, remarking at the same time that if it can be fully demonstrated that the surrounding country is fit for agricultural purposes the success of Calgary is beyond doubt only a question of a few short years; therefore in order that we might give our readers a true and reliable account of the farming prospects we determined to see for ourselves, and accordingly in company with some other gentlemen procured a rig and proceeded to visit some of the farms in the vicinity. The first place we drew up at was Mr. Glen's on Fish Creek about eight miles south, on the Fort McLeod trail, and found a fine, well cultivated farm with a comfortable 1½ storey house, out-buildings, and farm-yard which would compete favorably with many of the oldest settlements of Ontario. After inspecting the buildings, we repaired to the garden and was surprised and delighted with a view of the best vegetable garden it has ever been our privilege to inspect, of about 14 acres in extent, and containing potatoes, cabbage, cauliflower, turnips, carrots, beets, parsnips, and corn, all in the highest state of cultivation. On asking him, if the summer frosts affected anything in his garden, the reply was "look and see if you can find any trace of it," we looked but could find none, and, although this was the second week of August, Mr. Glen had been using garden produce for nearly a month. We brought home some samples, and after trying them can testify as to their excellent qualities.

Mr. Glen has also about 32 acres of Oats, 2 acres of Wheat and 5 acres of Barley, all of which notwithstanding the dry season, will compare favorably with the average crop of the best parts of Ontario.

We next visited the farm of Mr. James Vortier also on Fish Creek, and found about 40 acres under cultivation, consisting of Oats 27 acres, Barley 10 acres, and wheat 3½ acres. On inquiring why coarse grains were raised instead of wheat, we were informed that heretofore they had no market for wheat nor could they get it ground as there was no grist mill in the vicinity, therefore they raised coarse grains and potatoes, which sold readily at from 4 to 10 cents per lb., and bought their flour at from $15 to $25 per sack, of 96 lbs. We also inquired the yield per acre, of the different grains, and found that it was no uncommon thing for 70 to 75 bushels per acre, on land that had been broken the preceding year, while on spring breaking 40 to 50 was the usual yield. As to potatoes, Mr. Vortier informed us that last year he had on 1 acre under crop, that he used from it for his own table from the time the new potatoes came in till the fall, and after keeping enough for his winter supply he sold 11,000 lbs. at 4 cts. per lb., thus realizing $440 from his 1 acre, after keeping his years supply. This is a record we think hard to beat, in any country, but if any one can beat it we would certainly like to hear from him. The wheat we saw on those farms we candidly think will yield 25 to 30 bushels per acre. Messrs Glen and Vortier, informed us that other settlers on Pine Creek and vicinity viz: Messers Belconir, Campbell, Robb. Moss, Jacques Bros. and others, had crops equal, if not superior to their own and wished us very much to visit them; but our time

being limited we were obliged to defer the pleasure till a future occasion.

On our return we left the trail to see the surrounding country, and truly we find it impossible to give even an adequate description of the lovely rolling country over which we passed, thousands of acres just awaiting the hand of the settler to become the garden of the North-West. Before reaching Calgary we came upon the farm of Mr. S. Livingston, who has been 18 years in this country and is now devoting his energies to farming. We found a large farm of 640 acres, situated on the Elbow River about 3 miles from Calgary, enclosed by a wire fence, 5 feet high, well built, and capped with poles; with about 50 acres under cultivation, the crop consisting principally of Oats and Barley in equal quantities, averaging about 4 ft in height; and although Mr. Livingston assured us it had been but poorly put in from the want of proper implements, still in our judgment an average yield of 50 bushels per acre will be realized, while his root crops, of which he has about 2½ acres look equally well. Mr. L. has procured a self binder and is now busily engaged in harvesting. Samples of his grain will be on exhibition at out office.

On enquiring his previous success in farming he assured us that from 11 acres of oats, he had sold 950 bushels, an average of 86 bushels per acre, weighing 45 lbs to the bushel. With these facts before us we do not hesitate to assert that this vicinity with its ulimited supply of purest water in the world, its abundance of wood and coal, the geniality and salubrity of the climate render it one of the most desirable localities in the whole North-West Territory.

Space forbids us entering on the ranching interests this issue, but we purpose visiting the principal ranches in a short time, when we will be able to lay before our readers a full account of that industry.

MANITOBA HISTORICAL SOCIETY.

The Manitoba Historical Society of Winnipeg, sent a delegation to visit the Rocky Mountains, and report on the various items of interest seen on the route. The party consisted of the Rev. D. M. Gordon, the Rev Prof. Bryce, Messers T. C. L. Armstrong, R. E. W. Goodridge, W. H. Hugon, T. F. Stewart, and J. H. Panton, arrived here the other evening and started on their way to Padmore. The party succeeded in scaling one of the largest peaks of the Gap, and visited the beautiful falls of the Bow near Padmore. They attended Divine service with the Indians at Morleyville Mission, and were highly pleased with the comparative progress made by the Indians in civilization.

Quite a quantity of mineral geological and botanical specimens were collected including specimens of coal from the mines on the Bow. The party returned to Calgary, some of the members going south to Fort McLeod, while the remainder proceed to Winnipeg.

Armour and Braden also proclaimed their intention to uphold all the "rights and freedoms", and to remain free of all factions and parties.

Besides their editorial, there was also in that first issue a glowing article on Calgary and its prospects. They described its beauty of setting, its commercial outlook, the mining and lumbering potentials of the area, and the fertility of the surrounding farms. To illustrate the latter point they included detailed descriptions of the acreage and produce of John Glenn, Sam Livingston, and James Votier.

The rest of the paper was packed with local news and advertisements from its enterprising subscribers. G. C. King, I. S. Freeze, and Tim Dunne were among those first advertisers.

The first item of news was about the I. G. Baker & Co: "NEW STOCK — I. G. Baker & Co. have just received 180 wood and coal stoves which will be sold cheap." This piece of news was probably of primary interest to Calgarians that 31st day of August, 1883. The temperature that morning had dropped to forty degrees and the prospect of the long western winter ahead must have been alleviated somewhat by I. G. Baker & Co.'s announcement.

Prospecting news was always read with avid attention by the *Herald's* readers. The closest mining community to Calgary was Silver City at the foot of Castle Mountain. *Below:* A group of prospectors pose on the main street of the town. In 1883 it was a thriving centre, at least big enough and complex enough to require the services of a lawyer. Hugh St. Quentin Cayley *(opposite)* practised there for some months before becoming editor of the *Herald*.

Among the other items were included prospecting news; announcements of CPR schedules and facilities; notices of church services (the Catholics already boasted a chapel; the Presbyterians and Methodists still had to settle for tents); a favourable report on Calgary's first hotel; social and personal announcements; and an assortment of criminal offences — a house raiding, a theft (some uncharitable felon had stolen the ropes from the Elbow River bridge), and a "murderous assault".

The hot item of the day was a railway smashup that occurred just east of the town which was duly reported in great detail.

Armour and Braden continued as editors until December 1884 when they were succeeded by Hugh St. Quentin Cayley. Cayley had come to Calgary in 1883, journeyed west to Silver City at Castle Mountain, and hung up his lawyer's shingle. Returning to Calgary he accepted a job as a clerk in the Dominion Land Titles office. A few months later he associated himself with the *Herald*; he wrote the editorials, Braden collected news and advertisements, and Armour set type.

At the time Cayley assumed charge of the *Herald* it was still very much a ranching-oriented paper, and Cayley and his associates identified very strongly with the ranching interests. "I think we resented the illicit entries of settlers into the stock districts. They would fence in the springs and interfere with the range." But Cayley was also a strong advocate of western interests in general, and took a dim view of Easterners who tried to legislate and dominate the West. "Outside the stock interests we considered deeply the mysterious ways of the Department of the Interior in Ottawa. The late deputy minister A. M. Burgess never knew how largely he loomed, a portentous figure in the eyes of the West. He had, of course, the Eastern view that the East had bought the West and that we pioneers (we were not then represented in parliament) did not know what was good for us. Perhaps we did not.

Perhaps Westerners did not know what was good for them. Nevertheless, Cayley was always ready to fight for their opinions and rights in his editorials.

The year eighteen eighty-four was notable for the *Herald* in that it marked the launching of its first competitor, the *Nor'Wester*, published by George B. Elliott. Unfortunately the files of this newspaper have disappeared and we have no record of his side of the battle. But if his booklet *Calgary, Alberta* is any indication, Elliott was a fluent and persuasive journalist and no mean adversary. Certainly he evoked intense and vituperative rivalry from Armour and Braden: "Let us whisper a word in your ear, Mr. Nor'Wester. We conduct business on business principles. We pay our hands every Saturday night. We do not get credit from the stores and compel the proprietors to take their pay in printing. We do not make the boast that the government will see us through and that the people of Calgary can go to . . . ."

From the time the *Nor'Wester* was launched, life was never dull for the men of the *Herald*. For example, when Elliott accused a *Herald* reporter of attending a private party without an invitation, he provoked a blast from the *Herald* which declared,

We are compelled to say that in purity of tone and freshness of information, the Nor'Wester *is not a mode to be imitated. We have never seen equalled, among all our exchanges, good, bad or indifferent, the bombast, egotism, and literary bravado characteristic of that paper. From the first appearance of that sheet, there have pervaded its columns the emanations of a newspaper pugilist - the* Nor'Wester *is falling far below the ideal of a true newspaper . . . . Abundant proof can be given of the untruthfulness of the statements. Henceforth it is our intention to allow the wailing and whining of the* Nor'Wester *to die upon the air . . . . We have no time for scanning the dictionary for spiteful epithets . . . . A nobler mission and a grander ideal is ours than seeking to imitate the style or pander to the wants of the inferior intellectual that characterizes the effusions of the prejudiced mind that have lately been in the columns of our contemporary.*

This was strong fodder for newspaper readers but not too strong for palates of the day; in fact it was quite the mode. The public became suspicious if editors did not whack each other mercilessly.

Before Braden and Armour relinquished editorial control to Cayley they threw a parting shot at editor Elliott. "We shall wrap ourselves in the mantle of honourable solidity, leave others to digest the obnoxious sentiments and disreputable remarks that may be made and pursue our course for the benefit of our readers and the community at large. Adieu *Nor'Wester* Adieu."

In the spring of 1885 an event occurred that was to have lasting consequences for the Calgary *Herald* — the second Riel Rebellion. Although the uprising never amounted to much more than a scare in Alberta, it underlined for Westerners their isolation and vulnerability, and they were anxious for up-to-the-minute

news of the happenings. Cayley responded with "Extras" that carried daily reports on the various battles. This experience with daily reporting convinced him that Calgary was ready for something more than a weekly newspaper. In his edition of July 4, 1885, he announced:

Today marks the first issue of a daily paper in Calgary. Slight as the proportions of the first daily are, they are not very much less than Winnipeg's first daily, and it is hoped they will presently be enlarged as the Winnipeg Free Press was enlarged within a few months of its inception.

We are aware that it is not generally admitted that Calgary can support a daily paper. It is a pity its citizens have so little faith in the future of the town as to suppose it can undertake anything without carrying it through. Calgary has undertaken much bigger jobs already than the issuing of a daily paper, and in spite of a good many howling prophets it is today in a better position financially than any town in the Territories.

We have the utmost confidence that a daily newspaper cannot only exist here, but be a success, and we have not the slightest doubt the town will welcome its appearance.

In 1886 Cayley left Calgary to practise law in B.C. where he had been elected to the bench as Judge of the Vancouver County Court. He left the *Herald*, but not before he had engaged in his memorable conflict with Jeremiah Travis. Bob Edwards and Everett Marshall commented on this conflict in their article of 1903, "The History of a Western Newspaper":

During the fall of 1885 Jeremiah Travis was appointed stipendiary magistrate of the Calgary district, and H. S. Cayley, editor of the Herald, *became clerk of the court.*

Some indiscreet articles about the stipendiary having appeared in the paper, Mr. Cayley was summoned before his worship who promptly sent him to jail. The Herald, *thus for a time being deprived of its editor, practically suspended publication, appearing intermittently and coming up for an occasional gasp like a codfish* in extremis.

Cayley's own comment on the stormy days of his editorship was as follows:

Calgary's second daily paper, the Calgary *Albertan*, began April 10, 1902. *Left:* William M. Davidson, its founder and publisher, a 1916 view of the Albertan office, and the paper's printing job shop in 1912. *Above:* Mrs. Davidson (nee Ethyl Haydon) added a woman's page to the *Albertan* in 1911, becoming Alberta's first woman's editor.

Music and the Drama

THE revised version of Shakespeare's "Julius Cæsar," which was rendered in the town hall on Monday evening last, was a decided success. The cast of characters was as follows:

CÆSAR—Mr. R-i-l-y.
BRUTUS—Messrs. K-n-g, C-s-h-ng, D-u-g-l-s, T-p-p, L-c-s and B-n-r-m-n.

This is not according to the accepted version of this play, but, it is the Calgary version.

Cæsar and the Brutus' wore the Roman toga, sandals and striped shirts (all made out of the leavings of decorations of the Barbecue) and were, as our illustration shows, most effectually disguised, with wigs, burnt cork, &c.

The tragedy opened with the usual proceedings of a Roman senate, applications being read for positions as ceuturion, town constable, &c., and was admirably sustained. Cæsar then made his address, after which, with one accord, the numerous Brutus' drew daggers, labelled " want of confidence," " yer can't fool us," " Come off," etc., and made a break for the august personage. The finale was most affecting; attacked on all sides, Cæsar stood, and when at last the cue came for the immortal words, " Et tu Brute ! Then *die*, Cæsar," he exclaimed with dignity, " Scat you

Brutes ! never say die, Jimmy"; the excitement was so intense that in the general stillness many a crystal tear was heard to fall with a thump on the pine carpet . When at last the players adjourned, it was decided to hold a meeting on Tuesday, in the Opera House, where, if those present didn't feel like doing any business, they would probably give a rendition of "Muldoon's Picnic. As I was not able to attend the latter, I cannot say how it came off.

Hoping I have not trespassed too much on your space,

Yours truly,

MARK ANTONY.

Above: The *Prairie Illustrated* was a weekly publication put out by Armour and Braden, 1890-91. The page above displays a sketch by Calgary artist John Innis. The cartoon to the left caricatures some of the town's campaigning politicians, among them James Reilly, G. C. King and W. H. Cushing.

I really forget now what we thought so oppressive, but I think that the extremely slow growth of our personal fortune irritated us. I look back on the fierce squabbles and incendiary talks of those days with the kindly eyes of sixty. I wonder now why we heathens raged so furiously together.

The fortunes of the *Herald* continued to experience very slow growth after Cayley. There was a succession of editors and a succession of different locations about the town. Finally, under the ownership of J. J. Young, the paper achieved a sort of stability. Edwards and Marshall, looking back in 1903, commented on Young and the status of the *Herald:*

Nothing could jar the faith of "J. J." in the Herald *in the future of Calgary. Handling this newspaper in the wake of so many fallen heroes was like playing leapfrog in a cemetery, but he hung on and "wrestled" with it undismayed. Success looked at him invitingly from inside the show window with her full price marked up — hard work; and he made the purchase at that figure.*

Floundering in a sea of hard times and nonplussed by a wind it was difficult to raise when wanted, it took a bold navigator to keep the ship off the rocks. In this case the captain had a faithful crew who stood by him year in and year out with a loyalty that was most gratefully recognised.

The locale of the Herald's *usefulness in those days was confined pretty well within the city limits; now it wields a power and influence second to none throughout the West. It is a far cry from the dogfights of '83 to the up-to-date telegraphic service of today, the infinite variety of local happenings and editorial comment adapted to a refined and cultivated people.*

A promotional layout for the *Herald* during the reign of J. J. Young.

130

The Herald.

CALGARY, ALBERTA.

CALGARY, MAY 23, 1891

Bob Edwards

A caricature of Bob Edwards sketched by Randolph Bruce in 1904, the year the Calgary *Eye Opener* was born.

If any Calgarian has become a legend it is Bob Edwards. Born and educated in Scotland, he served his apprenticeship in a newspaper office in Boulougne, France. Feeling the urge to travel, he emigrated to America, where he worked for a time on a Texas ranch. Life in the saddle was not satisfying, however, and hero Edwards moved on, ending up on a farm in the Wetaskiwin area. But to Edwards, the grandson of a famous Scottish publisher, the lure of printers' ink was irresistible, and after making the necessary arrangements, he launched his career as editor of the first newspaper to be published in any town between Calgary and Edmonton. Almost immediately he encountered disapproval. Reluctantly, he changed the name of his paper from the Wetaskiwin *Bottling Works* (it was sure to be a corker) to the Wetaskiwin *Free Lance*.

In spite of this concession the paper was not a success; plain and unvarnished reporting was not appreciated. Edwards was on the move again, first to Leduc and then to Strathcona on the south side of the Saskatchewan River. His plans to found a new paper, the Strathcona *Strathcolic*, again were subjected to criticism, and so it became the Alberta *Sun*. The lot of a small town editor was not easy. From Strathcona he went to Winnipeg to work for a daily. Not surprisingly, his free spirit did not lend itself to regular hours or conventional methods, and shortly afterwards he decided to visit his friend Jerry Boyce, owner of the Astoria Hotel in High River.

There, on March 4, 1901, the *Eye Opener* was born. The citizens of High River at first accepted this mild-mannered man who dressed conservatively and spoke with a cultured Scottish accent. Edwards wrote that "High River is the greatest place on the Line . . . . Any town that pays the Preacher and supports the Editor is so close to heaven that a man can hardly sleep for the singing of angels." However, the carefree spirit of the range was not ready to accept the editorials which showed the other Edwards — a ruthless, hard-hitting extrovert conducting a fearless war against pretentious or highly placed individuals.

In 1904 Edwards and his *Eye Opener* moved to Calgary, where he became a potent force in the city's life. The popular, widely read and often quoted newspaper was published "now and then" between 1904 and 1922. Its originality, verve, and innuendo rather than journalistic content, attracted 33,000 subscribers — the largest circulation of any paper west of Winnipeg. In those days newspaper men had to eschew fancy and stick to the facts. Bob Edwards never allowed accepted guidelines to interfere with getting his paper out. He ignored deadlines, scarcity of news, and advertising rates; he had no employees, no printing plant, and never kept receipts or accounts.

Edwards was tireless and amusing in his attack on phonies and stuffed shirts in every walk of life — social, political, and fraternal. One example concerns a real-estate shark who defrauded a waitress of her savings. Edwards forced a refund by threatening to disclose the slicker's name in the columns of his paper.

He could never resist the opportunity for a good line. Once, after finishing a piece of pie in one of the cafes, he remarked to the proprietor, Roy Beavers, "Roy, there is one cook in this restaurant who really knows his business - I want to congratulate you." Elated, Roy replied, "Well thank you Mr. Edwards, who is that?" The answer, "That is the son-of-a-gun who counted the raisins that went into the pie."

Nor could Edwards resist a practical joke. The story goes that a gramophone salesman persuaded the minister to allow him to demonstrate his machine as a substitute for the choir for one of his church services. The first record, "Hark the Herald Angels Sing", was well received. The second, "Just Because She Made Those Goo-Goo Eyes At Me" did not pass as a sacred song. The finger of suspicion was pointed at Edwards as guilty of slipping jazz records among the sacred recordings.

Edwards often used make-believe names and incidents in the *Eye Opener*. Calgarians could often recognize themselves or their neighbors in his fictions. They usually knew who was meant in Society Notes like the following:

Mrs. Alex Mugsy, one of our delightful Westend Chatelaines, has notified her friends that her usual Friday Musicale has been called off this week. Her husband, old man Mugsy, has been entertaining his own friends with a boozical for a change and is in an ugly mood.

Or

A delightful pink whisky was given Wednesday evening at the hostelry of the Honourable John Mosley, the eminent Conservative Leader. The evening was spent in games, progressive black-jack, the prizes being boozonnieres and charming cigars. An elegant time was

Eye-Opener Bob.

had. (In this case the name was not fictional. John Mosley was a popular Calgary hotelman.)

A staunch defender of the honest and sincere, he often skated on thin ice. His greatest protection against libel was the fear of ridicule which would be sure to descend on the outraged protagonist. The *Eye Opener* was a journal in which fact and fancy were inextricably mixed. For example, Edwards once wrote that the three biggest liars in Alberta were "Robert Chalmers, Gentleman; Honourable A. L. Sifton, Premier; and Bob Edwards, Editor." Premier Sifton threatened court action. Robert Chalmers offered to collaborate in joint action as he had also been slandered by Bob Edwards, Editor.

"Peter McGonigle" was another Edwards creation, his most famous fictional character. Stories of his exploits occurred again and again over the years. A gullible Toronto editor, taking the *Eye Opener* literally, wired the following McGonigle item to his paper in London England: "A banquet was tendered by the Calgary Board of Trade last week to Mr. McGonigle of Midnapore on the occasion of his release from the Edmonton Penitentiary where he spent some time living down a conviction for horse stealing. A number of prominent citizens were present, and songs, toasts, and speeches passed off with all the eclat possible on such short notice. Letters of regret were read from Lord Strathcona, Earl Grey, Premier Rutherford, J. S. Seagram, W.F. McLean, Rev. John McDougall, and others."

Joseph Seagram's letter of regret according to the *Eye Opener* stated, "Though unable to be with you in the flesh, my spirit is with you. Wishing McGonigle all luck in his next venture." Priceless advertising!

Lord Strathcona's was even better: "I regret exceedingly that I shall be unable to attend the McGonigle banquet, but my sympathies go out to your honoured guest. The name of McGonigle will ever stand high of emminent confiscators. Once, long ago, I myself came near achieving distinction in that direction when I performed some dexterous financing. In consequence, however, of stocks going up instead of down I wound up in the House of Lords."

Lord Strathcona was outraged and ready to sue. Cooler heads prevailed, however. Although reluctant to accept the explanation that McGonigle was an *Eye Opener* brainchild, Lord Strathcona understood and withdrew his suit.

Nothing escaped Edwards's attention and nothing was too sacred to attack. Of Paddy Nolan, the great

In the event of Calgary's member, R. B. Bennett, moving to England, it is understood that a movement will be put in motion to erect a statue to his memory in Central Park, in front of the Carnegie Library. As we old-time Calgarians, when old men and women, stroll through this park we will pause to admire the radiant features of R. B. and will try to remember what it was he used to say about this glorious heritage of ours and our duty to the generations yet to follow in peopling these

fertile something or other. Many men of future ages will stand before the statue and argue as to whether the subject of the sculptor received all the honor due him for bringing about confederation, quelling the Riel rebellion and building the C. P. R. Then some one wiser than the rest will speak up in a superior tone to inform the throng that Mr. Bennett was the man who drove Van Wart crazy. Then the throng will move away, marvelling greatly.

* * *

Standing on tiptoe in the crowd to get a good look at the Duke, our imagination gets very busy. All the time we are thinking, "That man passing before me was born of Queen Victoria and is the brother of the lamented King Edward the Seventh." What a fascinating link with the past!

* * *

Sir Sam Hughes expects to leave for England before the end of the month. Oh well! Ho hum! (Business of yawning.)

* * *

The death of Major Stanley Jones has deeply affected the Calgary community. Here was a man, every inch of him.

* * *

Even a non-military observer can see that the Russians fight better with cannon and rifles and ammunition than without these articles.

* * *

SOCIETY NOTES

Mrs. P. Q. Shinkleblister, 1201 Twenty-sixth avenue west, will receive this afternoon. She will be glad to receive anything, preferably something in the bottled goods line.

Mrs. J. B. Clinktwister, 2896 Twenty-eighth avenue east, will receive the first Thursday of every month, the second Tuesday of every week, the fourth Friday before the last Saturday, and the second last Wednesday before each Monday.

Mrs. P. B. McSquatulum, Parsnip Lodge, was the hostess at a charming pink whiskey last Wednesday. Mrs. McSquatulum was gowned in a garniture of red curtain tassels and looked very chic.

As the tea gown has become the fashionable attire at Mrs. Jawkleblotter's sumptuous residence on Thirty-Fourth avenue west, Mrs. Jawkleblotter will not receive until further notice.

Miss Jemima O'Squatty, one of the buds of last season at Airdrie, eloped last Friday with a gentleman who sings sentimental songs in a moving picture show. The many friends and admirers of Miss O'Squatty hope that this delightful contretemps will not necessitate her breaking off her engagement to Mr. J. B. Slopp, the popular real estate agent. Mr. Slopp's ad. may be seen on the fourth page.

Mrs. Peter Ashby de la Smashe has emerged from the kimona stage and will shortly be able to pour tea. It is a fine youngster, with a great pair of lungs.

Mr. Hugh W. Warwick, the popular promoter, has returned to town from Lethbridge, where he has been spending a delightful six months' holiday in jail.

Mrs. J. P. Shufflebuster gave one of her charming bridges at Tripe Court last Tuesday afternoon. Old Shufflebuster returned home earlier than usual with a partial jag on and had the game turned into poker. To the mortification of the hostess, he cleaned out the bunch.

Mrs. Spiffe entertained informally at the tea hour yesterday in honor of Mrs. Miffe, of Vancouver. Mrs. Biffe poured the tea.

Mr. Harold J. McWhinney was the guest of honor at a dinner party given by Mrs. Jabez Chortleberry, of Forty-ninth avenue. Mr. McWhinney, who has been taking the Keeley cure at Harrison, Hot Springs, was the recipient of many congratulations. The popular guest unfortunately broke out again before the evening was over and had to be carried home on a shutter.

Our old college chum, Lil' Arthur Sifton, also has his meeting and substantially the same motions are passed. Immediately the great Sifton railroad policy is sprung on an unsuspecting public, and thus the merry game goes on. Great pickins these days, boys. Everybody works for Bill and Dan.

* * *

Wake up, farmers of Saskatchewan and Alberta. Get wise! Turn 'em out! Turn 'em out! Turn 'em out!

* * *

The telephone number of The Eye Opener will be found in the Addenda of the new telephone book. Remember, the Addenda, not the appendix or the errata, but the addenda.

* * *

The wise guy who knows it all is usually the first to get stung.

* * *

A free hand and a fair field for Cuddy.

* * *

No, Gertrude, we cannot conscientiously recommend 10-year-old Scotch as a bust developer.

* * *

The palmists at the Fair were placed under arrest the first day by way of necessary hint that they were to cut out grafting on the credulous. On giving an undertaking to be careful if they couldn't be good, they were allowed to resume. They were a tough looking bunch.

* * *

It is a wonder that Chief Cuddy did not try to arrest Katherine Stinson while up in the air on a charge of having no visible support.

* * *

The movie actor has one great advantage. He can never hear the audience whisper "punk."

* * *

Mr. and Mrs. Alexander P. Harkness have returned from their honeymoon at Banff and taken up housekeeping in

the bridegroom's heavily mortgaged residence on Fifteenth Ave. W. Mrs. Harkness will receive at her home later on, as soon as she has got fairly sick of Alexander. Which won't be long.

* * *

criminal lawyer and close personal friend, who was often retained to keep him out of libel suits, Edwards wrote, "There is a famous lawyer here by the name of Paddy Nolan. All the best murderers go to him." Of the Calgary Exhibition, the town's pride and joy, he observed, "One of the most interesting features of the Calgary Fair is an exhibit of the seedless prunes raised in the vicinity of Okotoks."

The CPR, a sacred cow if ever there was one, came in for its share of the attacks. Edwards felt that the CPR was negligent in safety precautions at their railway crossings, and spoke out accordingly: "Not a life lost or a buggy smashed at the CPR crossing this week." Or, "Calgary's luck is in the ascent. No tragedy occurred this week at the CPR crossing at First Street West. This is fool's luck."

The Calgary *Eye Opener* was published on Saturday. Edwards, as Circulation Manager, took particular delight in counting out the papers for his news boys - the highest bidder or the one ordering the greatest number of papers was served first. It is estimated that about five hundred issues were published between 1904 and 1922.

Confusion resulting from contradictions in his behaviour and the editorials appearing in the *Eye Opener* can at least be partially explained. Edwards was a heavy drinker, but he supported the "drys" in their fight for prohibition. In 1921 he successfully campaigned for a seat in the Provincial Legislature. After months of silence he finally mustered enough courage to give his one and only speech; the subject: three and one-half percent beer.

Through satire, Bob Edwards exercised a profound discipline on citizens living in early Calgary. He is one of our legends. Many stories written by and about him still circulate. He can truly be called one of Canada's great humourists.

Right: The Calgary *Herald* circulation pony cart. *Below:* Newsies and dog gathered outside the *Herald* building.

* * *

Moved to pity at the sight of a small boy lugging a monstrous bundle of newspapers, a man stopped and asked: "Don't all those papers make you tired?"

"Nope," the little newsie replied cheerfully. "I can't read."

Chapter 5   Range Men

CODE OF THE RANGE

Be independent but always ready to help your neighbor.

Ask nothing of the government boys or you'll find yourself in the rat-race.

Feed the stranger and his hoss; and ask no questions.

Say little, talk soft and keep your eyes skinned.

Don't argue with the wagon boss. If he's wrong he'll find out.

*Don't stare on the brand on a **stranger's** hoss. But make a note.*

Deal with the other fellow's cattle as you would your own. Feed the stray, help the bogged. He's doing the same for you.

Don't stick a plough in the land — it's catching.

If paper and pencil aren't handy back up your word as you would your signature.

Women come in two breeds — the ones like your Mother, and the one behind the lace curtain. And you don't talk about either kind.

If ranching in Alberta has inherited a rich personality, it is the reflected light from rangeland pioneers who were aristocrats in the realm of achievement. Their lives were full but not easy. One hundred years ago southern Alberta was a buffalo pasture, and where buffalo thrive so can horses and cattle. All the prime necessities are here: abundant grass, running water, and sheltering hills. In addition, Alberta provides warm chinook winds and a long, mountain-filled skyline. John R. Craig in *Ranching With Lords and Commons* held that it was the chinook that made the cattle industry possible in southern Alberta, as it alleviated winters that would otherwise have meant total destruction of herds:

The chinooks last for several days, or it may be only for a few hours at a time, generally followed by long intervals of calm, prairie clear of snow, warm, bright days. In this lies the superiority of Southern Alberta's climate over other portions of the Dominion. As winter is understood in other parts of Canada, there are from six to eight weeks in Southern Alberta, putting all the winter days together. The climate makes our country. The chinook makes our climate.

Only fearless high-hearted men were drawn to this wild, wide range one hundred years ago, and all sorts, colours, and sizes found themselves riding together. M. H. Cochrane was one of the first and one of the biggest. His Cochrane Ranch Company, ranging over one hundred thousand acres, was supplier of beef to the NWMP. To mention a few others, there was Pat Burns, the cattle king of the West who was known as "Burns with the Big Heart"; the Montana cowboy George Lane of the Bar U who built up the largest Percheron horse ranch in the world; John Ware, Alberta's black rancher, still remembered for his extraordinary horsemanship; W. W. Hunter of the Big Reed Ranching Outfit at Olds; and bluff Dan Riley of High River. There was shrewd, steady A. E. Cross of the A-7; the one and only Frank Collicut, with at one time the world's largest herd of purebred Herefords; Captain Gardner and his son Clem, a world champion all-round cowboy, of Pirmez Creek; T. C. Milne of Claresholm; George Ross of Aden; Angus C. Sparrow of Pine Creek; George Stringham of Magrath; and the McIntyre family.

Separately and together the ranchers have been linked with the growing-up of Alberta. The days of the open range are gone. No longer in the trial-and-error phase, raising beef cattle will always be an important industry making a valuable contribution to the economy of our country.

140

This lovely ranch nestled beside the Bow is the Bow River Horse Ranche near Cochrane, early 1900's. The Rockies can be seen silhouetted in the background.

Brands

When Alberta was a vast, unfenced rangeland, the ranchers had a hard time keeping track of their stock. The branding iron provided the simplest way to mark their cattle. Each stockman had his personal trade-mark fixed on his animal's hide with a sizzling iron.

Branding dates to early American days. The story goes that a man by the name of Maverick suggested this method of keeping track of stock. Because of his soft Irish heart he asked to be excused from using such a desperate method on his cattle, suggesting that if others marked theirs then naturally the unbranded would be his. For a time all went well, until it became obvious that Maverick's herd had increased beyond the possibilities of nature. Ultimately he too was forced to use the harsh methods he decried. To this day any unbranded animal on any range is known as a "Maverick".

Many of the old cattle brands are as famous as their owners' names. There is the "Q" for the Quirk Ranch, the Bar K-2 of the Knight spread at Cardston; George Lane's Bar-U; or the "71" issued to Percy R. Neale and Samuel B. Steele in January, 1880, the first brand to be registered in the North-West Territories. John Ware's "9999" and Pat Burns **ᴎ** also come to mind. The "A-7" belonging to the Cross family is the brand held longest by any one family in Alberta.

Some brands contain complicated designs that include hearts, hats, diamonds, wine glasses, and saddle bags. Today brands are usually composed of three letters to make for easy and quick identification.

Alberta's Brand Book records over twenty-five thousand brands used to identify cattle, horses, sheep, poultry, and foxes. Branding is not enforced in Alberta, but since animals are forbidden to run at large, if the ownership of an unmarked animal cannot be proven it is branded with a big "A" for Alberta. Branding is advised on the neck, cheek, hip, or jaw, thus leaving the hide, a valuable by-product, unblemished. Brands are necessary, important to owners of livestock, and, to say the least, a very interesting facet of western lore.

The Chipman Ranch

The waters of the Glenmore dam now cover part of what was once a prosperous ranch, a showplace for visitors to the Calgary area. Established in 1882, the ranch was originally owned by "The Chipman Ranche Co.", with J. E. Chipman, president, B. W. Chipman, treasurer, and C. E. Harris, manager. It was the largest ranch to be located within the boundaries of the present Calgary city limits.

In a diary written by Mr. Harris there is a description of how a group of Nova Scotia businessmen, "The Halifax Ranche Co.", took a gamble on cattle ranching, then an infant industry in the West: ". . . a few Halifax businessmen conceived the idea of being the first, or among the first to grasp, some one of the many chances then offering, at the very beginning, to reap a fortune, to say nothing of fame. Well do I remember the sly, quiet gatherings that were held by this chosen few, in the back office of the firm whose leading

Above: An enlargement of the Chipman Ranch letterhead.

members were the promoting spirits in this scheme."

Mr. Harris details the difficult trip he made out west in 1882, transporting some restless horses to the new ranch. For a salary of 1,200 dollars a year plus room and board, he was to take over the duties of manager. His destination was the one hundred thousand acres of land leased annually at ten dollars per thousand acres, located eight miles southeast of Pincher Creek, extending from the Kootenay to the Oldman River.

By 1884 twelve hundred cattle were on the range, and by 1885 the Chipman Ranch stock consisted of twenty Percheron stallions and stallion colts and five hundred brood mares, geldings, and fillies. An advertising catalogue gave the address as Elbow Park, Calgary, N.W.T., "located on the Elbow River, four and one-half miles from Calgary."

143

The Chipman brothers also operated a successful hardware store in Calgary, but by 1885 it was up for sale. An advertisement in the Calgary *Herald*, March 12, 1885 indicates the firm was also considering selling the ranch:

Horse and Cattle Ranch. The entire herds and property of the Halifax Ranch Co. Near Fort Macleod N.W.T. 500 brood mares, Stallions, Geldings, Fillies and Suckers, including 50 selected Norman Percheron Mares, 6 selected Norman Percheron Stallions, one of which is the well known imported Norman Colt Kimo, weight 1,700 lbs. at 3 years old.

And the finest lot of saddle horses in the Territory. 1200 stock cattle, 25 Hereford Bulls. It is expected the summer branding will add 350 calves to this herd. Bain Waggons, Cheyenne Saddles and Harness, Horse Blankets, complete set carpenter's tools, all kinds of implements, 200 pine house logs and lease of 100,000 acres of the finest grazing lands. Apply to C. E. Harris, Manager, Fort McLeod or J. E. Chipman, Calgary.

This stock will be sold in one lot, or in small bands to suit purchaser.

By July of 1885 the cattle, "among the finest in the country," had been bought by the Military Colonization Company. But the horses were retained, and concentration began on the improvement of the horse stock. "Breeders of pure bred and grade Percheron horses," the Chipman Ranch became well known for its first-class stock. Horses were a necessity in the early West, and the Chipman Ranch excelled at producing some of the area's finest.

In the late 1890's, Isaac Robinson, a wealthy English-born diamond miner who had made a fortune in South Africa, acquired the land now occupied by the Lakeview sub-division and some of the Glenmore dam. He sent for his brother R. G. Robinson, a San Francisco settler, to come and manage his new acquisition. Although officially the Robinson Ranch, it retained the old "Chipman" name for several years, until Mr. Robinson re-named it the Elbow Park Ranch.

It was with the spirit of adventure and a sense of optimism that the Robinson family set out for the foothills country from San Francisco, where they had been living. They arrived in the tiny frontier town of Calgary in July, 1888. Mrs. Robinson described the trip north:

And so we started out with four children. We came up the west coast by boat and took the CPR at Vancouver. It surely was a rough trip through the mountains. There were no dining cars in those days and we either took our own food along or got lunches at the various stations. I never stirred

Above: R. G. Robinson branding his stock, early 1900's. *Opposite above:* The Robinson household, 1894. From left to right: Mrs. Harry Walker with one of the Robinson children; unknown; Mrs. R. G. Robinson with baby; Isaac Robinson; Harry Walker; R. G. Robinson. In front: Johnny and Joe Robinson. *Below left:* A group of Robinson stallions in the 1890's. This is the part of the ranch that was later submerged by the Glenmore Reservoir. *Right:* One of Robinson's showpieces. *Overleaf:* A group at the Robinson Ranch in 1894.

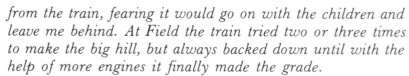

from the train, fearing it would go on with the children and leave me behind. At Field the train tried two or three times to make the big hill, but always backed down until with the help of more engines it finally made the grade.

It was rather a cold dark day when we arrived at Calgary, which was only a small village of about five hundred people then. The station was a red box-like building, a ticket and telegraph office being partitioned off, while in the centre of the general waiting room a large circular stove sent out a comfortable heat on that raw day.

We went over to the Royal hotel, a block north of the station, and what today is the southeast corner of Eighth Avenue and Centre Street. Between the station and it, there were only two or three little buildings near the hotel. Directly across the corner was the log store of the Hudson's Bay, while south and west across the railroad tracks there were no houses except a log shack inhabited by a family named Butler. The main general store of the village looked very odd to me after the big stores of San Francisco. I can see yet the piles of gaily colored prints and Hudson's Bay blankets. I remember, too, after a terrific hail storm, when the water from the melted hail leaked through the walls and got into the pile of red prints which did not have the fast colors of today, and consequently much damage was done by the running of the colors.

We stayed at the hotel three days and were then driven out to our future home, a ranch which my husband had bought from the Chipman Brothers at Halifax. All there was to it, was an old red barn and two log shacks. The larger one was the ranch house, which consisted of two rooms, one big room, in which a corner was partitioned off for a bedroom and another, a "lean-to" with a mud floor which was the kitchen. All the furniture was home-made and very rough and crude. There were no carpets, curtains, pictures. The walls were rough logs, which were not even chinked and through the cracks of which I could see outside, while the rafters that supported the ceiling were all visible. It was a bare uninviting-looking place. However, I had brought with me some curtains, some pictures, a carpet, and sewing machine, the high freight preventing us from bringing all our own furniture. We at once set to work to make the place look like home.

Those first months were hard months. I couldn't get used to the bad hail storms, when the hail beat in through the chinks of the house. I was afraid of the kerosene lamps; afraid they might explode and burn down the place.

Before I came I had been told a good deal about the Indians and that was another haunting fear - until after I had seen them. I did get several shocks those first months, when looking up from our table at mealtime I would see one

looking in at the windows, as it was their habit in the early days. Later I had an old squaw who worked for me for seventeen years.

Help was a great problem too. Especially did I find it so the first few months of life here, as on October 1 my fifth child was born. We had brought a man and his wife from San Francisco with us, but the woman proved almost useless. It was while lying in bed, helpless, and with a new baby - looking at the snow drifting in through the log chinks - in an early snow storm and anticipating one of the hard long cold winters I had been told about, that I nearly lost my courage. The woman left me three weeks after the baby was born - left me with clothes frozen in the wash tub. However, it turned out to be a beautiful winter. December and January were almost like summer, and every day I was able to take my little baby for a walk where I could see the blue mountains and the beautiful river valley. I was fortunate, too, in being able to get an English woman to help me while I had sent the older children to school, the girl to the convent at Calgary, and boys to St. Boniface, where they went for many years.

Next spring my husband started the building of the present ranch house, which was very roomy and comfortable. (The location was on a bench overlooking the Elbow River, part of the area which in 1961 became the Lakeview subdivision of the city of Calgary). He also bought several hundred head of cattle and horses from ranchers about, and in 1889 we were well away to a good start. The people, too, were so friendly - we were never lonely and even today I wish I was back on the ranch.

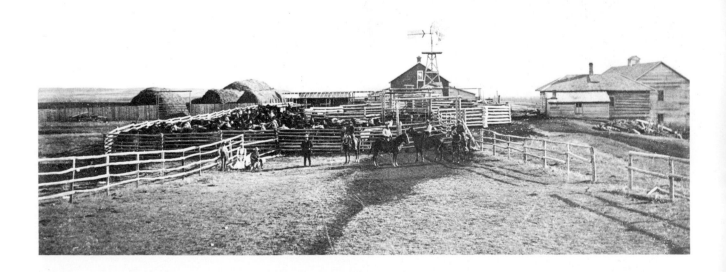

So it was under Robinson's ownership that the ranch achieved its greatest fame. His aim was breeding top-notch stock, and he purchased and imported famous purebreds. Among these fine horses was one he bought in 1892, top prize winner at the Toronto Industrial Exhibition in 1890 and 1891. This big chestnut imported Irish thoroughbred was named "Faughaballaugh" — a Gaelic word meaning "Clear the Way". He was only one of several noted stallions that included Clydesdales, Shires, Cleveland Bays and trotting horses. Cattle, numbering about three thousand, were added to the two thousand horses, and were likewise of prime quality. In 1896 he brought two carloads of short horn sires from Ontario, and in 1897 acquired twenty-three Durham bulls, all of pedigreed imported stock.

The "home ranch" became part of a chain of ranches owned by Mr. Robinson. Winter range was acquired a few miles west of Priddis at Fish Creek, and was known as "Robinson's Cow Camp". Charles Priddis, for whom that town was named, is said to have been Robinson's first stock man there. In the summer his stock grazed on miles of range at Melbourne in the Bragg Creek vicinity, and Pirmez Creek southwest of Calgary, which was also known as Moose Hill Ranch. The latter was subsequently owned by his son, Joseph Robinson. As well, six sections of land in Simon's Valley on Nose Creek were the location of Robinson's Horse Ranch.

Important as the Robinson Ranch was for stock raising in the 1890's and the early part of the 20th century, it was famous as a showplace for distinguished visitors, including the parties of at least two Canadian governors-general, Lord Aberdeen and Lord Minto. Such important visitors were usually driven to the spread in the most fashionable democrats escorted by colourfully uniformed NWMP.

Above: A Robinson stallion.   *Opposite:* The corral, circa 1890.

These were occasions for displays of wild bronc riding and steer roping by dexterous western cowboys. And the ranch was a favourite spot for Calgarians to spend Sundays looking over the fine stock and watching the ranch hands in action. For the ranch boasted some legendarily skillful cowboys, among them Jack Stewart, a famous Indian fighter and a crack revolver shot. Stewart later moved to South Africa, where he reportedly saved the life of Cecil Rhodes during the Matabele war, for which Rhodes presented him with two of the finest farms in Rhodesia.

The Robinson Ranch was known especially for its hospitality, and thirty or forty guests a night would be the rule rather than the exception. Ranchers and other westerners were always guaranteed a warm welcome and an invitation to make the ranch home while in the Calgary area.

Another interesting feature of the old Chipman Ranch was the cheese factory built on the property in 1889 by Isaac

Robinson. This plant was only the second in the district, constructed a year after Ebenezer Healy began his business in Springbank. The cheese sold for twelve cents a pound — a high price for those days.

R. G. Robinson himself was very active in town affairs. He gained recognition for his excellence in game and trap shooting, and won first prize in Calgary's first field trials in 1891. Mr. Robinson was also president of the Calgary Industrial Exhibition in 1896, and his children also took an active part in the affairs of early Calgary.

When the Glenmore dam project was begun in 1932, the Robinson estate received 80,000 dollars for 720 acres, and part of the once-famous ranch disappeared forever beneath the waters.

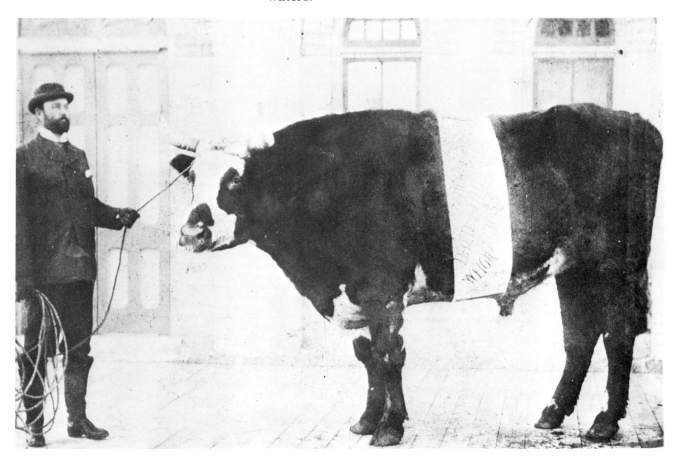

One of the most successful entrepreneurs in early Calgary was William Roper Hull. Hull came to the West in a roundabout fashion, in 1873. Having emigrated to America from England, he walked across the Panama isthmus with his brother and trecked up the west coast to Victoria. He then ranched in B.C., raising horses and cattle.

Hull made his debut in Calgary in 1883 with 1,200 horses he had driven over the Crowsnest Pass from his ranch in Kamloops. He did a roaring trade in horses, and furthermore secured a contract with the CPR to be the sole supplier of beef during their construction in B.C. In 1884 he opened a butcher shop in Calgary and in two years had expanded it to a chain of

William Roper Hull

fifteen outlets. To keep up with the steady demand that these outlets created, he started buying ranches in Alberta, among them the famous Oxley Ranch that ranged over one hundred thousand acres.

Hull contributed not only to the economic structure of the town but also to its visible appearance. His building ventures included the Grain Exchange and the Alberta, Victoria, and Albion blocks. Another, the Hull Opera House, was probably in its day the most imposing structure in town and its chief centre of social gatherings and functions.

Above: The Bow Valley Ranch when it belonged to William Roper Hull. Hull is the central figure in this merry group. He sports a straw boater and a jaunty manner and altogether looks quite pleased with himself. *Opposite:* Beefman Hull in 1903 with what was believed to be the largest steer in the area.

151

Pat Burns

The story of Pat Burns has all the action and romance associated with a successful pioneer. Burns was a superb example of the self-made man in the best traditions of the West. From the most modest of beginnings he built up his packing and provision business to what is known today as Burns Foods. In the intervening years he purchased or built packing plants at Edmonton, Vancouver, Prince Albert, Regina, Winnipeg, and Seattle. He bought out or started over one hundred retail meat shops in the provinces of Alberta and British Columbia. He established sixty-five creameries and cheese factories, eleven wholesale provision houses, and eighteen wholesale fruit houses. He extended his business overseas, and set up agencies in London, Liverpool, and Yokohama.

Hurling his energies into the livestock and ranching industry on the prairies, he became the owner of two of the best-known ranches in the West: The Bar U, and Willow Creek, which surrounded the E. P. owned by Edward, Prince of Wales. In addition to all these interests, Burns was a strong supporter of enterprises designed to develop Alberta. These included opening up the Turner Valley oil fields, as well as drilling oil wells on his own property. He also acquired real-estate holdings.

Born at Oshawa, Ontario, on July 6, 1846, Burns was the son of Michael and Bridget Gibson Burns, both of Irish birth. When he was an infant his parents moved to Kirkfield, Ontario, where he received a meagre education in the village school.

In Kirkfield at the same time lived William Mackenzie, afterwards to become famous as a member of the Mackenzie and Mann firm of railroad builders. Young Mackenzie and young Burns were great friends. This friendship later provided the opportunity for a business association which was the foundation of Burns's packing industry.

In 1878, when Pat Burns was twenty-three years of age, he and his brother John decided to come West during the emigration of Ontario farmers to Manitoba. They filed on homesteads near the present town of Minnedosa, and returned to Winnipeg to get work to "save a stake" which would enable them to prove up their homesteads.

Pat Burns got a job blasting rocks on the Canadian Pacific Railway right of way. For this he received twenty-five dollars per month and his board in a construction camp one hundred miles east of Winnipeg. He worked for a year and saved enough money to buy a yoke of oxen and then returned to his homestead.

In 1886, the Mackenzie and Mann firm of railroad builders was incorporated. Burns had always kept in touch with Mackenzie, and he was awarded the contract to supply

Opposite: Views of Burns's enterprises in the 1900's: the interior of his Calgary butchershop; a delivery wagon; and the abattoir on the east side of the Elbow.

meat to the construction camps. This was followed by similar contracts for the Qu'Appelle, Long Lake, and Saskatchewan Railway in 1888, and the Calgary and Edmonton Railway and the Calgary-to-Macleod branch of the CPR in the early nineties.

The railroad construction was finished and with it Burns's contracts. However, Burns used the facilities and connections he had established as a meat contractor to go into the business of wholesale distribution of livestock to retail meat-merchants in British Columbia. Although business grew quickly, he also had his setbacks. Twice the Calgary plant burned down — the original slaughter house in 1892, and his new plant in 1913. In the second instance he gave orders for the rebuilding before the fire was out (it took Calgary firemen a week in sub-zero winter weather to extinguish the blaze), and in the interim carried out regular business with very little delay or confusion.

During his personal administration of the business there were practically no labour troubles among the thousands of workers he employed. He put his resources at the service of the government in World War I by shipping livestock to France for the Food Conservation Campaign in World War One.

In 1928, he sold P. Burns and Company to Dominion Securities for fifteen million dollars, and turned his talents to directing his other interests under a company known as "The P. Burns Agencies."

The opening day of the 1931 Stampede, July 6, coincided with Burns's seventy-fifth birthday. As he was one of the four original subscribers to the first Calgary Stampede, a celebration was planned.

The following illuminated address was presented by Mayor Andrew Davidson in front of the grandstand.

Opposite: The abattoir and another Burns meatshop.

The City of Calgary is today celebrating with enthusiasm the seventy-fifth birthday of its best-loved citizen. It is the privilege of the undersigned to echo the unanimous and fervent wish of the men and women of the community that you reach many more milestones on the highroad of happiness. That wish is no mere casual expression of ordinary good-will. It comes, we believe, from the very innermost hearts of those who are proud to call you fellow-citizen, neighbor, and friend. Your experience as a humble pioneer, fortified by faith in your western home, taught you the broad tolerance, the simple kindliness, and human understanding, which have stimulated in us a lofty pride in your career, and the deepest respect for your character. Western hospitality has been defined and crystallized in your genial personality; private benevolence has received its greatest encouragement from your unselfish liberality; the business relations of men in this community have been exalted by the contemplation of a successful man unspoilt by success. Your life amongst us, is itself your most enduring monument. Your fellow-citizens wish you many more years of quiet joy, and on this happy occasion join in honouring and saluting a great-hearted gentleman who has deserved and gained the affectionate regard of us all. On behalf of the City of Calgary and its citizens.

Dated July 6, 1931
Andrew Davidson, Mayor
J. Miller, City Clerk.

For a man of Burns's stature and pre-eminence, such words of praise in no way constituted an exaggeration.

Famous Alberta cattlemen. *Right:* George Lane and the Prince of Wales. *Below:* The Prince with the Big Four. From left to right: Pat Burns; George Lane; Prince Edward; Archie McLean; A. E. Cross.

Archie McLean

One of Alberta's first large ranchers, a prominent politician, one of the "Big Four", and a pioneer oilman, Archie McLean played an important part in the province's early history.

McLean was born on a farm in Aldboro, Elgin County, Ontario, on September 25, 1860. Like many youngsters of the time, he was intrigued by the lure of the West, with its promises of vast stretches of wide open spaces. In 1881, the twenty-one-year-old Archie set out for Winnipeg, and settled on a farm in the Pipestone River district, which later became Virden. With a ready market in the CPR crews, contractors, and local farmers, he began importing horses from Ontario, and quickly built up a successful trade. During this time he met a man with whom he would share a common interest and lasting friendship — Patrick Burns.

Attracted by prospects in the foothills country, McLean moved on to southern Alberta in 1886. For a year he took his knocks as a cowpuncher and became skilled enough to take over as manager and partner of the Cypress Cattle Company about twenty miles northwest of Taber. Young McLean proved himself an intelligent and efficient administrator.

He also realized the need for more markets for the expanding cattle industry, so he organized an export company, Bater and McLean, and shipped cattle to the United Kingdom. Stock was also sent to eastern Canada, and the firm's offices in Lethbridge and Winnipeg earned an excellent reputation for fair dealing.

However, the situation was changing for Alberta's big ranchers. With the development of the wheat-growing industry, farmers began to encroach more and more on the former ranch holdings. Such was the case with the CY ranch. As Tom Primrose wrote in the Albertan many years later:

Archie McLean was the old time rancher type. He helped establish the beef industry in Alberta and with regrets saw the days of the open range change to a new and different era, that of the homesteader. He told my uncle of the very day when he knew for certain that the old range days were numbered. Riding one day on inspection of his cattle he met men and wagons near what is now the location of the town of Taber. The spokesman of the wagoneers was James S. Hull from Utah. He was looking for land to settle on. McLean told him this was unlikely country for anything but ranching. He put up what he felt was a convincing argument against settlement and when he was finsihed Hull looked at him and said quietly, "Looks to me like good country to raise a family in." McLean said no more but turned his saddle horse and rode back to the ranch. When he got back to the CY he said to some of his cowboys, "Boys, I guess we can start winding

This picture of a reclining cowboy is from an old postcard of Alberta entitled "Prairie Kitchen".

up operations here pretty soon, the settlers have started to move in." In 1903 James S. Hull built the first house in the townsite of Taber. Until then it had been only a watertank on the CPR. The days of the open range were at an end.

Thus in 1905 some of the CY's holdings were liquidated.

But Archie McLean still had many experiences ahead of him. In 1904 he had married Margaret Duncan, from Hamilton, Ontario. Tragically, Mrs. McLean died two years later, leaving an infant son, Duncan. The death of his wife was a severe blow to McLean who, already taciturn, became even more withdrawn after the incident. But his honesty and sincerity had won him many friends. And all who knew him trusted him. Thus when the provincial election of 1909 came around, the people around Taber knew who they wanted to represent them in the legislature.

But McLean was a rancher, not a politician, and wanted no part of such a life, despite the houndings and entreaties of his neighbours, especially the Liberal delegation. However, McLean was a man who put personal interest aside for the common good. Tom Primrose writes:

One day he came out of a Taber store, followed by the delegation, and met his friend Jim Fuller, manager of the big Cameron Ranch which was not far from McLean's CY Ranch. McLean jokingly told Fuller that the men following him were trying to get him to run for the Legislature. Fuller gave the matter some thought and told McLean that, if the people so much wanted him to be their man, it was his duty to run. McLean thought a great deal of Fuller and finding he favored the nomination, McLean finally agreed to stand.

But his conditions were somewhat unusual. Mr. Primrose continues:

He agreed to run on the condition that he would not have to do any campaigning, and would not make any campaign speeches, or promises. The Liberals at Taber agreed to this, and in the short time left before the election, McLean's running was advertised by democrat, buggy, and horse-back rider. Men rode through the country, making the simple announcement, "Archie McLean is running for the legislature - vote for him."

And these low-key tactics won the day, McLean easily taking the seat as an Independent Liberal for the Lethbridge constituency. In 1910, after the fall of the Rutherford government, McLean was elected by acclamation and invited to form part of Premier A. L. Sifton's cabinet. Again McLean was reluctant to accept a position, protesting that he had run as an independent and it would be unfair to the electors if he entered a Liberal cabinet. However, he was reassured by a majority of his supporters and thus became the Honourable A. J. McLean in 1910, with the office of provincial secretary.

In 1911 he took over the portfolio as minister of municipal affairs, and two years later was returned as Taber's representative to the Legislature. In 1917 he was appointed Minister of Public Works under Premier Charles Stewart. In this capacity he made no small contribution to the province's highway system. A significant tribute to his political career is the fact that he was known as "Honest Archie", a title seldom used in this context. He remained in the legislature until 1921 when the United Farmers of Alberta swept into power with a landslide victory.

With this release from politics, McLean returned to his first love, ranching. With two experienced partners, he started a new ranch, using the old CY brand. Eighteen thousand acres were leased on the Peigan reserve west of Macleod, and the ranch did quite well until 1929 when the Depression forced him to sell out his CY interests.

But he remained in the ranching business. When George Lane died, the Bar U bankers approached McLean to settle the estate's affairs and run the holdings. McLean took over the administration, eventually selling the Bar U ranch, the Flying E, and others to the Burns company.

McLean moved to the Namaka Farm of the Lane estate, dividing his time between it and two of his own at Macleod and Pincher Creek. In partnership with C. R. Mitchell he formed an oil company, with drilling operations near Coutts. However, in spite of sustained efforts, the rigs failed to strike a deposit. This was one venture in which he was less than successful.

Perhaps McLean's most famous venture was his investment in the Calgary Stampede. The 1912 Stampede owes its beginning to the generosity of Archie McLean, who along with Pat Burns, George Lane, and A. E. Cross, underwrote the affair's expenses. It is due to the financial commitment of these men that we today can still enjoy this magnificent Calgary Stampede.

On October 13, 1933, while on a trip to Macleod, A. McLean died, leaving behind a legacy rich in the colourful history of the Canadian west.

George Lane

The whole story of ranching in Southern Alberta can be read in the career of George Lane and his Bar U Ranch at Pekisko, south west of High River. When George Lane reached the top he could look over almost 150,000 acres supporting 10,000 head of cattle and hundreds of the world's finest Percheron horses. This was the famous Bar U which became the mecca for princes, politicians, industrialists, peddlers, acquaintances — in fact, everyone who wanted to visit the great livestock empire. Lane became known on this continent and abroad as a leading Canadian rancher; at home he was "George", the boss of the Bar U spread. He made visitors welcome, but no special regard was given to exalted rank.

Lane was born in Iowa in 1856. He started working for his living at thirteen, and spent the next fifteen years laying the ground work necessary for a prospective cattle king. His strong, enduring physique and alert faculties were developed from years of cowpunching, scouting, and Indian fighting. In 1884 the Montana Cattle Association recommended him as the best man for the job of foreman of the Bar U, then owned by the Northwest Cattle Company, at thirty-five dollars per month. He accepted at a fast gallop.

The following year Lane met and married Elizabeth Sexsmith, a daughter of a High River pioneer family. They raised a family of eight children. For the next seven years George Lane worked ceaselessly at building and improving the herds, bossing the annual round-ups, and saving his money. Then he resigned from the Bar U and went into ranching on his own.

In the ensuing years he traded in horses and cattle. He supplied beef to the Blood Indian Reserve on a government contract, shipped cattle to dealers on both the east and west coasts, and sold horses to the States and Mexico. He acquired more and more ranch land, until in 1902 he formed a company with other investors to buy out the Bar U ranch. In 1912 he engaged in wheat farming, shipping his grain across the mountains to the coast, at that time a daring and innovative undertaking.

Lane loved the life of the range. To him it was almost blasphemy to spit or even laugh within ten feet of a steer. But he was one of the first to recognize that ranching on the open range could not go on forever. When the homesteaders commenced building their fences, George Lane faced facts. He knew that the settlers would need horses to pull their ploughs, so he developed the greatest breeding farm for Percherons in the world. He foresaw and advocated mixed farming for greater agricultural security in Alberta. He gave practical assistance to many farmers and ranchers. To ensure the success of the first Stampede in 1912, he was one of the "Big Four" who put up the one hundred thousand dollars that got the venture off the ground.

George Lane looked the typical old-time cowman, with his slow drawl and shrewd humour. "Exercise may be fine for people," he used to say, "but every step a steer takes works a pound of beef off him." His motto was typical of the western old-timer: "Always keep yourself in a position to look any man straight in the eye and tell him to go to Hell."

Left: A team of the famous Bar U Percherons. *Below:* Bar U round-up 1901. From left to right: F. R. Pike; Charlie Lehr (at back); Charlie McKinnon; next four unknown; Joseph Brown; an unidentified North-West Mounted Policeman; Jewet Thorne; unknown; Ted Hills (sitting up); unknown; Milt Thorne.

Above: The A-7 Ranche. *Right:* A. E. Cross at the Calgary Brewing and Malting Company with his trained buffalo team.

Alfred Ernest Cross was born in Montreal on June 26, 1861, the fourth son of Mr. Justice Alexander Cross, Judge of the Queen's Bench. From 1875 to 1878, like many other boys of the day, he went to Hailebury College in England for formal schooling. On his return, his father thought he should learn the rudiments of business, so the young man was sent to Montreal Business College. But to a youth whose mind wandered along the gleaming railroad being built across the prairie, knowledge of agriculture seemed a necessity. His holidays were spent on his uncle's farm in the Eastern Townships. Then, majoring in animal husbandry, he graduated from the Ontario Agricultural College in 1881. On graduation, he enrolled in the School of Medicine at McGill University to study veterinary science under Sir William Osler. The great doctor and humanitarian made a profound impression on his pupil, who felt that those years, 1881-1884, constituted one of the great experiences of his life.

A. E. Cross

His career began to take form. In June of 1884 he came to Calgary as bookkeeper, veterinary, ranch hand and assistant-manager of a large ranch owned by Senator Cochrane, twenty-three miles west of Calgary. Of those days he recalled living in a sod-roofed shack where "it rained for two days inside after it stopped pouring outside."

In the severe winter of 1884, the stock, driven by the storms, bunched and froze. Cross's experiences with sheep that winter in all probability contributed to the future ranchman's decision to raise cattle.

Excellent as his opportunities were, he preferred to have a foot in the stirrup rather than a pen behind his ear. He took up a homestead fifty-five miles south of Calgary at the fork of Mosquito Creek and began his career in ranching. Observing that the rain belt along the foothills produced better pasture, he purchased a quarter section from his brother, William Heber Cross, and moved his belongings to what is now the Home Place of the A7 Ranche. His few possessions were transported to the new location in a wagon, but somehow a precious lamp chimney was left behind. As the article was only a small one, Mr. Cross went back for it on a saddle horse. On the return journey the paper wrapping rustled and his horse started to buck. It was always a matter of great pride that when he was eventually fired off he landed on his seat with the glass chimney intact.

Cross imported pedigreed Shorthorn bulls and cows from Ontario, and prior to 1905 brought in his first Herefords. A perfectionist, Mr. Cross's ambition was rewarded in 1917 when his grass-fed steers fetched the highest price ever paid on the world market in Chicago. The homestead was proved up and was increased in acreage until it became as we know it today, one of the largest ranch holdings in Alberta.

In 1888, while riding a particularly spirited horse, he was hurt by the horn of his saddle. Continuing pain forced him to return to Montreal for medical attention. The specialist observed his particularly healthy patient, diagnosed the illness as the new-fangled complaint called appendicitis, and recommended the young rancher live in town closer to a doctor. It was while recuperating in Montreal that Cross conceived and launched the enterprise that was to make him a wealthy man — the Calgary Brewing and Malting Company.

The well known A7 brand has an interesting origin. Mr. Cross reasoned that the finest cattle on the best ranch should wear a distinctive brand. The first brand he submitted, A1, was returned; the authorities advised it would be too easy "to get onto" — in other words, change the "1". Respecting their advice he resubmitted the A7 design — "A" being the first initial in his name and the "7" because he was one of a family of seven children. The word "Ranche" in the original documents, spelled with a final "e", in all probability is of Spanish origin via Mexico.

In 1898 a new challenge presented itself - politics. He was elected Conservative member for East Calgary in the Legislative Assembly of the North-West Territories. Sir Frederick W. G. Haultain was his campaign manager. Mr. Cross recalled that a very tall man and a very short man carried him on their shoulders through the city. On June 8, 1889, he married Helen Rothney Macleod, the eldest daughter of Colonel James Macleod the famous Assistant Commissioner of the NWMP. A. E. Cross like his father before him had seven children.

In the early days of Calgary, ranchers coming to town for supplies had no place to meet. Through the efforts of A. E. Cross, the "Wolves Club" was formed with a box car for a clubhouse. In 1890, along with other members of the Club, Cross organized the famous Ranchmen's Club. Cross was Vice-President from 1894 to 1900 and 1908 to 1910, and President from 1906 to 1908 and 1911 to 1912.

He was one of the "Big Four" who underwrote the first Calgary Stampede in 1912. To mention just a few of his many other diversified activities, he was Director and President of the Calgary General Hospital Board, founding member and Vice-President of the Western Stock Growers' Association, Director of the Western Canada Brewers' Association, President of the Western Canada Polo Association, an active member of the Alberta Fish and Game Protective Association, founding member and Director of the Western Irrigation System, and founding member and Director of The Calgary Board of Trade.

Above and opposite: Cross, McKid, and Hull having their membership photos taken for the Wolf Club. They are sitting before what appears to be a makeshift shrine festooned with pictures of other members, family snaps, and prairie scenes. The building shown housed the Ranchmen's Club.

H.G. McKid M.D.
"Surgeon
to the
Wolves."

Calgary 1893

W.C.F.R. Hull
"A Successful
Wolf!!"

Calgary 1893.

John Ware

A negro who had been born a slave in South Carolina before the American Civil War, John Ware arrived in the Highwood River area in 1882 with a cattle drive for the Bar U Ranch. When the cowboys were paid off, John Ware, described as "the best man in the crew," was recommended for permanent employment to ranch manager Fred Stimpson.

After working for several years with the Bar U, Ware left to become top hand with the Quorn outfit, whose ranch was situated in the area known today as the Turner Valley oil fields. The Quorn had many English traditions, boasted a pack of hounds, and, like the Cochrane Ranch to the north, was frequently hosts to British aristocracy. John Ware developed a taste for the sport of riding to hounds, and became a great favourite with visiting Lords and Earls as they rode over the prairie in pursuit of coyotes.

In the High River regional history *Leaves From the Medicine Tree*, an account of Ware's service with the Quorn ranch is given:

Above: John Ware and his family, 1896. From left to right: Mrs. Mildred Ware; Robert; Nettie; and John. *Opposite above:* The ranch at Millarville, 1896. *Below:* John Ware at the Red Deer River, circa 1901.

John was put in charge of the horse herd and of breaking broncs. No horse was too tough for the coloured Texan and indeed many old-timers claim they never saw a horse that could throw John. Weighing over two hundred pounds, standing six foot three inches, and agile as a panther, John could hang by his arms from the cross bar of the corral gate, drop onto a bronc as the horses rushed from the corral and ride the horse to a standstill without saddle or bridle.

In 1891, Ware took up a place of his own on the headwaters of Sheep Creek, a ranch with a herd of two hundred cattle branded with his own 9999 brand.

In 1902 Ware moved to the Rosebud district on the Red Deer River. Deciding that the obvious means of getting his herd across the Bow River was the east Calgary bridge, he planned his drive directly through the city. Cowtown or not, Calgary by 1902 was possessed of a certain grace and sophistication, or so the City Fathers believed. After all there were by-laws dealing with such matters. However, there wasn't a horse or a by-law that could throw John Ware. He simply held his peace till the middle of the night and proceeded directly on course. If the citizens of Calgary heard strange rumblings and rustlings from their beds that night they never reported it. Next morning Ware's herd was "ten miles east of Calgary and none had any Bow River water on their hides".

On the new place he built his herd to one thousand head. There John and Mildred Ware and their five children — Nettie, Bob, Willie, Mildred, and Arthur — gained an enviable reputation as one of Alberta's most noteworthy ranching families.

Ware was acknowledged as one of the greatest riders in the history of the Canadian range, and was equally well known as an excellent shot with both rifle and hand gun. He was genuinely respected throughout the range country; his honesty was as legendary as his great strength. He is commemorated in two places on the map of Alberta: Ware Creek and Mount Ware.

It was said the horse had not been born that Ware could not ride. However, due to a riding accident he met his death in 1905. His horse tripped in a badger hole, and Ware was thrown to the ground and broke his back. When carried to his last resting place in Calgary he was accompanied by many friends paying their last respects to one of the greatest cowboys and finest men who ever rode the range.

Below: A touch of Olde England at the Elbow River — coyote hunting near Weasel Head Bridge.

For forty-three years as Prince of Wales, and through his short reign as Edward VIII and Duke of Windsor, Edward owned a ranch southwest of Calgary.

In 1919, on his first visit to Canada, the then-Crown Prince fell in love with and purchased the E. P. Ranch on Pekisko Creek, sixty-five miles from Calgary. George Lane negotiated the sale.

Albertans regarded Edward as a member of the ranching community. The Duke was well known for his love of informality. "I want to be a Canadian along with them all," an article appearing in the Calgary *Herald* quotes him as saying. "I want that place to be just like any other ranch around here. I want to be a friend and a neighbour when I am there, and indeed a friend and neighbour all the time."

A story is told of a stockman whose property adjoined the ranch of the Duke of Windsor. A number of important people from Calgary and other towns in Alberta had arrived at the Prince of Wales Ranch to welcome the Prince as a newcomer to the ranching fraternity. The stockman was delighted to make the formal introduction but was slightly uncertain as to how to act as liaison between royalty and cowpunchers. His speech was short and to the point: "Boys, this is the Prince. He's a hell of a good fellow!" The Prince smiled and in his reply defined the difference between a "rancher" and a "rauncher". A rancher is one who made his money on the ranch and spent it in the town. A "rauncher" is one who made his money in town and spent it on the ranch. He confessed that he himself belonged decidedly in the "rauncher" class.

Breeding Galloway cattle, Welsh ponies, and Wessex hogs, the ranch prospered. During the forty-three years he visited "his spread" six times, the last occasion in 1951. Visitors to the ranch included Winston Churchill, and of course the "Big Four" — Senator Pat Burns, George Lane, A. E. Cross, and Archie McLean, as well as other prominent individuals such as Guy Weadick.

In 1929 and again in 1936 and 1940 it was rumoured by the British press that oil had been discovered on the "king rancher's property". The real story was not told until 1960, when the Duke confided to a magazine writer that oil was drilled for, but the result was a dry hole.

From 1951 to 1964, the newspapers ran yearly stories speculating on the Duke's next visit but he never made it. When the ranch was put up for sale there were so many eager buyers that the Duke retained the services of a Montreal firm to accept bids. The sale to Jim Cartwright was a popular one — High River residents had been afraid the buyers would be U.S. "dudes".

Royal Rauncher

Above: Prince Eddie on his front stoop with Calgary Mayor George Webster.

Opposite: Group at the British American Horse Ranch, Cochrane, 1886. One of the largest ranches in the province it was also one of the most luxuriously outfitted and furnished. To the serious minded rangeman such luxuries would have seemed excessive, as would the chic garb of the men in this group. They would have been much more in sympathy with the men pictured below, eating in their unpretentious bachelor's shack. *Below:* Three riders near Calgary; a round-up wagon; and the round-up crew of the Oxley Ranch.

Chapter 6 Ambitions

Calgary is beautifully situated in the valley of the Bow River, and is the largest town in the neighborhood of the Rocky Mountains, whose snow clad summits are always distinctly visible in clear weather rising away on the Western Horizon. They seem to enclose the valley with its low foothills in a species of amphitheatre circling from the north to south. The town which is daily growing in size and importance and spreading over the prairie in all directions, has a population of about 1,200, possesses several busy streets, a number of ambitious shops, beside a private bank — now doing such flourishing business that its proprietors have just erected a new and commodious building — and a very good hotel, the "Royal" by name, which is also undergoing an extensive addition. The accommodation is at present somewhat limited, but when the new wing is completed the "Royal" will compare very favourably with what Winnipeg can offer to the traveller in the hotel way.

From A Stranger's View of Calgary, *by* Ernest Smith, 1886

174

A person who perceived very clearly the impact the railroad would have on the West was Richard Hardisty, Chief Factor for the Hudson's Bay Company. Having served with the Company since 1849, Hardisty was well acquainted with western life and the western economy. He had served successively at Fort Garry, Cumberland House, Fort Carlton, Victoria (Alberta) and Fort Edmonton. He had three brothers who had also risen to responsible positions in the Company, and by the 1880's the Hardisty family had become somewhat of a dynasty and an institution. Hardisty's marriage to Eliza McDougall, daughter of the famous missionary George McDougall, strengthened this impression.

Hardisty's great strength was his consummate administrative ability. Operating from his base at Edmonton, the clearing station for the northern fur trade, his skill at scheduling supplies in and furs out from the districts of Athabasca, Peace, and Mackenzie impressed the natives and his superiors alike. Furthermore, as settlers began to homestead in the area, he persuaded the Company to erect lumber mills and flour mills, and, after the buffalo disappeared, to engage in ranching.

In 1874 Hardisty gave orders for a Hudson's Bay fort to be established on the Bow River. An abandoned post near Morley was re-opened, and the following year the Company moved to a new location some forty miles downstream near the newly established Fort Calgary. This post was named Bow River Fort.

For the next few years the post traded for buffalo robes with the natives and also competed against I. G. Baker & Co. for the NWMP business. The Baker organization proved a formidable competitor. With their vast transportation network throughout the West, they could offer goods of such a variety and at such a low price that they could generally dominate the trade with the Police and the surrounding white settlers. The Company was more or less content to accept this secondary role — after all they were in the fur trade, not the retail business. However in 1882 as the CPR slowly advanced across the prairie it became obvious to Hardisty that the retail trade was in for a boom. This is what he had to say about the changing economic picture in a letter to his superior at Fort Garry:

There appears to be a great change taking place in this part of the country. People are flocking in, in connection with the Canadian Pacific Railroad and cattle ranches, besides others going in for the purpose of settling down on farms. The Company will require a good supply of groceries and goods suited for the trade sent in there at an early date. No doubt I.G. Baker and Company will have in a large supply of

HBC

Above: Chief Factor Richard Hardisty. *Opposite above:* Calgary from the north, looking southwest in the late 1880's. *Below:* This Indian camp in East Calgary is said to be near the original Hudson's Bay store. None of the visible buildings, however, have been identified as the store and it may be obscured by the teepee in the foreground.

all kinds, and be able to undersell us in groceries etc. on account of the present means of transport, but if the Railroad comes to Calgary, we can then be better able to compete with them. As it is the people prefer dealing with the Company, being confident they get a superior article for their money. The Company's tea and blankets are greatly in demand and we cannot from Edmonton furnish the full supply.

We cannot now look to this Post for any return in fur since the disappearance of the buffalo, but we may look forward to a great cash business with the whites, provided the place is well equipped with a proper outfit. Angus Fraser, who is a trusty, reliable man, remains in charge of this place.

This letter, with its predictions of the new importance of Calgary, also spelled changes in Hardisty's own future; the Company immediately removed its district headquarters from Edmonton to Calgary, and Chief Factor Hardisty with it. The little log shacks on the east side of the Elbow continued as the Company's outlet in Calgary until 1884, when they were dragged over the river and re-located just behind their new building, where they were used for storage purposes. The new store, a rather grand building, was located in the heart of the new townsite on the northwest corner of Stephen Avenue and McTavish Street.

I. G. Baker and Co. also moved into town about that time, and set up shop on the northeast corner of the intersection. They were still the dominant traders in the town, and before long had raised an ornate sandstone building to house their wares. In 1891, however, the Hudson's Bay Company bought them out, and used their store as a temporary measure during the construction of their own premises, a fine new sandstone building that had its grand opening in September of the same year. The wooden store (or the better half of it) was sold to J. C. Linton, a local bookseller, who carted it off to his own lot a couple of blocks east, where its lovely windows did justice to his splendid selection of books and toys.

The new HBC building was the epitome of stolidity and establishment. By 1913 it had doubled the size of its sandstone building and then relocated altogether at its present spot on Eighth Avenue and First Street S.W. It had made the transition from the fur trade to the retail trade without a backward look.

Right: The first Hudson's Bay store on the west side. *Centre:* I.G. Baker & Co.'s sandstone building. *Below:* Employees of I.G. Baker & Co. at the Company's first location, about a mile south of the fort. One of the original log buildings can be seen in the background.

James C. Linton,

BOOKSELLER AND STATIONER,

—AND DEALER IN—

Fancy Goods, Wall Paper, Toys, &c.

CIGARS, : CIGARETTES, : TOBACCO, : PIPES, : ETC

The Latest Papers, Magazines and Novels always on hand.

Sign of the Big Book

178

Opposite: James C. Linton, Calgary bookseller; his advertisement; and the store he bought from the Hudson's Bay Company. *Left:* The Company's new building, built in 1891, was a solid and imposing affair. *Above:* An interior view of the store, taken in 1904, shows the grocery department. The "orange meat" advertised in the sign was cornflakes. *Overleaf:* A train of HBC Red River carts arrive in Calgary, 1888, laden with seventy-five thousand dollars worth of furs from the north.

997. H.B. CO'S, TRAIN OF CARTS FROM THE NORTH,

WITH 75,000 DOLLARS WORTH OF FURS, ARRIVIN

Boards and Nails

The I. G. Baker and Hudson's Bay companies supplied the first needs of the incoming settlers — food, clothing, stoves, and other household equipment. After that the most immediate concern of the new arrival was housing. Mostly, everyone was willing to suffer it out in a tent for a short while, but sooner or later it was necessary to build a house. There was a constant and pressing demand for building materials. At first Colonel Walker and his Bow River Mills had the monopoly on supplying this demand. Walker supplied lumber not only for houses but for CPR construction and the town sidewalks.

Then in 1886 the Eau Claire and Bow River Lumber Company erected their milling equipment on the Bow River, in the north corner of the town; and established logging camps on the Bow near Silver City, and on the Kananaskis. The company was financed by American interests from Eau Claire, Wisconsin.

The president of the company was I. K. Kerr, an Ontario man who had worked in the Wisconsin lumber business. In 1883 Kerr had been told by an Ottawa lawyer, Kutusoff MacFee, of the vast timber stands west of Calgary, and had come with two associates to inspect the area. Guided by an Indian named George Kananaskis they explored the Bow, Spray, and Kananaskis Rivers, noting stumpage of the various lumber stands, and charting water routes for getting the lumber out. They travelled on horseback for their survey. When they were finished they returned by canoe from Morley to Medicine Hat. On their recommendation MacFee obtained rights on a hundred square miles of timber in the area inspected, and the Eau Claire Lumber Company was formed to harvest the lumber.

The company employed over one hundred men. Each winter three to five million feet of timber — spruce, jackpine, and fir — were cut and hauled to the driving streams. In the

Above: Eau Claire Lumber Co. logs, somewhere west of Calgary. *Right:* A view of the mill. *Opposite above:* A distant view of the mill from across the Bow River. *Below:* The employees of Eau Claire Sawmill in the early 1890's.

184

spring the logs were floated down the Bow to the mills at Calgary where they were cut and processed into lumber products. The drives took up to two months every year, and required large gangs of men who patrolled the banks ready to forestall log jams. These drives were ten miles long and at their fastest rate travelled about three miles per day.

The Eau Claire Company, until the turn of the century, was one of the largest suppliers of lumber to the area and one of the biggest employers. During its regime in Calgary the company engaged in several enterprises quite apart from lumbering. They operated a ranch and two grocery firms, founded the Calgary Iron Works, and even ran a flour mill (I. K. Kerr had operated a flour mill in Ontario). Next to logging, probably their most important function in the early town was their Calgary Water Power Company, founded and run by Peter Prince, which provided the first dependable electric supply to the town.

Next to the lumber mills, the most important source of building materials were the hardware stores. The biggest store in town in 1885 was Rogers and Grants'. This is their description in Burns and Elliott's directory:

This firm opened out in May last. Their premises are situated on Stephen avenue opposite the post office. They carry on the business of dealers in shelf and heavy hardware, stoves, tin, sheet iron and copperware, silver and plated goods, cutlery, oils, glass, blacksmith supplies, carriage hardware, anvils, bar iron, bellows, forges, cast-steel, hammers, nails, barbed wire and so forth. They have had a long experience in their line and keep the largest hardware stock west of Winnipeg. Their present store is 20x30, they put up an addition last year, also a large warehouse in the rear of their lot as rapidly increasing trade made it necessary for them to increase their stock. Their bar iron and carriage hardware are a speciality. A special feature in their line is that they handle heating and cook stoves, barbed wire and heavy goods in car loads direct from the manufacturers.

Their establishment is one of the most useful among the mercantile firms in Calgary. In selecting Calgary as business place they have wisely seen that in the near future the town must become a distributing center. The firm comprises Mr. E. R. Rogers and Mr. Archibald Grant. Their advertisement will be found on the opposite page.

Does it sound like the handyman's heaven? Probably someone like George Murdoch, resourceful and able to turn his hand to anything, spent a great deal of time browsing through the Rogers and Grant store. But there were many people either less self-sufficient or who lacked the time or inclination to

185

build a house, or a store, or a chicken coop. Contractors and builders flourished. There are eight carpenter shops listed in the 1885 directory, who, taken together, could advertise a wide range of services. One, for instance, specialized in stairs and shop fronts. Some concentrated on stonework and plastering. Another, Jarrett and Cushing, produced sashes and doors; this company is also described in the directory:

This firm, during the past year erected, under contract, a large number of the principal buildings in town. They have recently put up some buildings on the Mission property; and they are about to erect a dwelling on the Mission property for Mr. J. Burland, one for Sergeant Hamilton, and one for Mr. Rozelle. They are now completing a residence for Messrs Rankin & Allan; and they are the contractors for the new two thousand dollar residence of Mr. Rogers of Rogers & Grant, which is to be erected on the Mission property, and another handsome residence for Mr. R. I. Hardisty to cost about four thousand dollars. The amount of their contracts during the present year will probably amount to one hundred thousand dollars for buildings alone.

Jarrett and Cushing was a perfect example of the adaptable and enterprising frontier business. Having experienced delays in obtaining finishing materials, they had decided to manufacture the materials for themselves. They purchased planing equipment and established a factory. This sort of enterprise was exactly the sort of thing the town was anxious to encourage. It not only provided employment but kept capital from going out to eastern producers. By 1892 the firm had achieved a creditable degree of success. As an inducement and encouragement to the operation, the town passed a by-law that year exempting them from paying taxes. Their success continued, and eventually they had a network of woodworking plants in Edmonton, Regina, and Saskatoon.

Above: A cartoon of Cushing's establishment, taken from the Prairie Illustrated, 1890-91.

Left: W.H. Cushing's mill.   *Below:* A group of Calgary carpenters, 1901, pause for a smoking break.

188

PROPRIETORS

Opposite above: Robert V. Hunt, owner of Chicago Outfitting Company. *Opposite below:* James Abel Hornby and his daughter Marion in the Bowness area, 1906. One of Calgary's entrepreneurs, he owned, among other things, the building that housed McClellan & Hawkes grocery store (left). *Right:* The Simon family in their confectionery shop. *Below:* "The Geisha", Olivier's bakery and confectionery.

Alberta Ice Man

With ranching and the beef industry such a thriving concern in Calgary, it was to be expected that there would be a considerable demand for ice. There were various sources of ice about Calgary, but the closest dependable source of uncontaminated ice was Lake Wabamum near Edmonton. It's cost, not surprisingly, was prohibitive. Sensing an opportunity, R. C. Thomas went into the ice business. This was not Thomas's first business venture in Calgary by any means — he had by this time engaged in a number of various enterprises. He was always ready to try something new, to take an outside chance.

Robert Cadogan Thomas was born in Wales in 1862. As a youth he became proficient in German and French and even in his eighties could speak in these languages "with precision and fluency." He also acquired the professional skills of the book-keeper, and an insight into business methods that would serve him well in later years. Thomas arrived in Calgary in 1884 with 575 dollars cash and a team, wagon, and harness. After working for ten days for the Hudson's Bay Company taking trial balances, he paid the usual ten dollar registration fee and took a homestead at the mouth of Pine Creek on the Bow River. He purchased additional land from the CPR which he farmed for several years. During this time, he married Egerie Louise Shaw, daughter of the Midnapore pioneer Samuel William Shaw.

In 1891 Thomas was lured away from his homestead to manage a ten-thousand-acre farm at Gull Lake for the Canadian Colonization Company. For this he received the sum of twenty dollars a month. Six months later the company went broke and Thomas was out of a job. Instead of returning to his own farm, which he still owned, he came to Calgary, where for fifteen hundred dollars he purchased a livery barn on the corner of Stephen Avenue and Hamilton Street. In the year 1892 this was considered a second-rate location. S. J. Clarke, proprietor of the Queen's Hotel at Drinkwater Street and Stephen Avenue, was attempting, along with his fellow councillors, to create the city centre east of McTavish Street. As an indication of their success, the barn Thomas bought on the west side had been out of business and vacant for three years. Thomas, however, confidently extended the structure, added dormers to the loft, and opened for business under the name of Frontier Stables. The venture was an unqualified success. In those days the livery stable was as much a gathering place as the hotel saloon or the barber shop, and Thomas's barn became one of the more popular hangouts of the local ranchers; George Lane, for example, used to hold court there during his trips into town from the Bar U, and no doubt a great deal of unofficial business took place within its walls.

It was natural that his business interests should expand. To keep his horses and equipment busy he operated a coal

Opposite above: R. C. Thomas's ice wagon at the Dominion Exhibition, 1908. *Above right:* The old Frontier Stables. *Below:* The Thomas Block on Seventh Avenue and Second Street S.W. By 1911, the year this picture was taken, Thomas was into coal, ice, lumber, and farm machinery.

P.O. BOX 138.
PHONE 20.

CALGARY, ALT
CANADA.

191

yard, a lumber yard, and a farm machinery agency. With the arrival of the motor car, however, the demand for a livery stable was bound to diminish, so in 1911, he directed his energies to other ventures.

Recognizing the need for improvement in the methods used for keeping perishable foods, Thomas decided to enter the ice business, and in 1911 formed the Alberta Ice Company. Alberta Ice secured land at Keith nine miles west of Calgary opposite Bowness Park, and created a nine-acre artificial lake connected to the Bow. In 1913, six ice houses, each forty-five feet high, thirty feet wide, and one hundred ten feet long, with a storage capacity of thirty thousand tons of ice, were constructed at a cost of ninety thousand dollars. A similar facility was built in the Sunalta District.

"Diversified ice farming" was introduced. Water from the Bow River was filtered over gravel beds into the reservoir. In the winter season six to eight "crops" could be "harvested". After the ice froze to a predetermined depth, it was cut by ice ploughs drawn by horses along lines formed by markers. Conveyor belts lifted the blocks from the lake into the storage houses. Modern machinery loaded the delivery wagons. The 75-man crew cut 1,500 tons per day.

A large portion of the crop was shipped directly to supply stations between Swift Current and Vancouver to be used by the CPR for its stations and passenger service, and by other corporations needing refrigeration. Ice was also supplied to communities in the greater Calgary area.

Below and Opposite: Views of the Alberta Ice Company.

But the ice business is not the field in which R. C. Thomas made his greatest impact on the life of Calgary. To an amazing degree, he was instrumental in transforming the face of the city through his numerous building projects. In 1911, the same year as the ice business was started, Thomas demolished his livery barn and on the same site built the Cadogan Block, a four-storey building containing forty-two offices, which was later renovated as an addition to his Royal Hotel. As further proof of his faith in the west side of the city, he built the Royal Hotel (not to be confused with James Reilly's old Royal Hotel), the Wales Hotel, the Frontier Block, and the Thomas Block, all on Second Street. To the time of his death he was still petitioning for a subway railway crossing at Fourth Street, but opposing political interests were able to prevent this. Such minor setbacks neither destroyed his optimism nor prevented his success. At one time he owned eight lots on Seventh Avenue between First and Second streets, as well as property on Third and Fourth avenues. One building site he purchased for 400 dollars; 15 years later, in 1915, he sold the property for 55,000 dollars cash. The money was used to finance the construction of an additional sixty rooms onto the Royal Hotel. The Thomas Block was removed to make way for the Wales Hotel.

While Thomas was an advocate of development and progress, he had a wealth of memories of early Calgary. In those early days before many bridges had been built in Alberta, almost everyone had a good fording-the-river story, and R. C. Thomas was no exception. In March 1885, during the Rebellion Scare, he was hauling supplies on the Calgary-Edmonton Trail. His party experienced difficulty fording Nose Creek before hitting the three-rut trail to Red Deer (the three ruts were cut by the one-horse, two-wheeled carts used by the Hudson's Bay Company). When they reached the Red Deer River crossing about three miles upstream from the present city of Red Deer, the river was in flood, so all hands laid into the task of building a ferry. The ferry, complete with cannon, was finally launched. Picket ropes were tied together to form a long line which was tied to the ferry and secured on the north bank of the flooding river. But the current proved too strong. The collection of ropes broke under the strain, and the ferry — cannon and all — floated downriver to strike ground opposite the present site of Red Deer. By the time the ferry was rescued the river had subsided, and the teamsters were able to cross unassisted.

Another of Thomas's favourite memories was of purchasing the Edmonton Coal Company in 1895, and personally canvassing his customers from door to door. He was so intent on his work that on one occasion he went into an office to sell coal only to discover that it was the headquarters of a competitor.

R. C. Thomas covered a lot of ground in his eighty-three years. Pioneer, homesteader, drayman, retailer, developer, hotel man, local politician, and ice-company president, he was typical of the kind of man who came to Calgary in those first years and gave it its particular civic and industrial character.

Fording the Bow River at Calgary, 1887. The spires of the Anglican Church and the Fire Hall predominated the skyline at this time.

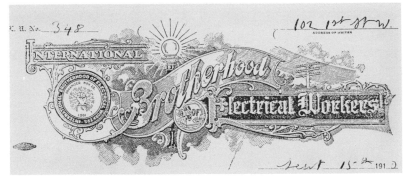

The story of the milling industry in Alberta begins with Father Albert Lacombe. Arriving at Fort Edmonton in the fall of 1852, the young French-Canadian priest established a mission at St. Albert. The settlement flourished. He organized the first cart brigade to transport tools, seed, grain, and machinery from Fort Garry to Fort Edmonton. In 1863 he built a tiny stone grist mill in the primitive frontier country to grind wheat into flour for local consumption. This was the first flour mill in the North-West Territories.

About the same time, Donald McLean, the son of a Lakefield, Ontario farmer, was serving his apprenticeship in a local flour mill. As was the custom, local farmers brought their grain to be ground into flour for bread and feed for their livestock. The water-powered stone mill ground the soft Ontario grains into products acceptable to the local market. Western grain growers started to ship their hard Manitoba wheat to Ontario. McLean experimented, blending western and eastern grain, hoping to produce a better flour, but it seemed that the western grain was not satisfactory.

Then fate played into his hand — the mill where he worked was destroyed by fire. The new mill built to replace the original was equipped with the newly invented steel rollers, purifiers, sifters, and the new centrifugal reels (it was only the second mill in Canada with this advanced equipment). Once again McLean tried blending the slightly frosted western wheat with Ontario wheat — and this time found to his surprise the new mill ground the best flour he had ever made.

Excited by the potential of western Canadian wheat, McLean sold his interests and in 1892 moved to Calgary, then a town of four thousand people. Supported by a petition signed by one-half of the resident ratepayers, he applied to the corporation of the Town of Calgary for a bonus towards the erection of a grist mill. The Town Solicitor drew up an agreement dated the tenth day of March, A.D. 1892, in which McLean:

Agreed forthwith to deposit with the Treasurer of the said Corporation the sum of one hundred dollars as a guarantee that he will, if the said By-Law when submitted to the said ratepayers is carried, proceed with all due diligence in the erection of such a mill, and that the same shall be completed within all respects by the First day of October, A.D. 1892.

McLean also agreed to "complete his said Mill with a capacity to reasonable satisfaction and shall have insured the same for the sum of three thousand dollars; and for . . . five years thereafter not remove such mill from the said town." The City for its part agreed that the mill should be tax-exempt for a period of ten years.

Flour Mills

Opposite: The labour force of Calgary. *Above:* CPR employees leaving work, 1912. *Centre:* Letterhead of the International Brotherhood of Electrical Workers. *Below:* Collective shots of Riverside Laundry employees, 1913; and of Local 496, Plumbers, Gas, and Steam Fitters, 1907.

R. C. Thomas later recalled that "McLean arrived in Calgary in 1892 with a team of horses and a wagon loaded down with milling machinery. He built his mill on Ninth Avenue W. near Fourth Street with stone from the old quarry on Seventeenth Avenue W."

Modern equipment was installed — including the all-important steel rollers — and the mill was ready to go into production. At that time not enough grain was grown in the Calgary area to keep the mill operating at its full capacity of fifty barrels per day, so McLean made arrangements to purchase wheat in Moose Jaw. The CPR agreed to freight the wheat to Calgary for thirty-five cents per bushel.

In the early milling processes the wheat was ground between a single set of stones in a single operation. The "chop" was then separated by sifting or bolting into the various mill classifications — flour, shorts, middlings, and bran. As tiny particles remained after the finest screening, pioneer milling processes produced a dark flour.

Today, modern milling is a process of "reduction" rather than grinding. The kernels of wheat are broken, and through a series of reduction rolls, screens, and reclaiming rolls, are progressively reduced in size. The screens vary in size from coarse metal screens to the finest silk or nylon. The object is to mill a flour with the least possible admixture of bran particles which impair baking qualities.

Right: Donald McLean's Calgary Milling Company, mill and elevator. *Above:* The mill as it looked in the '20's. *Opposite:* Aspects of the flour industry.

Robin Hood Mills   Calgary

On a typical grinding floor in a modern mill, there are thirty stands of rolls, each of which grinds a separate classification or size of stock. The thirty stands collectively are known as a "mill". There may be several "mills" in one plant.

McLean, after pioneering the milling industry in Calgary, sold his plant in 1898 to a group of local business men and moved to Moose Jaw where he started a second mill. In Calgary the operation was renamed the Calgary Milling Company. The new owners included I. K. Kerr and P. A. Prince of the Eau Claire and Bow River Lumber Company. Eau Claire at that time supplied electric power to the downtown section of Calgary; the steam engines at the flour mill were used to power the mill by day and at night to turn generators to supplement the electric power supply. William Carson, a grain-elevator operator from Maimi, Manitoba, was brought in to manage the mill, and Fred Brown was hired to manage their retail grocery store on Stephen Avenue. In 1911 the Calgary Milling Company sold its interests to Robin Hood Flour Mills, who, three years previously, had also purchased Donald McLean's Moose Jaw Mill.

In 1906, the Western Milling Company built a flour mill with a capacity of three hundred barrels per day. In the same year the Brackman-Ker Milling Company built a cereal mill in Calgary to produce rolled oats, oatmeal, graham and whole wheat flour, pearl barley and other cereals. The two companies amalgamated in 1913 to form Western Canada Flour Mills, which in turn was incorporated under the name of Purity Flour Mills Ltd.

Below: Harvesting Alberta grain. *Opposite:* Hauling the grain to the elevators.

ACCOMMODATIONS

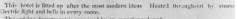

THE ALBERTA HOTEL

The Leading House in the Territories

This hotel is fitted up after the most modern ideas. Heated throughout by steam. Electric light and bells in every room.
The cuisine department is managed by an experienced cook.
All trains met. Sample rooms for commercial men. Rates sent on application.
A. W. BURGESS, Clerk.   H. A. PERLEY, Proprietor.

Grand Union Hotel, Calgary.

Anyone looking for digs in early Calgary had a number of choices. R. B. Bennett's was the Alberta Hotel. He was probably impressed by the sobriety and dignity of the lobby *(opposite)*; anyone alarmed by this could put his fears to rest in the bar, "the longest in the West", or so they claimed. Probably inspired by the Alberta's success, S. J. Clarke by the '90's had replaced his saloon with the Queen's Hotel. Its location at Stephen and Drinkwater was the busiest corner in town in those days. The Grand Union Hotel was built on Atlantic Avenue in full view of approaching trains. It probably looked like a good place to stay to incoming visitors. Certainly the patrons ranged along its balconies and steps seem very satisfied.

For those looking for home comforts there were always the boarding houses like the establishment of Mrs. Jean McWilliam, captured here in a pensive moment, and in a jollier mood with her first boarders.

Markets

The earliest reference made to a public market in Calgary was in 1885, when the city obtained sites for a town hall, fire hall, and market place. Under By-law 20, approved February 11 of that year, "the vacant space lying between Byers Blacksmith Shop and Drinkwater Street" was declared the Calgary Public Market. The new By-law stipulated that all hay, straw, coal, and firewood brought into Calgary for sale could be sold only at the city market. First, however, it had to be weighed and measured on the public weigh scales, operated by the superintendent of the market. Nor could any such load brought into the city for delivery be turned over to the owner until it was weighed. Likewise, horned cattle, calves, swine, sheep, horses or other livestock were to be weighed at the market before being offered for sale.

The market place was often a scene of uproar and confusion with rigs pulling in from all directions vying for position. It was the market superintendent's task to line up all the loaded wagons, carts, sleighs, or other vehicles. Once in place, the driver was instructed not to move out of order until his load was disposed of, unless he planned to leave the market completely. In that case he was not to loiter on the streets, but to take his load directly back out of town.

Penalties were imposed on anyone who refused to have his load weighed, or failed to pay the weighing or measuring fee. And anyone who dared to dupe the weigh-master or buyer of a load of hay, straw, coal or wood by adding heavy articles to the load or wetting or concealing wet or unmerchantable articles in the load was liable to be fined.

The following scale of weighing fees gives an indication of the sort of things sold in the market:

For weighing every load of hay, straw, coal or grain in bulk, per ton, when drawn by two animals, the sum of 25 cents
When drawn by one animal, the sum of 15 cents

For measuring every load of firewood when drawn by two animals, the sum of 25 cents
When drawn by one animal, the sum of 15 cents

For measuring wood when delivered on the premises of the purchaser or on the banks of the rivers within this Municipality 2 cords or under, the sum of 25 cents
5 cords or over 2 cords, the sum of 50 cents
10 cords or over 5 cords, the sum of 75 cents
Every additional cord over 10 cords, the sum of 02 cents

For weighing all articles not exceeding 100 pounds, the sum of 05 cents
Over 100 pounds and not exceeding 500 pounds, the sum of 10 cents

In a frontier town the horse was all important and there were a good number of establishments catering to their needs. *Above:* Shoeing a horse at Page's Blacksmith shop. Page is on the right; his partner Tom Oliver is the one with the pipe. *Opposite:* The employees of Carson's Saddlery.

*Over 500 pounds and not exceeding 2,000 pounds,
the sum of 25 cents
Every additional ton or fraction thereof,
the sum of 25 cents*

*For weighing every living horned cattle, horse, mare,
gelding, or mule, the sum of 15 cents*

*For weighing every live calf, sheep, or swine
the sum of 15 cents*

*For weighing every load of merchandise not otherwise
enumerated herein the sum of 25 cents.*

Two years later, the market site was moved. On March 12, 1887, a By-law was passed designating "the roadway on Atlantic Avenue from Bains Brothers Stables to Osler Street, in the Town of Calgary" as the public market. Somebody must have been tempted to start a lucrative business, for under the new regulations it was emphasized that making charges or fees for weighing as a source of profit was strictly forbidden.

The market at this time was not equipped for selling produce, and there was considerable delay in setting up the proper facilities. Two years later, on January 16, 1889, the *Herald* reported:

*The advisability of establishing a farmer's market in
Calgary has several times been pointed out but we appear no
nearer witnessing the accomplishment of the project than
when the necessity was first felt. As the town increases and
the country becomes settled up, the necessity for the
establishment of a market is more apparent. As things are
at present, there is a profitless competition between the
produce merchants and those country people who prefer to
market their own produce and peddle it about town. . .
Apart from this actual monetary consideration altogether,
the convenience a market would be to all concerned is a
powerful argument in favor of its establishment. If we had a
public market, the thrifty matron, instead of having to
ramble over half the town in search of the wherewithal to
judiciously and economically furnish her pantry and cellar,
probably to be disappointed after all, would be able in a few
minutes, at a public market, to secure exactly the supplies
she wanted, and at what she can easily satisfy herself are
fair prices.*

*This matter is such an important one that it is most sincerely
to be hoped that the new council will as soon as installed,
take steps towards filling this pressing want. There appears no
reason why any great expense should be incurred in*

Opposite: The growing panorama of Calgary. *Above:* The city in 1886. To the left can be seen the spire of The Church of the Redeemer, and a large gable that is probably Boynton Hall. These were the two most impressive buildings in town at the time. *Centre:* The same view five years later. The Fire Hall, built 1887, dominates the centre of the view. To the extreme right is the newly completed Alexander Corner. The Hudson's Bay now occupies that spot. *Below:* The city *circa* 1899. There has been considerable filling in of empty spaces over the years. For example Hull's barnlike Opera House can be seen to the left of Alexander Corner, and several large business blocks have sprung up in the background between the Church of the Redeemer and the Fire Hall.

carrying this project out. A rough platform similar to a station landing with some sort of a shed over it should fit the bill. It would certainly be advisable, if possible, to secure a more central site for the market than the land purchased for the purpose; but even if it had to be established there, it would be better there than nowhere.

Shortly thereafter plans for a market shed were drawn up, but things weren't progressing very smoothly. The first time a building motion was submitted to Council only four members showed up for the meeting, and the bill had to be reintroduced in July, 1889. Here the whole question of even going ahead with a market at all was argued, until one of the councillors pointed out that the matter of a market had already been decided, it was too late to be discussing its advisability, and it was time to consider the plans. Councillors Fitzgerald, Murdoch, and Orr voted in favour of calling for tenders to build a market, but the motion was overruled by Councillors King, Grant, and Bannerman, supported by Mayor Marsh.

The defeat of the market motion was a blow to district farmers, who were pressing for some kind of market house in Calgary. Meetings were held to draw up petitions, and some farmers even refused to trade with the councillors who opposed the building motion. Their pressure was successful, for the matter was resolved, and by December 1889 a new building was rising in town. A *Herald* article of December 18, 1889 reads:

The work on the new market shed, commenced in midsummer, is about completed. The building is 110 feet long and 20 feet wide, and a single story. The shed is open in the rear, but a portion is being enclosed, so that farmers can be protected against the inclemency of the weather when necessary. The front is enclosed with doors and windows. The shed is still unpainted. A set of scales to weigh as high as a quarter of beef will be supplied, and also shelf scales for smaller articles. The market, as our farmer readers in the vicinity of Calgary should remember, is free of tolls or charges of any kind, and it should be utilized accordingly. It is understood, of course, that no meat can be offered for sale in the market in less quantity than a quarter of a carcass, and only producers can exhibit goods for sale there.

A market bylaw provides that Thursday shall be the market day for the town of Calgary, the market being open on that day from six AM to six PM all the year round, except when Thursday will happen to be a statutory holiday. It is time something was being done to give effect to this decision. The day fixed seems suitable for an established market day, especially for persons driving long distances, although every day will be market day for those who choose to come on other days than Thursdays.

There will probably be a handsome revenue coming to the city from this quarter in the near future. The farmers ought to be satisfied with an arrangement which gives a free market, the only charge imposed on their products being for weighing hay, straw, cattle, etc., measuring wood, etc.

The article went on to quote the prices of country produce:

Hay is now selling at ten dollars to eleven dollars by the ton loose, thirteen dollars to fourteen pressed. Alberta oats have been better in quality this year than those of Manitoba and Ontario. They are selling at forty-five to fifty cents, according to weight and quality. Housekeepers are paying for potatoes ninety cents, turnips thirty cents, carrots two to three cents, per lb. Eggs are in demand. Packed Manitoba sell at thirty cents; fresh are very scarce at fifty cents. Butter retails at thirty-five cents for fresh; packed domestic twenty-seven to twenty-eight cents; Manitoba packed twenty-five cents.

And so for nine years the market ran satisfactorily, until new regulations were needed to tighten up its operation. On May 31, 1898 the city council passed By-law 359 "to establish a Public Market and Public Weigh Scales in the City of Calgary and for fixing the fees for weighing upon the said scales." A new site was chosen, the north side of McIntyre Avenue east of Drinkwater Street, and the market day was changed to Friday from eight in the morning until six P.M. It was reaffirmed that only producers could sell goods — these being fish, grain, roots, vegetables, hay, straw, and other produce, and meat in quantities more than the quarter of a carcass. Anyone selling fish, or meat in quantities of less than a quarter carcass had first to obtain a twenty-five-dollar license from the City Clerk and a ten-cent daily certificate from the market clerk attesting that such had been inspected. This meat and fish could be sold or displayed only after 10 A.M. The driver of any load of hay, straw, coal or other produce brought into the public market would now be required to supply his name and that of the owner of the goods to the market clerk. Every load had to be weighed, and a ticket of weight obtained before any delivery to a purchaser.

The varied duties of the market clerk were outlined in this By-law. These included weighing articles and vehicles; issuing a dated and signed weigh ticket to the person in charge of the load; weighing an unloaded wagon, if requested by the purchaser or seller; and keeping a record of the owner of all articles weighed, the person for whom the load was weighed, the weight of the articles, the day and hour of weighing, and a description of the wagon or other vehicle and its weight. These records were to be available for inspection whenever necessary.

The market clerk was also responsible for inspecting the hay and other produce on sale in the public market and for issuing a certificate if it was wet or otherwise not saleable. If he found that an article brought to be weighed was wet, or from any other cause was heavier than it should be, he could make a deduction according to his judgement. And he was appointed a special constable for the market, with the power to enforce market regulations and control the people frequenting the premises.

In 1907 the market was enlarged and improved, but there still was no substantial market building. The *Farmers and Ranchers Review* of September 1908 headlined, somewhat ironically, "Farmers Now Have a Market. They Can Now Se'l Their Produce in Comfort." According to the article,

Calgary has at last a creditable market, where farmers from the country and others can place their produce for sale. Alderman Manarey, chairman of the market and health committee, has had one of the old high school buildings fitted up with tables for the lighter produce, and seats arranged where ladies can sit down and rest. On the east side of the building is an open lot, where wagons can be arranged in rows.

By 1910, the Consumer's League which included among its supporters numerous women concerned with the prices and quality of foodstuffs, had become an active agent in the city. One of its most influential members was Mrs. Annie Gale, later a city alderwoman. She explained how her interest in a market had been aroused shortly after her arrival here in 1912:

I could not understand the poorness of the quality and the fearfully high price of vegetables; with millions of acres of as-yet unsurveyed land in the Province we poor immigrants were compelled to pay a quarter for two or three mouldy carrots, a quarter for a miserable, frost-bitten cabbage, which would only be fed to cows in the Old Country. Then I watched a friend of mine grow English vegetables, white turnips, etc. on her husband's ranch, and looked on while she vainly visited all the stores in Calgary to find a purchaser, but all merchants had contracts with B.C. growers and could not break them and encourage the settlers of their own Province. This short-sightedness surprised me greatly, also the want of control of the real estate boom exhibited by the

Some of

Above: Montage of the Spy Hill Dairy and Stock Farm. By 1915 the dairy business had become fairly modernized and sophisticated.

Right: This section of Sleepy Hollow High School was, for a while, used as the public market. *Below:* After considerable effort and agitation on the part of Calgary housewives they finally got their market. This handsome building was built in 1914 at the corner of Second Avenue and Third Street E.

*government of the city; so that when the first Consumers'
League was organized here you can readily understand that
I took the work of establishing a Municipal Market where
small producers could find purchasers for their products and
be independent of the short-sighted merchant. . . In
getting legislation for the market, I was again struck by the
selfishness of the merchants in protecting fully their
own little businesses. They had lost sight of the development of
their country for I saw at once that the Province must
depend for its development on its agriculture.*

Mrs. Gale worked hard to promote the idea of a better
market. She met with members of the City Board of Health to
have regulations eliminated from the Health Act to encourage
small producers, and she encouraged aldermen to have by-
laws made and amended. By 1913 interest in a public market
had grown and there was considerable agitation to get the

This group of Calgary officials, 1908, were
probably some of the people concerned with the
planning of Calgary's market. The man with the
spade is Commissioner S. J. Clarke. Beside him
with his hands on his hips, is Mayor Cameron.
Alderman Moodie is to his left in the little cart. The
man in uniform on the right is Mr. Shelley,
Haymarket and Pound Keeper. It is quite likely
that the occasion for this picture was the sod-
turning ceremony for the market shed that was
built in 1908. Certainly the load of hay parked
behind at the left would suggest some kind of
marketing location.

project underway. According to a *Herald* report published
almost twenty-five years later, "In 1913 it was made a public
issue and after five hundred Calgary housewives attended a
meeting and heckled the aldermanic candidates for four hours,
the city fathers decided that a market was necessary. It was
built the following year at a substantial cost on a site near Second Avenue and Third Street E."

Calgary Booms

The year 1912 saw the end of a great land boom in Calgary. In the three previous years the population of Calgary increased by more than thirty thousand, and promoters spoke of the city reaching beyond the then level of eighty-five thousand to five hundred thousand. Nearly everyone played the land boom and farms five miles beyond Ogden were surveyed as home sites.

Astronomical prices were paid for city lots. The Royal Bank paid four thousand dollars per foot for the old Hudson's Bay property on Centre Street and Eighth Avenue. The Canada Life Assurance Co. paid two thousand per foot for the site of its present premises. The Hudson's Bay Co. paid 750,000 dollars for the Seventh Avenue site of the original portion of the new store. The Merchants Bank paid two hundred thousand dollars for the seventy by one hundred foot site of the old Royal Hotel, located on the site of the Treasury House. The Dominion Bank paid one hundred thousand dollars for its site opposite the Post Office.

The land boom had just subsided when the Dingman Well blew in about May 14, 1914. During the following few weeks five hundred oil companies were formed. Anyone who had no oil stock was considered an outcast, and the orgy of speculation reached such heights that some brokers used wastepaper baskets to hold the money thrown at them by the speculators. Mr. Vance Graveley remembers seeing baskets full of money being carried across the street from brokerage offices to the bank.

The outbreak of war in August, 1914, brought the oil boom to an end. Today few of the companies then formed are in existence. Few of them ever drilled for oil. By 1916, the population of Calgary had receded to 56,000.

Scenes of boom-town. *Right:* Barrelling oil at Dingman Well. *Opposite:* Oil and real estate offices; and a hoax postcard of 1914 proclaiming Calgary's prosperity.

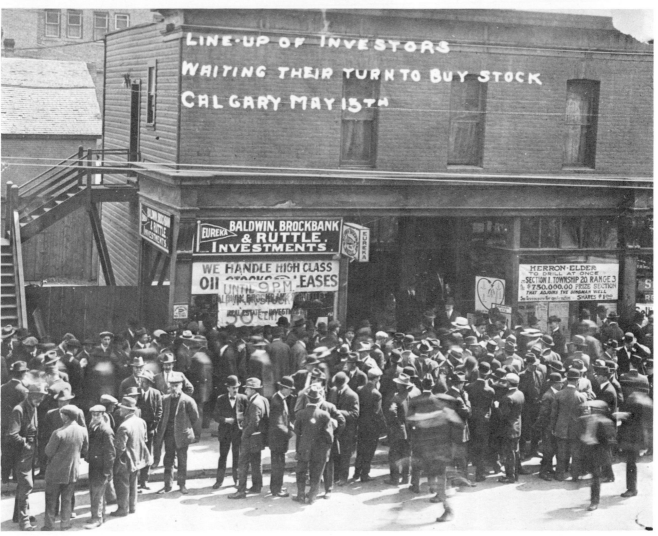

Chapter 7 Moving

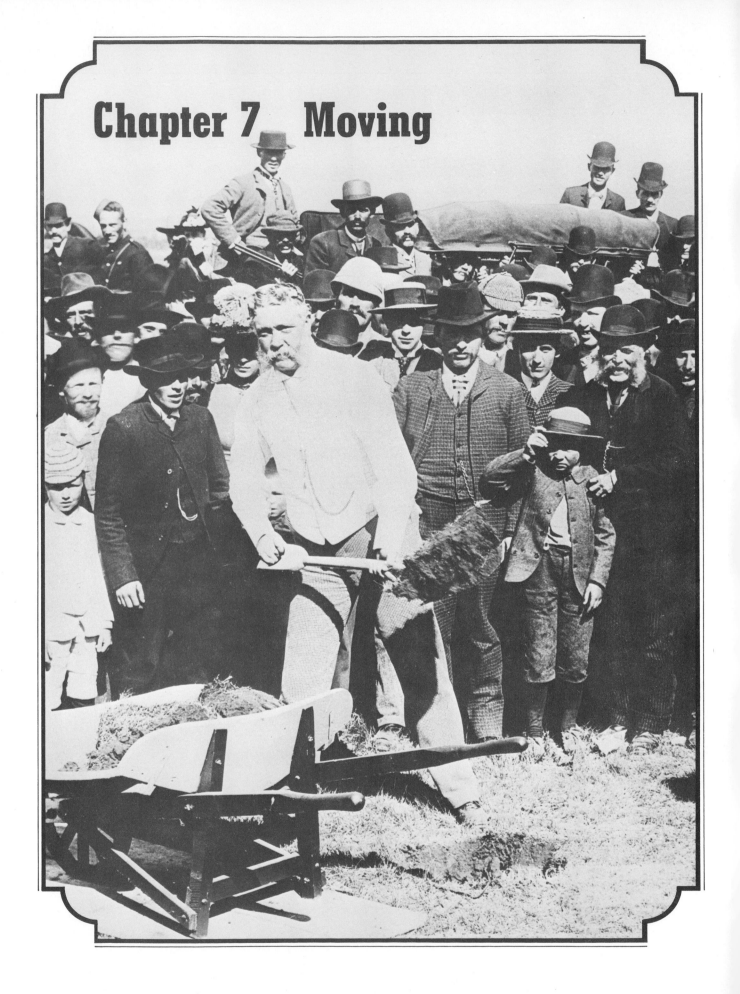

The car line runs up a hill on the other side of the city. Last winter when the ground was very slippery, a car started from the top, leaving the conductor behind, without the motorman being aware of it. The conductor just chased it by sitting down on the snow and toboganning down; but he hadn't gone very far before he had taken on a passenger. A lady who emerged from a side street, sat on him suddenly, and went along.

An ordinary man would have complained about being used in that way; but the lady's luck was in when she dropped on a streetcar conductor because he just couldn't help being polite and actually apologized to her for not being able to take her further than the bottom of the hill. "I'm very sorry, ma'am," he said, as soon as he could get enough breath to speak, "but you will have to change here. I ain't carrying passengers any further!"

Related by William Dunlop, 1914

Prairie Freighters

Before the railway came to Calgary, most of the freight arrived via Missouri River steamboats to Benton, Montana, and thence over the trail to Fort Macleod and Fort Calgary. The freight trains of those days were pulled by bull teams and horse and mule teams. Three or four big covered wagons coupled together were hauled by ten or twelve yoke of oxen, or ten or twelve teams of horses or mules. They travelled an average speed of twelve miles per day. Each bull team was driven by a "bull whacker" who walked alongside his team, handling a heavy rawhide whip with a fifteen-foot lash and "popper" which cracked like a rifle when thrown over the teams. The horse and mule teams were driven by a "mule skinner" who rode the near wheeler, guiding the team with a jerkline running from his hand through rings on the head stall of each near horse. The horses were trained to turn to the right by a succession of sharp jerks on the line and to the left by a steady pull. Several of these teams travelling together were called a train. Bull whackers and mule skinners excelled all other classes in the country, including cow punchers, the police, and stage-coach drivers in the picturesqueness of their vocabulary. The round-up cooks almost ran them a dead heat.

Because of the soft mud of the northern prairies which made the heavy bull teams unsuitable, the chief freighting vehicle north of Calgary was the Red River cart. *Below:* a donkey-drawn cart at Wetaskiwin, 1895. *Opposite:* Bull teams en route from Fort Benton to Fort Macleod, 1879.

When the bull whackers, the mule skinners, the stage-coach drivers, and cow punchers congregated, the frontier town became a lively place. A pleasant time was had by all, especially if there was a generous supply of Montana 40-ROD contraband whisky available.

The Edmonton Trail

Above: George K. Leeson, who ran the Royal Mail Line. His advertisement appears *(opposite)* next to a picture of the stage. *Below:* The stage, mired in one of the many mudholes between Calgary and Edmonton.

The true Calgary-Edmonton Trail as we know it today was made in 1875 — the same year that Fort Calgary was established by the North-West Mounted Police.

The credit for opening the trail should go to the Reverend John McDougall and his brother David, who cut out the northern half of the route in 1873, while making a cart road from Fort Edmonton to Morley. This route was roughly the same as the old fur trail made by the North West Company in 1803, between Fort Augustus and the old Bow Fort. It followed an old Indian trail past the Bear Hills, across the Battle River north of Red Deer, over the Red Deer River west of the present city, and turned southwest at Olds to travel in almost a straight line to Morley. After the establishment of Fort Calgary, this route branched at Olds and went directly south over the Didsbury Coulee to Nose Creek, and on down to the new Police post.

By 1881, the use of the trail had developed to the point where local citizens began demanding mail service, and to back up their claim, an *ad hoc* census was taken. According to this survey, between Edmonton and the Red Deer River the population was as follows: "Peace Hills Indian Farm (Wetaskiwin), ten whites and fifty half-breeds; Battle River Station (Ponoka), three whites and three hundred Indians; Red River Crossing, no population."

Their request was granted. The first mail service between Calgary and Edmonton started in July, 1883, with Al McPherson and John Coleman obtaining the contract. They made regular fortnightly trips carrying light freight, Royal Mail, and passengers. Heavy freight was handled by wagon trains. The first stage-coach passenger service was started in the following month by D. McLeod of Fort Edmonton. The weekly stage made the two-hundred-mile journey (as it was then) in five days, stopping at Peace Hills, Battle River, and Red Deer River, and at other points on request.

On January 10, 1885, a bridge was built across the Battle River about one and one-half miles downstream from the old ford. It measured forty feet long, and was complete with piers and stone-fortified approaches. The bridge necessitated a change in route; the new road swerved east about four miles south of the river and rejoined the old trail six miles beyond the ford.

The first survey of the Calgary-Edmonton Trail was made in 1886, with C. A. Bigger laying out the route from Calgary to the Red Deer River, and George P. Roy surveying the portion north to Fort Edmonton. If the comments made in his report are any criterion, surveyor

Right: William G. Gilmore, a driver for the Calgary-Macleod Stage photographed in 1896. *Below:* The Millarville Stage in front of the Calgary Fire Hall. It ran a twice-weekly service, leaving Millarville on Tuesdays and Thursdays and returning from Calgary Wednesdays and Saturdays.

Roy must have been something of a prophet who could foresee the future. His predictions of great things in the pioneer days of wagons and stage-coaches have come true. The most interesting was his statement about the selection of a roadway: "In view of the great traffic and immense travel which some day may be done this way, my intention was to make the road as straight as the actual direction of the trail between the two extreme points Red Deer and Edmonton would allow."

And straight it was. Over small hillocks, through corduroyed muskeg, and across small streams in the parkland, the surveyor laid the trail, always making sure that it would be easily passable. "A little ditching, a small culvert, a slight cut or a few branches thrown on a soft spot" were all that was needed to make the road passable at all times.

He also made predictions about the maintenance: "After settlement, farmers will improve the road to satisfy the public." This indeed became a fact at the turn of the century — when the land seekers churned the trail into an almost impossible quagmire, the farmers in the locality voluntarily doubled the road tax on themselves.

After the completion of the Calgary and Edmonton Railway in 1891, the old trail lost much of its popularity. Nevertheless, it did not fall into total disuse; commenting on the high freight rates charged by the railway, the Edmonton *Bulletin* had this to say: "The Old Trail is not as deserted as it might have been expected. From Red Deer south a great deal of freight is being handled by wagons, as it can be done more cheaply than by train. Elliot and McCue of Wolf Creek, and W. MacDonald of Bear Hills Plain are bringing in freight by wagon." And eventually, of course, the Calgary-Edmonton Trail progressed from a crude pathway in an unexplored wilderness to a strategic highway serving a modern civilization.

The Calgary-Edmonton Stage at Blindman.

Ike Ruttle

Calgary history is replete with instances of men who, endowed with that business acumen and ability to make good, started into business on a small scale, and through constant attention to commercial principles and an earnest endeavour to serve the public in a satisfying manner, gained positions of esteem in the community, and built up a fortune in their business. Isaac G. Ruttle was one of these.

Ruttle came to Calgary from Grand Forks, North Dakota, and immediately entered the livery business. Starting on a small scale, his business soon increased by leaps and bounds. Shortly after his arrival he entered into partnership with James Young to operate the Bain Stables, one of the first barns in the pioneer town. A few years later he displayed his confidence in the growth and future of Calgary by forming the Elk Livery Company with John Hamilton and F. H. Birmingham, two other pioneer liverymen. The company erected some of the most efficient facilities in Alberta. The stables and barns boasted such advanced features as concrete floors, absolutely sanitary systems of drainage, and the most modern equipment for feeding and caring for the stock. Twelve men, all expert drivers, were employed to drive the sixty-five blooded horses.

Ruttle bought out Hamilton's interests in Elk Livery and purchased a ranch of 283 acres six miles from town. The company's horses were taken to the farm to rest at frequent intervals; animals were never over-worked or driven longer than fixed periods at a time. Well lighted sanitary barns were erected to house the horses, and part of the land was cultivated to grow the feed required by the sixty-five horses in town and the ten resting. Every animal was regularly inspected by a veterinary surgeon.

With the coming of the automobile, Ruttle abandoned the livery business and converted his stables into a garage, but after several years he dropped this project and returned to his earlier occupation. He operated the livery until 1933. Ruttle also played an important role in Calgary politics. He was an alderman for four years and was a director of the Calgary Stampede for almost twenty-five years.

Right: The Elk Livery Building, 1910. In front are displayed some of Ruttle & Co.'s rigs — and various horse-drawn carriages, and a hearse. Hearses were usually rented from livery companies. The one below, however, belonged to the mortician, G. L. Jacques, who is the man standing in formal attire.

Above: The Honourable Edgar Dewdney turns the first sod for the Calgary and Edmonton Railway, Calgary, July 21, 1890.   *Right:* A group of surveyors for the railroad.

C & E Railway

P. Turner Bone.

The decade before the turn of the century was a stirring time in the country between the young communities, Edmonton and Calgary. Railway's "Big Four", of James Ross, Herbert Holt, William Mackenzie, and Donald Mann, had moved in to build the Calgary and Edmonton Railway.

The right of way surveyed by the locating engineers (M. Macleod from Red Deer Crossing to Edmonton, and P. Turner Bone from Red Deer Crossing south) followed the old Indian pathway skirting the eastern foothills from the Saskatchewan Valley southwards.

Construction started in April, 1890. A temporary trestle was built across the Bow. The Calgary-Red Deer section following the Nose Creek Valley north was completed in eighteen working days.

On the completion of the Red Deer Bridge in January 1891, the crew returned to Calgary to build the Bow River Bridge to replace the temporary span that had been thrown across to accommodate the supply trains.

The south branch of the C & E from Calgary to Macleod was dubbed "Bone's Line" - partly after its locating engineer P. Turner Bone, and also because part of its route was staked out with buffalo bones. A prairie fire near High River had left part of this section a blackened ruin. Survey crews ran out of stakes, and there was no available wood. To save time the men collected pile after pile of buffalo bones. From these piles of bones came the locating stakes. One engineer later recalled that the white bones showed up "like a streak across the blackened prairie."

Food was hauled to work crews once a month, and fresh meat was added as a supplement when supplies were available. A typical food list for a build-in crew reads:

Two sacks flour; 125 lbs. bacon; 65 lbs. ham; half barrel of corned beef; 26 lbs. sugar; 10 lbs. tea; 5 lbs. coffee; 1 keg syrup; 30 lbs. oatmeal; 25 lbs. beans; 12 lbs. split peas; 25 lbs. dried apples; 1 lb. baking powder; 1 pkg. yeast cakes; 20 lbs. rice; 1 lb. hops. One bag of salt; 1/2 lb. pepper; 1/4 lb. mustard; 10 bars soap; 12 lbs. wax candles; 1/4 gross matches; 1/2 dozen mixed pickles; 1 case tomatoes; 6 lbs. cheese; 1 tub butter; 1 pail lard; 6 lbs. currants; 25 lbs. raisins; 1 dozen corn; 1 dozen peas; 1 dozen canned milk; 1 case canned apples; and one case canned plums.

It is noted there were no CPR strawberries (prunes) on the list.

229

Some of Alberta's first settlers and merchants got their start with the railway construction gangs. When the steel was laid many of the railroad workers turned to pioneering of another sort, and became permanent residents in the area.

"Cappy" Smart, in his *Herald* memoirs, described the first excursion by rail from Calgary to Edmonton, on August, 1891:

The first railway excursion from Calgary to Edmonton which was held during the month of August, 1891, was the red-letter event of the summer, and when the train pulled out of the makeshift Calgary depot, no less than 110 Calgarians were aboard, including the mayor and members of the town council. Only a small percentage of the excursionists had ever been farther north of Calgary than the Big Hill (Crescent Heights), so the 200-mile trip was eagerly looked forward to.

As I remember it, the train proceeded north at the rate of about 25 miles an hour, but to give the passengers an extra thrill, the engineer steamed up to as high as 30 miles when the going was good. Red Deer was reached shortly after noon, and although the train stopped half an hour for lunch, it was discovered that the Red Deer residents had not been aware of the excursion and had not prepared any dinner. A number of the excursionists, however, had provided themselves with sandwiches and lemonade and the more fortunate ones very kindly shared their lunch with those who had not come prepared for such an eventuality.

The train arrived at Edmonton in the early evening. The end of track was about one mile south of the Saskatchewan River, and the travellers had to be ferried across the stream before finally reaching the town. Calgarians were surprised to find that Edmonton was a real busy and thriving centre, while the surrounding district was also being built up. The busiest little town, as I recall it, was the French settlement of St. Albert, some distance from Edmonton. The excursionists were driven there in rigs of all descriptions, returning to Edmonton the following day.

A Sports day was held on Wednesday, the feature event being the baseball game between Calgary and Edmonton. I umpired the struggle and we won by two runs. Foot races followed and then a match race was held between a Calgary runner and one from Edmonton. When all bets had been made and the ground marked off and checked, the Edmontonians trotted out a long lean Indian, clad only in a loin cloth, and what he did

Views of the survey and construction teams for the Calgary and Edmonton Railway, both on and off the job.

The day they changed to coal. Historic meeting of coal and woodburning engines on the Calgary and Edmonton Railway, at Innisfail, 1900.

to the Calgary runner was terrible. We dropped a lot of money on this event, but before leaving we invited our northern neighbours to bring their man down to Calgary in the autumn, and we would have a suitable opponent for him. They agreed to do this, but that is another story.

The excursion train finally arrived back in Calgary, with everyone singing the praises of the north country. Many persons took up farm lands in the northern districts as a direct result of this trip, and several businessmen also decided that the northern country also held better openings than many of the districts south of Calgary, and they accordingly transferred their business to the north. Strangely enough, however, when Edmontonians paid Calgary a return visit, they were equally enthusiastic over the prospects here.

It was about this time that the Edmonton baseball team came to Calgary for a return match . . . . It was a free-hitting game, and Calgary won by a score of 26 - 19. I was again umpire-in-chief of the contest, with a chap named Clark of Edmonton as base umpire.

It was this series that really started the friendly rivalry in sports between Calgary and Edmonton. Having been beaten twice in baseball, the Edmontonians switched to another branch of sport. Quietly and efficiently they organized a rugby football team. A Calgarian, who happened to be in Edmonton while the organization meeting was being held, promptly notified the local sports, and they in turn decided to organize a rugby team in preparation for the challenge that was sure to come.

Sure enough, less than a month later Calgary was challenged to a football game, and the bid was accepted. The game was to be played in Calgary, and a special train containing about five hundred Edmontonians arrived here late in October. More than two thousand dollars was bet on the game, and the northerners experienced the shock of their lives when Calgary trotted out a husky team that ran rough-shod over the Edmontonians. It was several months before another sports challenge was hurled in this direction.

Street Railway

The City of Calgary did not enter into the street railway business so much as a matter of choice as of exigency. The first franchise for a transit system was applied for when the town had a population of about four thousand. During the six years prior to 1910, Council received many applications for the right to operate a railway within the city. In 1906 a company negotiated with the City for a franchise, but being unable to come to terms, the company refused to accept the conditions required. Consequently, a municipal system was proposed. In 1907 the ratepayers approved a 250,000-dollar by-law for the construction of such a system.

In December, 1908, a paid commission was organized, composed of two members elected for one and two years and the mayor as ex officio chairman. The ratepayers also approved another by-law in the amount of 266,000 dollars, making a total sum to construct and equip the proposed railway of 516,000 dollars on the estimates provided.

Tenders were called for twelve modern "pay-as-you-enter" cars forty-one by six feet in size, with cross seats, the latest car construction, and seating-room for forty passengers. An experienced superintendent was appointed. Rails, special poles, line material, power equipment, and rolling stock were ordered, although washouts on the railway delayed delivery. Contracts were let to five paving contractors and one track-construction company. The City was to do all the "special work", including the installation of steel rails at the intersections and the installation of the overhead wiring.

Under the supervision of engineer Childs and Superintendent T. H. McCauley, crews worked to meet the deadline, which was to have part of the system in operation for the opening of the Alberta Fair in 1909. The power generator arrived on July 1st and two streetcars on July 3rd. The Calgary Municipal Street Railway officially opened at eight a.m. on the first day of the Alberta Fair, July 5th, 1909, with two cars operating from the city centre to the exhibition grounds. A total of 35,460 passengers were carried during the week without an accident and without any service interruption.

After "the Fair", construction continued in earnest. By September 15th, twelve cars were in operation on sixteen and one-half miles of track. The eighty-pound, sixty-foot-long rails were spiked to six-inch fir ties spaced four feet apart. The ties were laid on a sub-base of four inches of concrete, and grouted to within four inches of the top of the rail in the wood block sections and to the top of the rail on the paved sections, making

A second-hand horse-drawn bus from England still bearing the names of London streets on its sides. Calgary railway station, 1906.

Left: Mayor Jamieson, his aldermen, and Supt. McCauley stand with civic pride in front of Calgary's first streetcar. This picture, dated 1909, might well have been taken on July 5 of that year, which was the promised delivery date of the new street railway. Having met their deadline with time to spare the Council gathered at 8 a.m. for the inaugural ride from the Alberta Hotel to Victoria Park.

The street railway was the ideal means of transportation for a frontier town like Calgary. Once the tracks were laid there was virtually no maintenance, no paved roads to keep up, no mechanical breakdowns to worry about (that is, as long as the steam plant kept working). Buses like the one at the right were occasionally tried but were seldom successful.

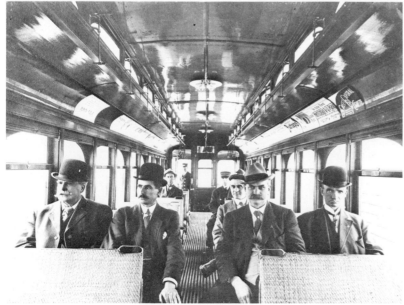

Left: An interior view of the car. A local paper reported of the maiden trip: *They travelled at a fairly good speed down the main street and made the grade at the Second Street subway successfully.* The passengers enjoyed themselves so much that they voted themselves free passes as soon as they got back.

a solid bed of seventeen inches of concrete. Solid manganese tonques and centres supplied by the United States Steel Corporation, the Montreal Steel Works, and Hadfields of Manchester, England, were used in the construction of switches and intersections.

One hundred and thirty-nine extra-strong steel poles were put in to carry the overhead cable in the business section. Another twelve three-section tubular steel poles were used in heavy traffic areas. Cedar poles set in concrete were used in the residential areas. By extensive use of copper and aluminum in the overhead cable system, the City was able to effect a saving sufficient to purchase six additional streetcars.

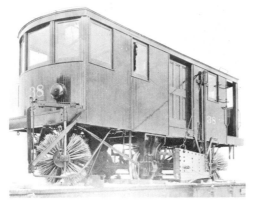

The specifications for the semi-convertible cars, which were set out in ten typewritten pages, state "all materials entering into the construction of these car bodies to be of first-class quality, well seasoned and adapted to the purpose which it is intended, all work to be done and finished in a skilled workmanlike manner." White ash was used in vestibule framing and sheeted with "well seasoned narrow tongued and grooved yellow poplar sheeting." Other features included bronze railings, standard PAYE fare boxes, bevel-plate bulkheads, and door sashes. The cars were equipped with fenders, scrapers, brakes, heaters, and bells.

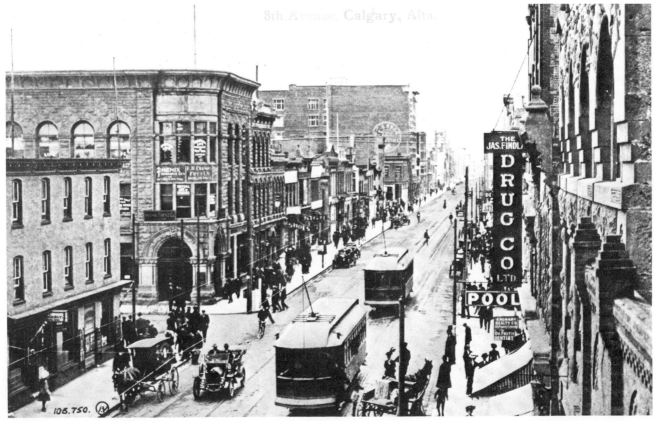

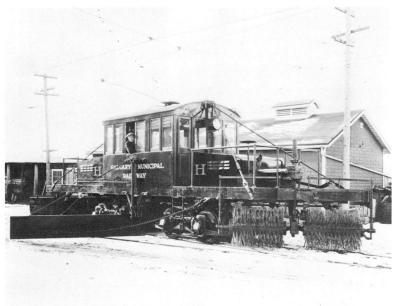

The era of the street railway. *Above:* A streetcar terminal at Sarcee military camp, 1916, and a tramcar passing over Louise Bridge. *Left:* "Mary Ann", Calgary's large snow remover, necessary equipment in the winter months. This one was built by the CPR for a mere thirty thousand dollars. *Opposite above:* A small snow remover. *Below:* A postcard view of Eighth Avenue, 1912, a transitional period in Calgary's transportation history.

Below and *Opposite:* Construction of the street railway.

Several different routes were in operation, with each route named after the colour of the illuminated signs on the streetcars. In 1910, the line was extended twenty-four miles, and twelve additional cars and more equipment were purchased to improve service by providing a total of forty miles of track and thirty streetcars. The following year, ratepayers approved the expenditure of another 375,000 dollars to finance construction of twelve additional miles of track; purchase eighteen additional passenger cars, one scenic car, and one sprinkler car; build an addition to the car barn; and equip the system with modern appliances.

The Calgary Municipal Street Railway even assumed responsibility for operating a park. John Hextall offered to donate eighty-six acres of land for a park as part of a plan to promote interest and sales in his Bowness Land Development Company. In return, he stipulated that the city would build a bridge over the Bow River (Shouldice Bridge), construct a subway under the Canadian Pacific Railway right of way, and extend the street railway service to Bowness. The offer was accepted, and it was further agreed that the Street Railway would schedule an hourly run to Bowness by June 30th, 1912. Under supervision of the Parks Department, work started to develop "a wooded and watered" park featuring "excellent scenery and boating." A bridge was built to the island, picnic facilities were developed, and a circular drive around the island and a soccer pitch were constructed to attract citizens to the recreational park. The Calgary Municipal Street Railway took over management of Bowness Park in 1917, and continued to operate it until the Town of Bowness was annexed by the City in 1961. The Bowness Land Development Company folded up in 1914.

With the decision of the Canadian Pacific Railway to locate their western shops in Calgary, a further three miles of line were constructed to Ogden, and more cars were purchased. By 1912 the System consisted of fifty-four passenger cars, an observation car, two sprinkler cars, and fifty-nine miles of track with one mile of siding.

Four classes of tickets were available: "School" (good to and from school for adults and any time for children), ten tickets for twenty-five cents; "Work" (good during the morning and evening), eight tickets for twenty-five cents; "Ordinary" (good anytime), six tickets for twenty-five cents; and "Ordinary", twenty-five in book form for one dollar. Civic employees could also purchase pads of thirty tickets for one dollar, the cost being charged to the departments in which they were used. No free passes were issued to anyone. Transfers were made between the different routes at ten different points in the city.

Politics were not permitted to enter into the operation of the system. Superintendent T. H. McCauley was sole judge of qualifications for employment, and dismissals were made subject to the employee concerned having the right to appeal to a committee composed of the officers of the Street Railway's Sick-Benefit Association to arbitrate with the Superintendent in the event of dispute.

All in all, the Municipal Street Railway was an extremely successful operation. In an article published in the Calgary *Herald*, Alderman Samis commented:

Calgary's Street Railway is her greatest advertisement. The remarkable success that has attended the City's operation of this publicly owned utility is a live topic for discussion in municipal circles all over America, the reason being that so many of the cities of this continent are cursed with politics and graft, that their citizens regard it as little less than miraculous when they see a city publicly operating any concern, and particularly a street railway, with sufficient honesty to make it pay. It is quite natural, therefore, that the annual surpluses that are being piled up by the Calgary system are regarded with admiration and wonder by 'our envious neighbours'.

Similarly, Commissioner A. G. Graves prepared a report on the operation of public utilities in Calgary, which was published and made available to councils in other cities. The concluding paragraphs read as follows:

The great evils of Municipal controls, such as politics, lack of experience by those in executive positions, incompetent labour and lack of incentive have found no place in the services of the City. The aforesaid utility is under the control of the Mayor and two paid Commissioners who are responsible to City Council.

It can be truly said that the operation of Public Utilities has been a success in Calgary, and there are few people who would be willing to hand them over to private control.

Indeed the Calgary system *was* the envy of other cities throughout North America. In an article appearing in the Calgary *Herald* in September, 1914, M. T. Stanton, an electrical engineer from Cleveland, Ohio - the city of the three-cent streetcar fares — is quoted as saying

Calgary has the best street railway system of any city its size on the continent. As a matter of fact, your street railway system here is much better than in other cities, American or Canadian, many times the size of Calgary . . . . You will often hear municipal ownership of public utilities, especially street railways, attacked in the United States, but assailants of the municipal ownership of the street railway lines are always careful to except Calgary, Alberta, as the one place on the continent where municipally operated lines have proved an entire success . . . . Perhaps one of the most characteristic things a visitor notices about your lines is the uniform courtesy of the employees. It is refreshing after some of the bullying methods one meets on street railway lines in some other cities.

One of Calgary's most extraordinary accidents, at the corner of Seventeenth Avenue and Fourteenth Street S.W.

Touring the Town

On a beautiful Indian-summer day in October 1914 William Dunlop decided to tour the city on the "Seeing Calgary" streetcar. The only one of its kind, the "Pride of the Fleet" boasted elevated seats, bronze fittings and bevelled glass sides. Along with the other sight-seers he paid the twenty-five cent fare for the one-hour tour.

Dunlop described how the conductor greeted his passengers with "This is a town where tram-men smile and look on life as well worthwhile . . . . The City of Calgary, commercial capital of the Province of Alberta, never has any tramway disputes, because the motor men and conductors couldn't find anything to strike about, even if they found themselves bound to conform to fashion."

"It is a treat in these days to hear a man extol his job," Mr. Dunlop was moved to say when recalling his experiences on the tour.

As the car started towards Eighth Avenue, the conductor put a megaphone to his lips to give the passengers his opening address (as related by Dunlop):

Ladies and Gentlemen, on behalf of the city government, I welcome you heartily to our fair city. With a view to making your stay with us as pleasant as possible, gentlemen have permission to smoke and ladies may chew gum. While you are enjoying yourselves in that way, I will entertain you to the best of my ability.

We will start with this car, Ladies and Gentlemen. It is supposed to be the finest thing of its kind on the North American continent, and being so there is no finer car anywhere else. It cost 7,500 dollars and the money is well invested, for I often take over 100 dollars a day on it in fares. I hope to take something more from each of you, for you cannot see the whole of the town in one trip.

A gentleman has just remarked that I am 'a good business getter'. I hope that every streetcar man in Calgary is that, for we all try to boost the receipts, because the better the cars pay, the more wages we get. They gave us an increase of two cents an hour last year, and promised us another rise this year if the receipts justify it. We are nearly the best paid and certainly the best treated of any streetcar men in the world, although our system only started on July 5th, 1909, with two cars running over three miles of track.

At present we have seventy-eight cars and seventy-one miles of rails. Nine hours counts a day's work for us, and the lowest rate of pay after three

SEEING CALGARY . ALBER[T]

Above and *Opposite:* Calgary's sight-seeing car 1912 to 1914.

months probation is twenty-eight cents an hour. In the second year a man gets thirty-two cents an hour, which rises to thirty-four cents in the third year and thirty-five cents thereafter. As I have said, these rates will be increased, for our bosses don't wait to be asked for increases if they can afford to give 'em. We pay half the cost of our first year's uniform, except the winter coat which is free from the start, and after that our work clothes cost us nothing. The corporation pays half our sick-benefit subscription, and provides us with a furnished clubhouse, where we can enjoy ourselves with a tune on the piano or a game of billiards.

If any man is dismissed, he has the right to have his case referred to the arbitration of the officials of our sick-benefit society. Conductors and motormen are sworn in as constables to give them authority over people who don't behave themselves in the cars.

I believe that we are the most polite streetcar men in the world. I will tell you a little story that illustrates our politeness, and when you have heard it I will bet that you also will say that our politeness cannot be matched anywhere else in the world. The story I am going to tell you has made a bit of noise and it has been meanly appreciated by people who have fitted it to different places and other circumstances; but you may *take it from me that the real thing happened right here in Calgary.*

The car line runs up a hill on the other side of the city. Last winter when the ground was very slippery, a car started from the top, leaving the conductor behind, without the motorman being aware of it. The conductor just chased it by sitting down on the snow and tobogganing down; but he hadn't gone very far before he had taken on a passenger: a lady who emerged from a side street, sat on him suddenly, and went along.

An ordinary man would have complained about being used in that way; but that lady's luck was in when she dropped on a streetcar conductor because he just couldn't help being polite and actually apologized to her for not being able to take her any further than the bottom of the hill. "I'm very sorry, ma'am," he said, as soon as he could get enough breath to speak, "but you will have to change here. I ain't carrying passengers any further!"

That building there is one of our most foremost hotels. It is run on the American or 'eat on contract' plan, which was a new thing to an Englishman who put up there a short while ago. The waiter brought him his dinner, which was on a dozen or so little dishes, more or less, ranged all around him, and left him to it. The Englishman sat looking at the food for about ten minutes without attempting to get to work. Then he shouted for the "waitah"! "Waitah!" he said, "I really cannot wait much longah for my dinnah. If you don't bring it soon I shall eat your bally samples!"

Calgary. Alta.

See that big white skyscraper up there? Well, that's the new Hudson's Bay Company store. When it was opened you couldn't buy a streetcar ride in Calgary. The Hudson's Bay people hired the whole system for the day, and everybody rode where they liked for nothing. Never heard of anything like that before, have you? My Friends, there's lots of things to see in Calgary that you can't see in any other place.

Calgary is just IT!

244

HORSE
AND BUGGY
DAYS

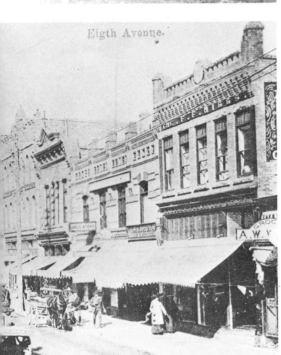

Eigth Avenue.

Chapter 8   Smoke Eater

At 4:15 this morning the Fire Department responded to an alarm of fire. It was at a house down by the Bow and was caused by a stovepipe. The householder had a chicken house attached to his kitchen. A passage led from the hen residence to the kitchen and the hens passed through this passage to the kitchen where they laid their eggs. The fire chief was unable to learn if the hens laid their eggs to order or not. A stovepipe from the kitchen stove passed through the hen-house and kept it warm. A pup dog alarmed the household or they might have all perished. Most of the hens died in the flames. Damage was estimated at 75 dollars.

From *The Calgary* Herald, *1907*

"Cappy's" Calgary

It has been said by many old-timers in the North-West that two events in the transformation of Calgary into a modern city occurred in 1883 - the arrival of the CPR, and the arrival of "Cappy" Smart.

The life of James Smart personifies the spirit of early Calgary. The last of a valiant breed of "shirt-sleeve" fire chiefs, he believed that his place at a fire was in the midst of the smoke and water. It was always "Come on in here boys." It was never "Go in there." Rough-and-ready "Cappy" was a fearless smoke-eater.

"He swallowed an awful lot of smoke - more than a man could stand - but it never got him down," said his successor, Chief Carr. Dangerous, yes, no-one knew it better than "Cappy". But he believed a firefighter, like any other fighter, to be effective, must get in close.

Colonel G. C. Porter once recalled seeing "Cappy" in action:

This long-armed, short-coupled body with enormous shoulders astride the roof of a burning building trying to chop a hole through which a nozzle could be inserted. Flames were all around and he was bellowing out orders, while his men directed streams of water to the scene in order to save his life.

James Smart was eighteen years old when he came from Scotland to western Canada. The journey, by cattle boat and train, took nearly a month. At Winnipeg he was met by his uncle, Thomas Swain, a forest ranger in the North-West Territories. They continued west together by train, arriving in Calgary on October 19, 1883. "When we got off the train east of the Elbow River it was a cold raw day, and as far as we could see Calgary was nothing but a village of tents. They were every-where - on the flats, on the hillsides, on the river bank." James and his uncle pitched a tent too, in some woods on the bank of the Bow River. After tidying up the campsite, young Smart took a walk. The first person he met was Dr. N. J. Lindsay, pioneer physician, whose tent, a short distance away, was his home and surgery.

The "No Help Wanted" sign was out at the railway construction camp. James Walker, formerly of the North-West Mounted Police, gave Smart a job in his sawmill. First a sawmill worker, then a carpenter, the young Scot worked hard in the frontier town. He made friends among the early residents of Calgary: George Murdoch, George King, and George Jacques, the first jeweller in Alberta, among others. In the evenings he enjoyed the barn dances and concerts, with Jack Munro

"Cappy" in his business clothes.

Left: The first steam engine. *Below:* "Cappy" with the fire-department rig outside Firehall Number One.

playing the bag pipes and Archie McNeill, a fiddling cattleman, playing an ancient violin with a sadly bent bow.

In 1885 rumours drifted in of trouble between Louis Riel's followers and the government. Calgarians, alarmed at the news, bought guns and ammunition. On May 20, Major James Walker received orders to mobilize and swear in a company of Home Guards, and 106 men volunteered. Lee-Enfield rifles were issued to those who did not have their own firearms. The Home Guard, of which Cappy was a member, were drafted as guides, teamsters, and bull-wackers. "Cappy" only got as far as Wetaskiwin. The rebellion was quelled while his unit was plodding north.

On his discharge from the Guard he apprenticed to another of his uncles, a mortician. On completion of his apprenticeship, he established his own undertaking business under the name of "Smart and Company". Up to this time funerals had been conducted through the co-operation of a druggist and the church. In 1891 he sold out to devote his time and energy to what had become his all-consuming passion — the fire department.

Fire protection was a spontaneous affair in Calgary's first years. When the residence of J. L. Bowen burned down on January 18, 1885, for example, citizens threw snowballs at the frame house in their efforts to save it. On March 4th of the same year Mayor Murdoch, who was also a member of the Fire Committee and could appreciate the pressing need for more adequate water supplies, submitted the following report to himself and Council:

This old building, built by G. C. King in 1889, housed "Cappy" Smart's funeral home.

His Worship the Mayor and Council.

Your Committee has had under consideration for some time the question of Fire Protection, and, after the answer received from the Waterons Company, decided that a suitable system of Water Works for this Municipality is without our reach at the present time, except a loan were negotiated to defray the expense of such works. We find that wells can be sunk and cribbed at a cost of $1.50 per foot, and that the average depth necessary to sink for a plentiful supply of water will be about 25 feet, making each well cost for work, sinking and cribbing $37.50, Boards and Nails for cribbing $15.00, Platform over well, $8.50, making the total cost per well when ready for pump $60.00 . . . . Rowells patent lift pump No. 1, made of best wood with iron lever, and claimed to be anti-freezing with sufficient power to fill a pail by three strokes, Cost of Pump above platform $4.00, Tubing at forty cents per foot under $10.00. Freight from Factory, $7.00. Total of Pump and 25 feet Tubing $21.00. Force attachment extra $3.00. This pump is highly recommended by different parties throughout Canada as being anti-freezing and the most easily worked of any made by the Owens Manufacturing Co. of Peterborough, Ontario.

The total of a well as above described with this pump will cost $82.00 without the force attachment.

The heaviest and best of the Standard Lift Pumps costs here at Calgary over platform $12.00, 25 feet of Tubing $15.00, making a total of $27.00. This pump is manufactured at Toronto and is highly spoken of by Mr. Ramsay, agent for Calgary.

The cost of a well with this pump would be $87.00.

Your Committee considered these figures a fair estimate of the cost as full enquiry has been made of different practical men, and in three cases the difference was under five dollars.

We would therefore recommend that as soon as possible steps be taken by this Council to have a sufficient number of wells sunk and pumps placed in each, and that the wells be located at the corners of the most thickly settled blocks . . . .

In conclusion we would urge that the first available funds at the disposal of the Municipality be appropriated for this purpose, as the property of the place is entirely unprotected in this respect.

Geo. Murdoch,
Chairman.

Overleaf: The fire that brought corporate awareness to Calgary. The fire of **1886** is still smouldering in this extraordinary view of Atlantic Avenue, but the worst appears to be over. At any rate the bucket brigade seems to think so, if the row of pails outside the Grand Central and the group of men crowding into the hotel are any indication. Nearly everybody in Calgary is in this picture. Most are surveying the remains of the fire. The rest are taking inventory of the salvaged goods and possessions.

This proposal was accepted and nine wells were sunk at various points in the town. Murdoch immediately campaigned for further organization and equipment. In his own words:

The next thing required after water was a body of men as a Fire Brigade. This was done. Rubber buckets, etc. were procured for the Corps. Well buckets in addition in case the pumps froze up. This outlay exhausted our allowance: but we fully realized that we were not sufficiently protected against fire: at the same time we did not consider the rate payers of the present should bear all the burden of supplying permanent and expensive machinery for the benefit of those who came here years after, so the matter of a loan was recommended to the Council, but as this would make a delay of over 3 months we called a meeting to feel the rate payers on the engine matter . . . .

On August 25th, 1885, a number of spirited citizens congregated to organize the Calgary Fire Brigade. George Constantine was the first Captain. Ed Donahue was Lieutenant, and W. H. Cushing the Treasurer. Laddermen Joe Rodway and James Smart, hookmen Jack Summers and Walter Jarrett, and axemen S. N. Jordan and S. J. Clarke, were the other members of the first Brigade. J. H. Millward, J. Lambert, J. Sullas, Arthur Turnbull, J. Ellis, and Mr. Shaw were the members of the finance committee. A chemical engine and hook and ladder equipment were secured from Winnipeg. Four months later Chief Constantine resigned and Steve Jarrett succeeded him as Chief. Only members of the Voluntary Brigade could vote on election of officers. According to one of the fire eaters in charge of roll call, there was one hundred percent attendance at every fire, for which they were each paid seventy-five cents a time.

But Calgary was still woefully ill-equipped for fighting major fires. This was demonstrated in the fall of 1886 when the town was decimated by a great conflagration. "Cappy" recalled this fire in his memoirs that were published years later in the *Herald:*

At 2 o'clock in the morning on October 15 (a Sunday) someone noticed that a small shack just east of the Windsor Hotel, which was located near the intersection of Ninth Avenue and Centre Street where the Palace Hotel now stands, was on fire. The wind was blowing from the southwest, and when the volunteer fire brigade

was notified, several shacks were blazing. The bucket brigade was immediately organized, and although they worked with might and main, it was soon seen that there was danger of the whole townsite being destroyed.

The town council had some few months previously purchased a chemical engine and hose reel, but when the equipment arrived there was not enough money in the treasury to pay for it, so the manufacturers prevailed upon customs authorities to keep it in storage until the payment was made. It was, accordingly, taken from the railway station and put under lock and key in a small building nearby. When the fire was at its height, and with a real danger of the whole town burning down, the volunteer fire brigade, reinforced by a number of citizens, smashed open the door of the building, wheeled out the hose, reel, and chemical, and in a short time the value of the "modern" equipment was seen.

Fanned by a heavy wind, the fire spread east to the Grand Central Hotel, eating up all the small buildings between this building and Centre Street. The wind then veered, and the fire started to eat its way north. It jumped the alley between what is now Eighth and Ninth Avenue and attacked the I. G. Baker store where the Bank of Commerce now stands. It was not until Monday noon that the fire was finally extinguished. There is no record of damage in the present fire records, but I know that a large number of one-and two-storey buildings were destroyed. The bucket brigade and the volunteer firefighters were reduced to a state of exhaustion by the time the fire was extinguished.

The following day members of the volunteer brigade gathered informally around one of the bars, and after agreeing that fire-fighting with primitive equipment was no fun, decided to get the town council and the towns people interested in the purchase of some modern fire-fighting equipment. They pointed out that Calgary was growing fast, but another disastrous fire such as had recently been experienced would retard the development of the little frontier town.

Shortly afterwards the town council met and, after damage reports had been perused, voted to purchase a Ronald Fire Engine, two hand-drawn fire-reels, and two thousand feet of hose. On November 1, 1886, the fire board met, and under the chairmanship of Archie Grant, the hardware merchant, it was decided to elect new officers and appoint new firemen in place of those who had resigned in disgust when compelled to fight

Opposite above: The first firehall was built in 1887, on Seventh Avenue. That's "Cappy" Smart's house right next door. *Below:* The second hall was erected on Twelfth Avenue. Here, members of the CFD, human and equine, pose proudly with their rigs. *Above:* A display of ladder techniques in the early 1900's.

fires with practically no equipment. From then on the department gradually grew. More equipment was purchased, and within a very short time the town of Calgary had one of the best-manned and best-equipped fire-fighting forces in the west. The firemen had a great time practising, and their fire drills were watched with great interest by the towns people.

In 1886, Council agreed to build a properly equipped fire hall, which was located on McIntyre Avenue (present-day Seventh Avenue W.). Furnished through donations, the premises became a show place of the town. A big dance and concert formally opened the new fire hall. Impressed by its luxurious fittings, City Council decided they also would use the new hall and make it a general place for civic business. This did not meet with the approval of the volunteer brigade - the Chief and his firemen resigned, sold the furniture, and donated the proceeds to the hospital. The Mayor and Council in turn formed their own fire department, appointing a high-salaried chief and a brigade made up of the Mayor, councilmen, and would-be firefighters. On paper the new department was well organized, but their control of fires left much to be desired. Citizens clamoring for reinstatement of the old brigade prompted a meeting in E. L. Rogers's office on July 23, 1887, where a decision was reached to have the original team take charge again.

By 1888 the policy on the use of the hall had been ironed out to the satisfaction of all, as is shown in Report Number Six appearing on the Council Agenda for February 10, 1888:

Your Committee appointed to draft a code of rules in connection with Fire Hall and Fire Brigade, beg to submit the following:

1. Resolved that the Assembly Room of the Fire Hall shall not be rented for any purpose.
2. Resolved that the Regular and Special Meetings of the Council and such public meetings as the Mayor shall consider proper, shall be held in the Assembly Room of the Fire Hall.
3. Resolved that the Council shall allow the Fire Brigade the free use of the Assembly Room of the Fire Hall for their regular Thursday night meetings, also for their own balls, their own musical and literary entertainments, for reading room and gymnasium purposes when not required by the Council or for public meetings and not inconsistent with the conditions of the Insurance and the safety of the building.

Opposite: Immediately after the disastrous fire of '86 the Town Council voted to buy a Ronald engine, two hand-drawn hose-reels, and two thousand feet of hose. Here the new equipment is tested before Fire Hall Number One. Obviously pollution was not one of the concerns of those innocent days. The gleaming engine belches magnificently, totally stealing the show from the firemen at the left who are demonstrating the new hoses.

810 THE CALGARY FIRE BRIGADE. 1887.

Over the years the equipment improved but the water supply did not keep pace. By the 1920's the Fire Department still had occasion to pump from the Bow River.

4. Resolved that no ball or public entertainment shall be given by the Fire Brigade in the Assembly Room other than their Tuesday night weekly meeting without first learning from the Mayor that the Assembly Room is not needed by the Council or for public meetings at the time the Brigade wish to have such meetings.

5. Resolved that the Council do not approve of private persons visiting the Assembly Room of the Fire Hall except at Council or Public Meetings to the annoyance of the Fire Brigade.

6. Resolved that a grant of $100,000 be made to the Fire Brigade to assist them in their musical, literary or gymnasium pursuits with the understanding that such grant is to the Fire Brigade and not to individual members of the Brigade.

Another famous fire that happened in these years, which "Cappy" Smart recalled in a *Herald* article, was the Boynton Hall fire of 1889:

Nothing of an eventful nature happened during the balance of January, but on the afternoon of February 5, 1889, the fire alarm bell sounded and word was received that Boynton Hall, which was located on Eighth Avenue E. where the old Samis Block now stands, was on fire.

At that time the building was being occupied as a Salvation Army barracks. When the volunteer fire brigade arrived on the scene, flames were shooting out of the roof and although the Ronald engine was brought into play, and bucket brigades quickly formed, the fire had secured such a hold that all efforts of the brigade were unavailing, and the building was practically destroyed.

One building immediately to the west was also destroyed. The Boynton Hall was originally built and used as an opera house. When it looked as if the fire was going to spread, further detachments of volunteers were asked for. Storekeepers and professional men left their places of business to fight the fire. In those days the majority of the buildings were of frame construction, dried out by the sun, and business buildings were imperilized by the flames. When the blaze was at its height, a detachment of the Royal Northwest Mounted Police was also pressed into service and did fine work.

When the fire had been finally extinguished, the roll call of all volunteer fire fighters was called and those who took an active part were credited with fire pay at the rate of seventy-five cents an hour. This money was paid over at the semi-monthly meeting of the fire brigade, after which the men usually adjourned to the nearest "palm garden" where a pleasant time was had.

Meanwhile the department progressed and "Cappy" progressed with it. From ladderman he graduated to hoseman, and on December 1, 1891 he was elected Captain of the hose company. Three years later he was elected Secretary. He became Assistant Chief on January 23, 1898, and two months later he was named Chief - a very popular appointment. He remained Chief of the Calgary Fire Department for thirty-five years.

In 1892, Cappy Smart married Agnes Leishman, an Ontario girl. The marriage was blessed with two children - a son, "Bud", who died in 1905, and a daughter, Minnie, who was his secretary in what is now the old Number One Fire Hall.

Through forty-eight years of fire fighting, "Cappy"

Opposite above: Chief Smart. *Below:* A picture of the Boynton Hall fire, 1889. The Ronald engine and the concerted effort of firemen and townspeople saved this fire from repeating the disaster of 1886.

Right: Dwarfed by trophies, mementos, and family portraits, Minnie Smart helps her father with his paperwork.   *Below:* The grand occasion of the First Annual Firemen's Convention, Calgary, 1909. "Cappy" is behind the drums.

survived two serious accidents and scores of minor mishaps. He was often trapped in smoke and flame. He swallowed a lot of smoke - it never got him down. On occasion, travelling to the fire was more hazardous than the fire. In 1909, while driving the "department car" - a horse and buggy - he collided with a lumber wagon and broke his wrist. Again in 1912, responding to a minor fire in Elbow Park, he climbed on the engine with driver Carr and two Calgary architects with whom he had been discussing plans for a new fire hall. At the top of the subway at Second Street and Ninth Avenue S.E., the fire wagon collided almost head-on with a street car. Seriously injured, he was rushed to the General Hospital. Far from well, he was released two months later. The greater part of the next two years was spent convalescing in Honolulu, California, and New York.

His only regret in his career was that while he had been connected with the Calgary Fire Department since its organization, he missed the biggest fire the city ever knew. That fire took place in January, 1913, when the P. Burns Packing Plant in East Calgary was reduced

Below: The Chief's car after his accident. *Overleaf:* The Burns fire — the one that "Cappy" missed.

to ashes in a one-million-dollar blaze. It was not until two weeks later that the fire was finally tapped out.

One of "Cappy's" toughest fires occurred outside Calgary. Receiving word that a CPR freight train loaded with merchandise was on fire near Keith, seven miles west of the city, Council authorized Chief Smart to take the steam engine to the scene. About seven P.M. on November 4, 1909, a team of men rushed the engine from the old headquarters to the CPR depot where it was literally bundled into a freight car. The Chief and his two assistants climbed on board and the train pulled out for Keith. It was thirty degrees below zero. The firemen had to chop holes through ice over a foot thick to get water. Eighteen hundred feet of hose was laid from the Bow to the steam-operated pumper engine. At three P.M. the next day the fire was tapped out. Eight freight cars were completely destroyed and most of the others damaged. The fire was attributed to a hot journal on one of the cars which caused a derailment, and led to a fire in the overturned box cars.

Acutely aware in those early days that the smallest fire had the potential of destroying the entire town but for the vigilance of the volunteers, "Cappy" initiated campaigns against carelessness with fire. For his work in fire prevention he was honoured many times. In 1904, he was elected President of the Pacific Coast Fire Chiefs' Association. In 1906, he was elected Vice President of the Western Canada Firemen's Association. From 1909 to 1914 he was President of the Alberta Firemen's Association. In 1910, he was Vice President of the International Fire Chiefs' Association, and in 1932, he was named President of the Dominion Association of Fire Chiefs.

After every Fire Chiefs' convention, he came home with a suitcase full of blueprints and persuasive arguments for buying a new reel, a water tower, or smoke helmets for the staff. The Council of the young city - there were four thousand on the census returns - could refuse other Departments' requests for money, but not "Cappy's". He had a way with him which carried conviction, and when Council hesitated, the Chief's roar could be heard on both sides of the Bow River. Every modern device that would help reduce fire losses Smart wanted - and in one way or another managed to get. Because of this skill, energy, and loyalty, Calgary today has the most modern fire-fighting system in proportion to its population on the continent.

The Fire Brigade, 1903.

Left: The Calgary Fire Brigade Band in 1902 when it was under the direction of Crispin Smith. *Below:* The band in 1906.

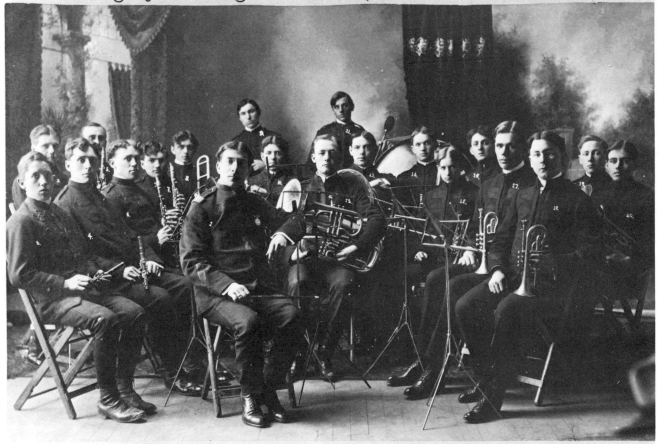

Calgary Fire Brigade Band, 1906.—W. H. Lewis, Bandmaster.

1. W. H. LEWIS.
2. M. GILL.
L. KERR.
4. F. O. BOULTON

5. H. VAIL.
6. H. L. FLUMMERFELT.
7. L. HAUTZINGER.
8. A. ANDERSON.

9. W. BOSTOCK.
10. A. J. CALHOUN.
11. A. C. THORPE.
12. I. FOSS.

13. W. EMMETT.
14. L. F. BARNES.
15. F. THORPE.
16. C. RODENIZER.

17. C. E. CARR.
18. W. I. SHAW.
19. T. BRYANT.
20. M. ANDERSON.

E. B. CURLETTE, PHOTO
CALGARY.

FIRE FIGHTERS

270

SHERMAN
RINK
FIRE

Chapter 9   Law & Order

The city did not own a patrol wagon in the early days but officers who gathered up the inebriates along Ninth Avenue soon hit upon a scheme to transport them to the cells.

"There were plenty of drays in front of the CPR station in those days," Dave Richardson claims. "We just loaded the drunks aboard and sat on them during the trip to the station."

From The Calgary Herald

Keeping the Peace

J. Ingram, Calgary's first Chief of Police.

Calgary originated as a police post, so it isn't surprising that law and order were strictly maintained by the NWMP for the first ten years. Yet, with the continual arrival of strangers after the completion of the railway, the town began to experience the problems of any quickly growing community.

Certain "undesirable" characters were automatically attracted to the advantages of a bustling boom town. In the shanties that sprang up beside the railway tracks on Atlantic Avenue, numerous gamblers and prostitutes were doing a lucrative business. Initially the NWMP had tried to prevent such a situation by meeting trains, weeding out any suspects, and sending them on their way. But there were so many newcomers that it was clearly impossible to screen everyone effectively.

With so many strangers around, some uneasy settlers demanded extra protection, and early in 1884 a town constable, Jack Campbell, was appointed. He was little more than a night watchman, however, since there were no municipal by-laws to enforce. The NWMP were already handling serious crimes and violations of federal laws. Cases were being heard by the Stipendiary Magistrate of the North-West Territories, and offenders worked out their terms at the NWMP barracks, planting gardens, cleaning stables, and clearing snow. If the sentence was more than two years, they were sent to Stony Mountain Penitentiary in Manitoba.

Things were about to change, however. Later that year, with a population of about five hundred, Calgary was incorporated as a town. By-laws were enacted as guidelines for behavior to protect the welfare and rights of the citizens. Armed with a fresh set of rules, City Council was quick to realize it was missing out on an important source of revenue. Money from fines, which could mount up to a considerable sum, was going straight to the federal government coffers. The only way any of it could be channeled into the City's purse was if the City itself enforced the regulations. And this couldn't be done without a municipal police force.

On February 7, 1885 the Council approved By-law Eleven to create the new position of Chief Constable. Among his duties the Chief Constable had "To arrest all drunken and disorderly people; to stop all fast driving and riding in the town; and to attend all fires and to attend all meetings of the Council." The man who got the job was the no-nonsense J. S. Ingram, who had earlier been the first police chief in Winnipeg. Two constables were hired: Robert Barker, who also served as the local truant officer, and Robert Barton.

For the first decade the NWMP held the monopoly on peace-keeping. *Above:* The guard house at the NWMP barracks, the town lockup for several years. *Below:* Some of the peace-keepers.

Serious as their duties were, the Force did find time for recreation. *Left:* Members of the Fort Calgary football team strike manly attitudes for posterity. *Below:* This quaint building is reputed to be the town's first jail, supposedly built by two lawyers. Legend has it that on its completion they got drunk and consequently were the first to be locked up in their creation. But, being the builders, they knew its weak points and escaped at the spot marked X.

And there was plenty to keep the three-man force busy. Their various responsibilities included inspecting licenses, fruit, vegetables, bread, meat, weights and measures, and buildings. They were also made keepers of the local pound, which in those days held something more than wandering cats and dogs. The constables were expected to perform as agile horse-chasers and artful stock-catchers. Above all the three had the policeman's mammoth task of "keeping the peace".

Regular foot patrols were made along the busy Stephen and Atlantic avenues. In an emergency the rest of the town could be reached only by riding in a democrat drawn by "Black Charger", the lone horse on the force. But the downtown area kept the policemen on their toes. Traffic problems were numerous, although substantially different than today. Horse-drawn carriages and rigs jammed the streets and jostled one another as they were manoeuvered into parking places. Stray stock either milled capriciously in the midst of impatient commuters, or caused even more havoc by stubbornly lying in the middle of the road contentedly oblivious to the stalled traffic. It was the constables' unenviable job to corral the elusive animals and shut them safely up in the pound.

It's doubtful that anyone looked forward to the night shift either. The constable had to prowl the streets in darkness brightened only dimly by the fitful flickering of gas lights on the street corners. He was sure to stumble in pot-holes, trip on steps, or walk into invisible wires, if nothing worse. Since he didn't have a flashlight, the only way he could investigate suspicious noises was with the unreliable and far-from-adequate light of sulphur matches. More than one lawbreaker took advantage of the dark, an ideal cover for a fugitive.

Ironically, Calgary's first jail is best remembered for its conspicuous failures, which began when its first inmates also made the first successful jail break! A one-room log hut on Stephen Avenue, it was apparently built by two Calgary lawyers. The day it was finished, they celebrated the occasion in such style that they were charged with drunkenness and incarcerated in their own creation. But the builders knew their product, and were intimately familiar with the weak spots in its construction. It didn't take them long to capitalize on their inefficiency and make their getaway!

Another spectacular jail break was made by a notorious local character, "Calgary's Strongest Man" (whose actual name, oddly enough, has disappeared from the record). He aimed a few well-placed kicks at the gable

This structure is also said to be Calgary's first jail — and probably was. At any rate it was the first to be "officially" built by the city. It was also the town hall, a part-time fire department, and a public school. In addition, the building served as headquarters of the Police Department - here arranged neatly before its front door.

Being called on to give emergency aid during floods was part of the policeman's lot in the early days.

end of the roof and liberated not only himself, but also two fellow inmates. But he wasn't free for long, falling victim to the skills the police had perfected nabbing wily strays. The police chased him to the Elbow River near the present Mission Bridge. Then followed a scene reminiscent of a bizarre rodeo event. After a violent struggle the fugitive was roped and hog-tied with a lariat, and ignominiously carted away.

Late in 1885 the police moved their operations out of the back room of a billiard parlor into more compatible and less distracting surroundings. A long, low, wooden City Hall was built immediately west of today's sandstone structure. At the north end of the complex was a double-storied portion topped by a bell tower, and here could be found the Police Department and four jail cells. The animal pound was convenient - it was directly opposite the police office on the southwest corner of the intersection of McIntyre Avenue and Drinkwater Street.

From here the force conducted another awkward assignment, patrol of the river banks during potential flood periods. As it wasn't until 1900 that the Bow River was diked, the evacuation of residents of the low-lying areas by rowboats was an annual undertaking. But if high water was an exasperating problem, fires could be even more bothersome. Wooden frame buildings heated by oil and coal-burning stoves were extremely flammable, and in 1886 a fire almost completely destroyed the downtown business district. Besides fire-fighting alongside the volunteer fire brigade, the police had to protect the property that had been rescued from the endangered buildings and piled in the streets. They also had to hold back the crowds of curious onlookers and keep them from blocking the roads.

But the busiest time of all was the typical rowdy Saturday night in the frontier town. The force was sure to have its hands full as thirsty ranchers and cowboys hit town for a good time at the local oases. More than one enthusiastic patron charged his horse right up the steps of the Alberta Hotel and reined in at the "longest bar in the west". Drinking has always presented the police force with problems. Ex-Inspector David Richardson, a constable in 1909, recalled that in the days before patrol wagons, the police lined the inebriated up along Atlantic Avenue. "There were plenty of drays in front of the CPR station in those days. We just loaded the drunks aboard and sat on them during the trip to the station."

In the early days crafty faces leered down from "wanted" posters strategically hung on the walls of

278

public places. Naturally, in a ranching area during the time of horses and buggies, the district abounded with horse thieves, who could receive stiff sentences of up to twenty years in jail. And from time to time a posse would set out after the outlaws who held up the Calgary-to-Edmonton stagecoach. This precarious situation which continued until the rail link was completed in 1891, was a hair-raising experience for unsuspecting passengers.

In 1888, Chief Constable Ingram, who later met a violent death in Rossland B.C. in a dynamite explosion, left the Calgary force. Matthew Sylvester (Tom) Dillabough became the new chief, and because the crime rate was relatively stable, the force was reduced by one constable.

Two years later Thomas English assumed command of the Calgary force which he was to lead for nineteen years. Associated with him during his early term were two constables, Jim Fraser and Tom Lippington; and in time English had twenty-six men under him. Justice was dispensed in the Police Courts by various justices of the peace, including Colonel Walker, George Murdoch, T.J. Boswell, and J. Creagh, proprieter of the "Tribune".

During English's term, the police office became a popular meeting place, where townspeople would pass the time of day with the sociable Chief. Chairs were set up on the sidewalk in front of the station, and pictures from the time show the Chief surrounded by companions and chatting comfortably.

He wasn't always in an amicable mood, however. A 1920 police publication relates the story of how Chief English and "Cappy" Smart almost came to blows over a football game. The Fire Brigade team was playing one organized by Chief English. When Smart "somewhat damaged" one of his opponents, the Chief started waving his famous shillelagh around his head, promising "Cappy" a sudden and violent death if he could get at him. Of course the peppery little Fire Chief invited him to "get on with it" and it looked like the outbreak of an historic fist fight. But the efforts of the crowd and the inherent good sense of the would-be combatants put an end to the confrontation. The following day the two Chiefs were seen strolling up Atlantic Avenue arm-in-arm, laughing heartily over the previous evening's entertainment.

Among the by-laws English and his men had to enforce was one passed in 1890 forbidding the firing of revolvers on main streets and the grazing of cattle on Stephen Avenue. Livestock were restricted still further

The only known likeness of Mother Fulham, one of early Calgary's more notorious malefactors.

In Chief English's day the front stoop of the police office was a favourite hangout for local dignitaries. *Above:* In this view taken in 1898 we have, left to right, Paddy Nolan, Chief English, Constable Fraser, ——, Senator Lougheed. Seated on the left is W. Orr, one of Calgary's mayors. The other two are unknown but the man right of Orr looks remarkably like George Murdoch. *Opposite:* Chief English poses again, flanked by his men and another group of citizens. The man third from the right is S. J. Clarke, who probably recurs more frequently than any other citizen in early photographs of Calgary.

in 1893 when a by-law made it illegal for them to run at large anywhere within the town limits. Until that time "cattle roaming at night over public streets caused considerable damage to fences, lawns, and shrubs."

The crime that attracted the most interest in 1891 was the robbery of Jacques Jewellery Store. Watches and rings valued at four thousand dollars were taken. Later two men received sentences of ten years for the crime. But two nights after they were jailed, one of them worked the bolts of the cell door loose and left. The escape was not noticed for several hours, but once it was, the red-faced policemen quickly recaptured the prisoner.

In 1909 English was succeeded by Thomas Mackie, under whom the force was enlarged to an inspector, three sergeants, five detectives, and forty-three constables. A unique new detachment was formed - the Mounted Police Branch - a practical addition to a force responsible for a stock-raising district spread over a wide area. The men patrolled the outskirts of town, especially the Roxboro and South Mount Royal districts where half-breeds camped below the hills were constantly fighting.

These officers were also a boon to ranchers, tracing strayed and stolen stock. One constable, Jim Miller, recalled how the men had once rounded up eighty-two horses near Ogden and were driving them to the pound. Suddenly three streetcars heading for Ogden rattled by. It took hours to get the spooked animals altogether again. This time the police weren't about to take any chances. They took the long way into town by way of Forest Lawn and the roadway past the dump at Nose Creek.

In town the mounted police branch regulated traffic, maintained order in crowds, and made a striking appearance at parades on their wellgroomed horses. This effective company remained active until 1922.

Nineteen eleven was a year of changes for the Calgary police force. "Black Charger" was retired, superseded by the first motorized wagon, "Black Maria". The newspapers boasted about the prestigious new acquisition: "the patrol wagon will even be ahead of Toronto." Offices were moved from their old home, which had come to be called somewhat disparagingly the "red barn", to the basement of the newly completed City Hall. Mackie resigned, and William Nutt took over as Acting Chief Constable until the appointment of the new Chief, Alfred Cuddy, the following year. A thirty-year veteran of the Toronto Police Force and a member of the Victorian Order, Cuddy's arrival was hailed in a local newspaper as "one more glittering gem to sparkle in the Prairie Diamond." He had the reputation of being mild-mannered, good-natured, thoughtful on behalf of his men, and fair in his dealing with criminals. He was just the man Calgary was looking for.

Above: Chief Alfred Cuddy. He cleaned up the town and created a scientific police force. *Below* and *Opposite below:* Views of the mounted city police. *Opposite above:* Sunday sightseers strolling through the Nose Creek red light district.

When Cuddy arrived in town, the city was celebrated for its bars, brothels, and gambling dens in east downtown, Hillhurst, and Nose Creek. The chief quickly got down to business. He "declared war" on Chinatown, which was considered a haven for "hop-heads", as opium addicts were called at the time. "Chief Cuddy Cleaning the City" became a familiar headline in the daily press. He was praised for his efforts in "inaugurating an energetic campaign against the operators of 'blind pigs' and gambling dens."

Cuddy had a somewhat unusual method of dealing with such places. "I believe in sending for people and telling them to quit," he said. But if after these "little talks" the Chief's word still wasn't heeded, the offender could be sure of persistent raids on his establishment until he closed its doors for good.

One such invasion of a gambling den was described by Inspector Richardson. "Cuddy was a great one to use 'stool pigeons'. They told us about a game but offered the advice we couldn't get into make a raid because the windows of the building had been barred and steel plates had been built into the doors. I borrowed a fire axe from "Cappy" Smart, crawled to the roof, and chopped my way through a dome and dropped into the centre of the gambling table. It wasn't such a bright idea, however, as I lit on my face and broke my nose."

Richardson also told of his capture of an opium peddlar wanted from Los Angeles to Vancouver. The inspector arrested the man on his arrival at the train station and seized his trunk. It was full of small tins marked with Chinese inscriptions. The officer selected one and had its contents analyzed. Sure enough the powder was opium, and the smuggler was sentenced to six months in prison and ordered deported. After the trial he told his captor, "Richardson, you're just lucky. You selected the only tin in the whole trunk that contained opium. The others are all full of flour which I sold as opium."

The policeman's success wasn't all luck, however, for Cuddy worked constantly to improve the efficiency of the police force. He was determined to organize his men into an effective unit suitable for policing an emerging cosmopolitan centre. To this end he issued a weighty manual of regulations, explicitly setting forth the proper response to any possible crisis. Police officers could find systematic advice for handling any problem, from children trundling hoops through the streets to acrobats performing in them. The constable was told how to escort prisoners to the cells (unobtru-

Opposite: Calgary's police force moves into the Twentieth Century, dealing with motorized traffic and instant communications instead of chasing runaway rigs and impounding stray cattle. The constable pictured at the top is Dave Ritchie, later Chief of Police. *Below:* Switchboard and signal station at Calgary Police Headquarters, 1920.

sively and down back streets); and how to deal with open-air preachers (to be left undisturbed unless causing "an actual obstruction to a public thoroughfare").

But since the best proof of a policeman's efficiency is the absence of crime, the emphasis was on preventing it. And to anticipate it the patrolman had to be particularly vigilant. Not only was he absolutely forbidden to abandon his beat, but he had to walk continually and at a regular pace, on the lookout for anything unusual or unlawful. Loitering or stopping for an informal chat, even with a fellow officer, were frowned upon. He was expected to be thoroughly acquainted with every part of the city and know everyone on his beat by sight so that suspicious people could be noticed and carefully watched. At night he was warned to be especially alert to anyone who was up and about, and was ordered to inspect any noise or disturbance immediately.

The list of regulations extended to the policeman's private life. His conduct was carefully prescribed, and he was urged to set an example of "sobriety, discretion, skill, industry, and promptness." To restrict any temptation toward corruption, he was forbidden to attend political meetings or befriend the proprietor of a public house. And he needed departmental approval to go to a movie or the theatre. He was encouraged to go to church regularly, and cautioned against using "harsh, violent, coarse, and profane language."

The constable was also told how to look - his hair cut had to be smart and clean, his beard kept trimmed, and his uniform neat. And of course he could never smoke in a public place while in uniform.

The manual wasn't the only innovation Cuddy introduced during his term. He tried other experiments to increase the efficiency of the force. Police personnel was growing with the expanding city. So some men were assigned to sub-stations set up in fire-stations on Sixteenth Avenue N.W. and on Second Street E. near Victoria Park, and in east Calgary and Ogden. These decentralized stations were abandoned, however, when the police moved into their modern brick headquarters in 1914. The new building included sixteen jail cells with accommodation for sixty prisoners, and was located just east of City Hall. Police offices remained in the new premises until 1961.

The year 1914 also brought technology to the aid of the isolated patrolman. Work began on a sophisticated police signal system. The system consisted of sixty bells and sixty green lights designed to alert constables by day or night. These were strategically placed on posts

Tug of war team, Calgary City Police, 1924. *Opposite:* Views of Calgary's Constabulary.

so as to be within seeing or hearing distance of an officer at all times. To be capable of instant communication with the switchboard at headquarters must have been a tremendous relief to the solitary patrolman.

And Cuddy also began a Criminal Identification Bureau. Lawbreakers were photographed and fingerprinted, and records and descriptions were filed and transmitted to other centres. The system was enlarged through the years, and became known as one of the finest in the country.

When World War I broke out there were ninety-two men on the Calgary Police Force. This number was reduced when twenty-five men enlisted and no substitutes were recruited. The remaining officers worked extra-long hours in their place. Among the twenty-one men who returned from the front was Captain David Ritchie, a former detective. Ritchie was promoted to the position of Police Chief in 1919, an office he held for twenty-two years. During this period he did much to strengthen the force and bring it to its high standards of today.

From its inception the Calgary Police Force was a major influence on the constructive development and progress of the city. It continues to be an outstanding contributor to the confidence and comfort of the citizens of today.

Ingenious Contrivances

In a series of articles published in the Calgary *Herald*, "Cappy" Smart recalled the wild and woolly days of early Calgary. Some of the highlights and reproduced below.

Calgary's appetite for hard liquors, whetted by the New Year's celebration on the eve of January 1, 1887, improved considerably within the next few weeks until it reached the stage that a new high record for the number of liquor permits issued had been reached. Officials of the town began to get a little anxious. Scotch whisky flowed freely, and the brand of liquor which appeared at numerous places led the authorities to believe that cheap liquor was being smuggled in and bootlegged by a number of persons who held government liquor permits.

Possession of the permits was used to cover up the illicit traffic. Mounted police and town police strove mightily to bring a halt to the trade but without much success. Calgary, enjoying its first boom, was in a gay mood, and its liquor proved amazing.

About this time Mayor G. C. King called a meeting of his town council; and, after reviewing the situation, the councillors decided that they should appeal to the Lieutenant-Governor of the North-West Territories to cease issuing permits for a time. The Governor agreed that the situation was a serious one, so on April 6, 1887, it was decreed that no more permits should be sold in Calgary for a three-month's period. With the new order in effect, the bootleggers redoubled their efforts. All sorts of ingenious contrivances were used to transport liquor into the city. One well known citizen, famous for of quart bottles, painted them blue-black, labelled them "ink", and then peddled them to the thirsty. gentleman went on a "toot" that lasted for a few weeks, it generally became known that the coal-oil barrels were fitted up with eight-gallon kegs, which contained real Scotch whisky.

By the time the Mounted Police got wise to the dodge, the Calgarian and his friends had almost emptied the kegs. Another favorite dodge of the bootleggers was to retail ducks' eggs which had been emptied and refilled with whisky. They retailed at about fifty cents apiece, and each one contained a fair-sized snifter. Then all of a sudden, tin imitation photograph albums became popular. There wasn't three cameras in the whole town, but many persons evinced a sudden interest in albums. Scores of them were purchased before the police discovered that they

THE CRITERION SALOON
STEPHEN AVENUE

PROPRIETORS :
BURLAND & SAUNDERS.

Reputed to have the longest bar in the West, the saloon at the Alberta Hotel *(above)* served most of Calgary's famous wits and drinkers, among them Paddy Nolan, "Cappy" Smart, Mother Fulham, and Bob Edwards.

contained whisky. Nothing daunted, the bootleggers thought up another dodge. They secured a large number of quart bottles, painted them blue-black, labelled them "ink", and then peddled them to the thirsty. When the post office didn't show any increase in business, in spite of the copious quantities of ink sold, the police again stepped in, and this little dodge was stopped. After several months of effort, the police finally managed to get the illicit liquor trade under control. Deprived of their liquor, the thirsty ones were forced to turn to water, and old John Brennan, who peddled water to the residents at twenty-five cents a barrel, experienced a sudden boom in business after being almost bankrupt during the few months that the bootleggers held sway.

In the autumn of 1888, complaints began to filter into the headquarters of the Calgary division of the Royal North-West Mounted Police concerning the increasing boldness of bootleggers. For several months prior to this time there was an unusually large flow of hard liquor into the district, and although the Mounted Police disliked the job, they exerted every means at their command to cut off the flow. As in previous days, it was being shipped into the city in every conceivable receptacle.

Calgary merchants used to ship in their supplies around the month of October, but when an unusually large shipment of jams, pickles, and jellies in tins and barrels was received by the local CPR railway agent, some of the police became suspicious and secured a magistrate's warrant to examine the shipment. Barrels which were supposed to contain pickles were found to be provided with false interiors. There was a layer of pickles on top and a layer of pickles at the bottom end of the barrel, but in the middle another receptacle contained a large amount of Scotch whisky, brandy, or sherry.

After the whole shipment had been examined, it was found that some one hundred gallons of liquor had been smuggled in. Strangely enough the "goods" were consigned to a reputable grocery firm, the manager of which, of course, denied all knowledge of the transaction. After investigation it transpired that the whisky smugglers had shipped the whisky to Calgary, using the name of the grocery firm. They had hoped to be at the depot when the freight shipment arrived, take charge of the consignment, and spirit it away before the authorities got wise to what was going on. The presence of the Mounted Police officers at the depot when the freight train arrived upset their plans, and they were forced to stand by and watch the liquor being poured down the gutters.

The quest for strong drink displayed by some early Calgarians did not go unopposed, and vigorous campaigns to "close the saloons" were organized by the more sober citizens of the town. Here the Hillhurst Presbyterian Sunday School leads the dry campaign about the year 1912.

Paddy Nolan

Paddy Nolan was another Irishman who made Calgary his home, and like John Glenn, Sam Livingston, and others before him, was noted for his wit, geniality, and eloquent command of the English language. He was revered as one of the most brilliant criminal advocates ever admitted to the Canadian Bar.

Patrick James Nolan was born in Limerick, Ireland, and was educated at Sacred Heart College and Trinity College in Dublin, and at London University. An Honours graduate in classics, a Bachelor of Arts, and a Bachelor of Laws, he also won the Gold Medal for Oratory. When called to the Irish Bar his ability was immediately recognized. After four years a restless longing for adventure drove him to seek his fortune in the colonies.

Nolan settled in Calgary, and in 1889 was called to the Bar of the North-West Territories. This land was ripe for a man of his gifts. There were many underdogs in the wild frontier community who were continually getting themselves in trouble with the law. Nolan's facile mind and silver tongue succeeded in extricating many an accused by persuading judge and jury that the prisoner at the bar was indeed innocent of criminal intent. Many of Calgary's early residents were successfully defended by this famous lawyer.

Paddy Nolan, 1904.

Nolan was born with a nose for news, and for a short time around the turn of the century acted as editor of the then-pioneer newspaper, the Calgary *Herald.* He could always spot a good story and build it into a newsworthy item. During his years of travelling through the West in the practice of his profession he passed on many items to his journalistic friends.

Nolan was also one of the first lawyers to be appointed King's Council in the new Province of Alberta. About the same time, 1907, he was made senator on the first Board of the newly formed University of Alberta.

In Calgary, Paddy Nolan's talents as a speaker were without parallel; crowds would gather to hear him whether he was appearing as an after-dinner speaker, at a political rally, or in court. On one occasion, when he was acting as delegate to the Knights of Columbus meeting in New York City, out of courtesy he was asked to speak to the delegation. His speech was so brilliant, witty, and imaginative that the New York *Sun* featured it on the front page as the work of "P. J. Nolan, K.C., from Calgary (wherever that might be)."

Nolan, with his keen sense of the rights of the small man, took delight in pulling down the mighty and puncturing an inflated ego. A well known court case found R. B. Bennett, later to become prime minister of

Canada, and Paddy Nolan on opposite sides. Picture, if you will, the impeccable Bennett laden with books containing his law references, commanding his assistant, "Boy, give me Phips on evidence," and in the course of his presentation ordering, "Boy, give me Lewin on trusts." Nolan on arising to present his argument turned to a young man seated in the court room and said, "Boy, give me Bennett on bologna."

On February 11, 1913, a young man of forty-nine riding the crest of a brilliant career, Paddy Nolan died. His staunch and loyal friend Bob Edwards wrote, "His faculty of keeping a crowd in a sustained roar of laughter for hours at a stretch was a constant source of wonderment. He never repeated himself. Paddy's well of fun never ran dry and the rapidity with which he would drive away the blues from the mind of a worried friend was not the least of his endearing qualities."

Below: The Nolans, pooch and all, pose for a family portrait in front of their home on Sixth Ave. S.W.

Right: Randolph Bruce's sketch of Nolan. *Below:* Paddy dandles a visiting baby on his knee. Mrs. Nolan is in the left foreground.

Rebellion Days

A particularly interesting account of Calgary's involvement in the North-West Rebellion is given in "Cappy" Smart's articles in the *Herald:*

By the middle of May, 1885, the North-West Rebellion scare was in full swing. Every night the little frontier town seethed with rumors of Indian uprisings. The powerful Blackfoot tribe on their reservation east of Calgary were reported to be uneasy. Calgarians knew Chief Crowfoot as a man of great courage and resolve, and a section of the population became nervous. The Sarcees, who lived in close proximity to Calgary, were becoming bolder, and it looked as if trouble might flare up.

On May 20, General Strange of Gleichen, an old Imperial army officer, received orders from Ottawa to mobilize a company of mounted scouts. On the same day Major James Walker, formerly of the Royal North-West Mounted Police, received orders to mobilize and swear in a company of home guards. One hundred and six able-bodied men answered the call, and they brought their own arms and ammunition with them. Those who did not possess their own rifles were furnished with Lee-Enfield rifles. Every man carried a six-shooter at his belt. If the Indians intended to go on the war-path they were going to be sure of a warm reception.

I still have in my possession the roster of all those who answered the call to arms in 1885. The names of some of Calgary's best-known citizens were included in the list. The "troops" were put through various military drills. There was one company of infantry, and one company of mounted men. Parades were held frequently, and even the most faint-hearted became courageous again when they saw the well-armed company of determined men.

March to Edmonton

No sooner had Quebec troops become settled down in their encampment than the officers professed a desire to see some of the surrounding country, and they decided to go touring via the horseback route. The good townspeople volunteered to provide them with mounts, but the day before the ride some practical joker slipped in several head of unbroken Indian cayuses instead of quiet saddle horses, and the result was laughable in the extreme. To see the natty French-Canadian officers on the hurricane deck of a bucking broncho tickled Calgarians, and after the soldiers had recovered from their "terrifying" experience, they took the joke in good part. From that time on, however, they were very wary about saddle horses.

About a week after the arrival of the troops, word filtered through that Fort Edmonton was in danger of being attacked by Indians and half-breeds, and the 65th Regiment was immediately ordered north. A number of the Home Guards, including myself, were drafted as guides, teamsters, and "bull whackers". We looked after the wagon and transport train, and drove peacefully along, while the foot soldiers plodded the 206 miles overland to Edmonton. When we arrived at Red Deer, where a detachment of northern guides and teamsters were supposed to take over, it was almost dark.

The taking over of the transport at Red Deer almost ended in tragedy. When the teamsters and bull whackers from the north slipped into Red Deer at dead of night they decided to have a little fun with the easterners; baiting tenderfeet seemed to be the prime sport in those days. The cowboys and teamsters crept into the sleeping camp and then, to the accompaniment of guns, let loose a few hideous yells. In ten seconds the camp was in an uproar. Bugles sounded, the troops poured out of their tents. There were yells of "The Indians are upon us," and a brisk rifle fire broke out. I ran for the nearest cart and hid under it. We suspected a practical joke of some kind because we knew there were no wild or even tame Indians within miles of us.

When the camp finally quieted down it was found to be a practical joke, but, although the commander of the regiment was furious, he was unable to lay the blame at the door of any individual or group of individuals. The northerners adopted a very innocent and shocked look when accused of the "crime" and the inquiry was finally dropped. The next day found us on the trail to Battle River, and from there on to Wetaskiwin. That was as near to the "front" as we ever got. After taking leave of the troops we hit the trail back to Calgary, arriving home about a week later. We were paid by the day, so we decided that it had been an enjoyable and profitable outing.

General Strange's company and Major Walker's home guards were not the only defences that were organized during the Rebellion Scare. Feeling that he could be of assistance, Captain John Stewart made a special visit to the Minister of Militia in Ottawa seeking authorization to form "a Mounted Force in the Southern District

Major-General Thomas Bland Strange was a compulsive soldier. He came out of retirement to organize the anti-Rebellion troops, even though it meant forfeiting his pension with the British Army. He consequently gave up his Military Colonization Company ranch, and to support himself became a sales representative for a machine-gun company.

Rocky Mountain Rangers

of Alberta." The force would be composed of ranchers, cowboys, and ex-members of the NWMP who would be assigned the three-fold task of guarding the two-hundred-mile frontier between Lethbridge and the Cypress Hills; protecting the cattle herds from thieves and rustlers; and acting as a buffer to keep warlike American Indians from surging north to join their Canadian cousins.

Authority was granted on March 25th, 1885, by Adolphe P. Caron, Minister of Militia and Defence "to raise four troops of Rocky Mountain Rangers on basis and conditions contained in report submitted by Captain Stewart to me." Included among these conditions were the following:

— *Each Officer, N.C.O. and Trooper to supply his own horse and horse appointments (Mexican) consisting of bridle, lariat, saddle and saddle blanket;*

— *the uniform of Officers to be that of an undress cavalry officer supplied at their own expense. The uniform of N.C.O.'s and Troopers to consist during provisional enlistment and whilst undergoing preliminary drill of their own serviceable Western apparel;*

— *arms to consist of one revolver Mounted Police pattern, one cartridge belt with knife attached;*

— *blankets 3 per man of* NWMP *weight and quality;*

— *all ranks to be allowed 50¢ per day for rations;*

— *the forage per horse to be allowed at rate of 50¢ per day;*

— *the pay for horse at the rate of 75¢ per day;*

— *the pay of Officers to be that of the respective rank of Canadian Cavalry Officers;*

— *the pay of* NCO*'s to be that of the* NWMP. *Non-Commissioned Police, Sgt.-Major $1.50, Sgt. $1.00 and Corporal 90¢;*

— *the pay of a Trooper to be the same as a N.W.M.P. Constable, 75¢ per day which with allowances totalled $2.50 per man and horse per day.*

Equipment was procured from the Hudson's Bay Company in Winnipeg, and soon the Rocky Mountain Rangers were up to strength and in active service under the leadership of Captain John Stewart.

Left: Major John Stewart, 1885. Stewart's Rocky Mountain Rangers patrolled the area from Fort Macleod to the international border during the Rebellion Scare. *Right:* This sketch of the cowboy cavalry riding down Stephen Avenue appeared in the *Illustrated War News,* June 20, 1885. The artist, J. Douglas White, was proprietor of the Rockies Paint Shop and obviously couldn't resist the opportunity to get in a plug for his business.

The Herald.

EXTRA.

2,000 More Troops Coming.

BAD NEWS FROM BATTLEFORD.

CITIZENS FIRED On.

H. B. Store Raided.

QU'APPELLE, March 31.—Lt. Governor Dewdney has just arrived here from Regina. He and Gen. Middleton had a conference together, at which, it is stated, they decided to ask the government immediately for 2,000 more troops.

The reports from Battleford are bad. The Indians are raiding the stores for food and firing on the citizens. A man named Haynes, and another not known, were killed. Indian Agent Rae went out to confer with them, but was fired on. The Hudson Bay store was gutted. The Industrial school has been burnt. The citizens are all housed in the barracks for refuge.

Four doctors leave for Prince Albert by one of Leeson & Scott's teams this morning.

MATTAWA, Ont., March 31.—300 troops passed here on Sunday, and 700 are here en route now.

NOTE.—Mattawa is 200 miles west of Ottawa on the C.P.R.

MEDICINE HAT, March 31.—Col. Herchimer is now here, waiting to go down the river by steamer. He may possibly come up to Calgary on Thursday. The government is sending a large supply of stores here to go to Prince Albert by steamer.

☞ The Home Guard will meet this afternoon at two o'clock in Theatre Hall. Those whose names are enrolled are expected to attend.   BY ORDER.

The Herald.

EXTRA.

Riel Corral'd

Gen. Middleton Surrounds the Half-Breeds.

A Hard Day's Fighting.

The Calgary Scouts.

The following dispatch was received by Lt. Col. Osborne Smith last night:—

QU'APPELLE, April 24.—Riel is surrounded in a ravine. "A" Battery having shelled them out of their houses. About 30 of our fellows are killed and 2 wounded. Gen. Middleton's cap was shot off, and his aide's horse killed. Hard fighting all day. Hostilities are supposed to have ceased for the night.

By the expression "our fellows" it may be meant that 30 killed belong to the Winnipeg 90th.—Ed. Herald.

Col. Smith's regiment leaves for the north to-morrow forenoon. One company will be left in Calgary and the companies now at Gleichen and MacLeod will remain where they are until the arrival of fresh troops when it is probable the rest of the light infantry will go to Edmonton.

Capt. Hamilton accompanies the Winnipeg regiment.

On the departure of Col. Smith, Inspector Dowling will remain in command of the district under the general order of Major-General Strange. Major Walker assists Inspector Dowling.

Chief Crowfoot, Commissioner Denny and Interpreter Gladstone went to the Sarcee Reserve this morning to have a pow-wow. Crowfoot re-affirms the loyalty of the Blackfeet.

Major Walker says that the ravine in which Riel is corralled is well known to him, and that if it was properly guarded last night, the rebellion may be considered settled as not a man could escape.

General Strange camps at Red Deer tonight. Major Steele's scouts are 40 miles ahead of him. No casualty of any kind has yet occurred.

The roads are bad and the snow reported deep.

Father Lacombe reports that Edmonton Indians are evidently restless.

The men were garrisoned at the Mounted Police barracks in Fort Macleod. One observer described the uniform as a "broad-brimmed felt hat with wide leather band; coat of Montana broadcloth or brown duck lined with flannel; a buckskin shirt; breeches of the same or Bedford cord; a cartridge belt attached to which is a large sheath knife; and the indispensable leather chaps. Topboots with huge Mexican spurs completed the equipment."

The cowboys, accustomed to a comparatively free and easy life on the range, did not take kindly to military discipline and training. The following description appeared in the local newspaper:

Combined with the order which they had obtained by their brief period of discipline and drill was that free and easy manner and action which is so characteristic of a border corps and which attaches itself to them, a charm not felt in the rigid movements of the strictly drilled military of the east. Troops for service in the west only require enough drill to be able to act in unison and any effort to make them mere drilling machines only trammels them and detracts from their efficiency.

Below: The Rocky Mountain Rangers in formation led by chief scout Kootenai Brown.

By the latter part of April the Rebellion was in full force, and the situation in the West looked desperate. Men working on a railway and telegraph line from Medicine Hat refused to work unless they had protection. The Bloods openly opposed construction of the railway in the vicinity of their reserve.

On April 29th the Rocky Mountain Rangers set out from Fort Macleod led by Captain Stewart and flanked by "Kootenai" Brown and his second scout, A. Vice. The departure is described by a contemporary newspaper reporter:

Rocky Mountain Rangers at Medicine Hat. *Left to right:* Commanding Officer Stewart; Captain Gilpin Brown; unknown; Lord Boyle and his brother; and Kootenai Brown.

Headed by their youthful but intrepid commander, Captain (later Major) Stewart, the Rocky Mountain Rangers presented quite a formidable appearance as they left Macleod amid the loud huzzas of the garrison. Their tanned faces were almost hidden beneath the shade of their huge Spanish sombreros, strapped on for "grim death". Around many of their necks were silk handkerchiefs, which, beside being an embellishment, prevented the irritation of their coarse brown duck or 'Montana Broadcloth' coats. Over pants of the same material were drawn a pair of chaps (leather overalls). Crossbelts pregnant with cartridges, a "six shooter", sheath knife, a Winchester slung across the pommel of the saddle, and a "lariat" coiled at the tree, completed the belligerent outfit; mounted on Bronchos, good for from sixty to a hundred miles a day, they soon disappeared in the distance; a loud clanking of bits and jingling of their huge Mexican spurs now gave place to the clatter of hoofs and the rattling of transportation wagons.

Travelling eastward, a troop was stationed for duty at Lethbridge, one at Woodpecker Island where a crew were cutting poles, and another at Cherry Coulee, the end of the telegraph line. Headquarters and the fourth troop, consisting of about forty men, arrived at Medicine Hat on May 3rd, 1885. From here a detachment was sent to the Cypress Hills while the remainder patrolled the area.

The force "earned three battle honours." The first action came when a man herding cattle was attacked by Indians and half-breeds; the Rangers pursued but did not locate the raiders. The second occurred when a scout by the name of Jackson on patrol in the Cypress Hills was attacked by Indians; patrols were sent out but could not find the wily marauders. The last is best described by the following report which appeared in the Macleod Gazette: "A message was received by Major Cotton from Major Stewart to the effect that some of his men had run across thirty or forty Indians and that shots had been exchanged. To the disgust of many in the Force who had enlisted to fight Indians, action throughout the remainder of the Rebellion was limited to 'patrolling with patient regularity'."

Understandably disappointed, the officers and men who had expected and prepared to fight for their country returned to Fort Macleod on July 8th, tired and dusty after three months of duty. The next day the Rangers paraded into the town and lined up in front of the Post Office, where William Black welcomed them back:

That your Corps has no record of battles lost or won is a matter of sincere congratulation, and we assure you that the absence of such a record detracts in no wise from the sense of obligation we feel for the protection afforded us. We are well aware that the country so faithfully watched over by you, offered, by its exposed condition and peculiar resources, great inducements to savage marauders who wrought such havoc to the north of us, and that our district was not in the theatre of such scenes of pillage and murder as there prevailed, is due to the alacrity with which you responded to the Call of Duty at the first intimation of danger.

On July 17th the men were paid off and the Rangers were disbanded. Captain Stewart obtained two rewards for his men - the Riel Rebellion Medal and the Rebellion Scrip, which, if applied for, was worth eighty dollars or three hundred and twenty acres of land.

The only major international military event that involved early Calgarians was the Boer War. *Below:* Recruits drilling at NWMP barracks in 1899. *Left:* A parade of homecoming veterans on Stephen Avenue, 1901.

Chapter 10 Power

On a nippy September evening in 1889 Theodore Strom, chief engineer of the newly chartered company, proudly opened the throttle of his new 100 h.p. steam engine. Thereupon, in some 300 light bulbs in the little prairie town, a thin wirey filament glowed redly.

Mr. Freeman felt satisfied. Mr. Strom was pleased. But the customers over in Calgary, who were paying for the 300 lamps, saw the matter in a different light.

"So that's what electricity is," they snorted, pointing to the dully glowing lamps. "Well we'd rather use candles."

Protests flowed down to the power house at the foot of Third Street west next day. Paddy Nolan, pioneer citizen, went over to see Mr. Freeman about it.

"Why didn't you put her on full strength?" he asked. "Everyone's making a fuss."

"Would you expect a new-born baby to walk the first day?" asked Mr. Freeman, and that was that.

From The Herald

Lighting the Town

In the early days of Calgary's history, crude oil and gas lamps afforded the only source of lighting both in the home and in the streets. For many years Calgarians generally went to bed with the dark, and pedestrians grumbled at the dim light as they groped their way down the streets in darkness. More lamps were installed, but they were neither brilliant nor steady enough to brighten things adequately. Continuous complaints eventually led to Calgary's introduction to the modern phenomenon — electricity.

In 1887, some eight years after the invention of the first commercial incandescent lamp, electricity first appeared in Calgary. Set up in the lane behind the Bank of Montreal were two dynamos owned by local men using the name the Electric Light Company. To drive the dynamos they had two steam engines with leaky boilers. Coal for fuel was proving expensive and the owners approached the Eau Claire Company about furnishing power. The lumber company had cheap fuel in the form of sawdust and at once ordered new boilers and a hundred horsepower steam engine which would run the mill's planer during the daytime and the dynamos at night. But when the new machinery arrived and was being set up at the mill site beside the river, the owners of the dynamos argued for the location behind the Bank of Montreal. Being denied this they refused to use the engine.

With more engine power than was now needed in the mill, Peter A. Prince, the enterprising manager of the Eau Claire Company, resolved to operate a light plant on behalf of his own firm. At this point, in June 1889, he petitioned the Town Council for permission to erect poles and supply street lights for a term of ten years.

The Electric Light Company took exception to this and did their best to block the Prince plan. Their first ploy was to circulate rumours that alternating current, the kind Prince was supplying, was highly dangerous. Wasn't it the kind used to electrocute criminals?

D. W. Marsh, mayor at the time, called a meeting at which members of the public would have opportunity of hearing both sides. I. K. Kerr and Peter Prince of the Eau Claire Company were invited, as were the owners of the Electric Light Company. The debate was long and loud. Finally, the mayor asked all citizens favoring the Eau Claire system to go to the east wall of the room and those favoring the other to go to the west wall. According to Theodore Strom, an Eau Claire engineer present at the meeting, the only ones at the west wall were the directors of the opposing company.

When the electric street lights went on in Calgary, in 1889, it was a big day for the town. *Below:* Sarcee Indians who danced at the turning on ceremony. *Right:* The Peter Prince family.

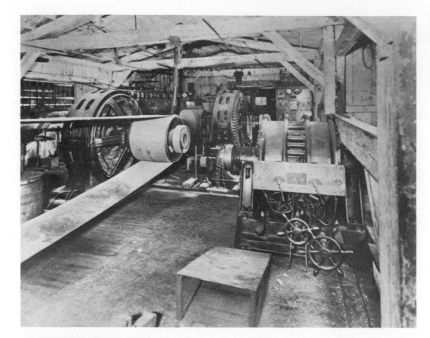

The Eau Claire Light and Power Plant. *Left:* An interior view of the plant. *Right:* The spillway. *Below left:* The sluice gates. *Below right:* The office. Standing on its steps left to right are: Margaret Eide; Charles E. Carr; and Theodore Strom.

On August 20, 1889, the Town Council passed a resolution: "That the solicitor be authorized to prepare for the next meeting of Council, a by-law and agreement authorizing Mr. Prince to erect poles and string wire within the municipality on conditions agreed upon." It was a Western Canadian landmark.

But the owners of the Electric Light Company, still wishing to create obstacles for the Prince plan, prevailed upon the Council to declare a date when street lights had to be in operation. If Prince couldn't meet the deadline, the contract would be void.

Being a spectator, Theodore Strom was in a good position to relate the events following. "As they knew that poles couldn't be cut and hauled to the railroad in the short time allowed, they thought they had already won their case. But the Eau Claire Company was also figuring. They went to Vancouver for three carloads of cedar square timbers, six inches by twelve, and thirty feet long."

According to the Calgary *Herald* of September 27, 1889, "The cedar poles have arrived for the Prince Electric Light Company and they will be planted on the streets in a short time."

The timbers were duly "planted"; the wire was strung and the lights were on, three days in advance of the scheduled time limit.

"The night we started," Strom related, "we had the hotels along Ninth Avenue. Our load was 200 16-candle-power lamps. As our lights were bright, we finally got all the hotels except the Alberta. When the bar rooms were full at night, our lights would go out and the crowds would move over to the Alberta Hotel. Mr. Freeman knew there was something wrong and finally caught two of the old company's linemen climbing the poles and pulling the transformer fuses. The men were arrested, heavily fined and ordered to leave town. Then things went along fine."

At first there were five customers in addition to the municipal corporation. Many citizens were still suspicious, and worried about this powerful force they could not understand. Men had been known to meet death from it and who could be sure the killing force would not leap from the wires and strike people around it? Prince was pioneering, and problems took many forms.

In spite of the initial problems, the new power venture was immensely successful. Within a year the Eau Claire shareholders, who had previously refused to back Prince's venture, could see a good thing and decided to change their minds. They agreed to support the operation, and the Calgary Water Power Company was organized in 1890. The same year the Electric Light Company folded, and the Eau Claire Company took over its customers and the sole responsibility for the supplying of power to all customers in Calgary.

These were the days before electric meters, and Theodore Strom, the above-mentioned engineer, got the job of driving through town in a buggy after midnight every night to see who was burning up electricity. He would count the number of lights still burning and make a record of where they were. Offices that left lights on after three a.m. had to pay extra or their power would be cut off.

Now the streets of Calgary were no longer a danger, and in fact, became a major attraction of the town. Citizens proudly promenaded at night knowing their city boasted one of the few electrically-lit roadway systems in Canada. Of course visitors had to be prepared for Calgary's sophistication. A sign in a local hotel in 1892 read:

This room is equipped with Edison electric light. Do not attempt to light with match. Simply turn key on wall by the door. The use of electricity for lighting is in no way harmful to health, nor does it affect the soundness of sleep.

But as the demand for power increased, the Calgary Water Power Company had to find new sources. In 1893 the company was granted Dominion Government Water Power Licence No. Six; it was thus a true pioneer in the industry, and the precursor of hydro development in the province.

For the first time the swift but unpredictable Bow River was to be harnessed. A dam was built across the river near Tenth Street W. to raise and regulate the water level. From here water was directed down a channel along the south bank to the power plant near the Eau Claire mill around Third Street W. and First Avenue. The twelve-foot fall powered two water wheels and generated 280 horsepower. Used in conjunction with the original steam plant, the water-power auxiliary was eventually increased to seven wheels.

But the new system was successful only when the water flow was high. A place for storage was needed, and the Hillhurst Dam was begun in the fall of 1894. According to Strom, the crews had built scaffolding across the river to carry the pile driver and engine, and workers were driving piles, when suddenly a wall of water

Calgary will now be not only the best lighted but the cheapest lighted town in Canada. The contract with the Calgary Electric Light Company has been closed and signed by Mayor Lafferty. The contract is for 40 lights each of 50 candle power to be placed on the streets and bridges in town.
Calgary *Herald* - January 25, 1890

Right: The Kananaskis Dam on its completion, 1912. *Below:* Stringing electric cable with horsedrawn equipment.

and ice five feet high swept down the river. The men reached shore just as the ice struck the span. They watched as the flood tossed the big, square, thirty-four-foot timbers about like matches. It was Thanksgiving Day- and the men had added reason to be thankful for their narrow escape as they went home to their suppers that night.

Yet even after the addition of the dam, the erratic water supply continued to present problems. When the water level was high, lights were bright; when it was low they dimmed. In the winter ice jams were bad, and for weeks at a time the old steam plant, fuelled mostly by sawdust and partly by coal, carried the entire power load. It couldn't cope with the demand, and residents sometimes had their supply cut off so that businesses could remain lighted. Power customers gloomily tolerated the situation until the city had grown so large that immediate expansion was necessary.

The first municipal generating plant was opened in December 1905 at Ninth Avenue and Fifth Street S. W. The plant consisted of two water-tube boilers — the first of their kind in western Canada — and an engine to run a 260 kilowatt generator. The system could then put out enough power, even if the water plant was not running. A second station, the Victoria plant, was built in 1911 and remained in operation until 1928, when the Ghost Dam was finished. And the Calgary Water Power Company, the first to bring hydro power to the city, continued to serve Calgary until 1938 when the city took over its distribution system and it became a subsidiary of another company, the Calgary Power Company.

But all this was in the future, and in the meantime Eau Claire was Calgary's only source of electricity. In 1904 its contract with the city expired. Larger and more extensive street-lighting units were needed, but terms could not be negotiated. So the city started a competing distribution system. Two 250 horsepower water-tube boilers and an engine were purchased and installed in a steam plant at the corner of Ninth Avenue and Fifth Street W., and went into operation late in 1905. The 350 horsepower generated was used mainly for lighting streets and some city buildings, and the surplus was sold to small consumers.

From the beginning the municipal plant expanded rapidly and continually. In 1906 the original plant was duplicated, and in the following year more boilers were added, bringing the total output up to one thousand horsepower. The enterprise thrived, and it was possible to offer reduced rates to customers. Further extensions

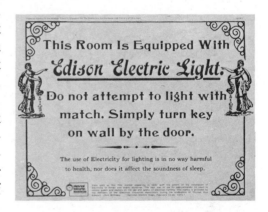

This Room Is Equipped With

Edison Electric Light.

Do not attempt to light with match. Simply turn key on wall by the door.

The use of Electricity for lighting is in no way harmful to health, nor does it affect the soundness of sleep.

were made in the next two years, and the operation was moved to Victoria Park in 1911. There was more room for extensions and coal storage at the new location, and an added advantage was a convenient water supply. A turbo generator of 1,600 kilowatt capacity was installed in the new plant when it was built, and the following year another generator of 2,500 kilowatts was added. Extensions continued to be made as needed, as the city grew into a modern urban centre. Power was required to move railway cars, operate pumps for the waterworks, provide current for street and private lighting, and supply businesses and manufacturing.

But power development on a large scale really stems from the formation of the Calgary Power Company in 1909. The Bow, never used extensively for navigation, was ideally suited for water power — an even more essential service in modern times. Not only was it a fast-running and clear river, but it also flowed through geological formations suitable for dam building. For years people talked of using the river to give Calgary the "power to grow" at a reasonable cost. Such a project, however, demanded advanced engineering skill and enormous capital outlay. But the ambitious plans were slowly developing into reality.

In 1906 the Calgary Power and Transmission Company, whose backers included R. B. Bennett and W. Max Aitken (Lord Beaverbrook), was drafting a plan to dam the Bow and supply power to Calgary. By 1909 the company had bought one thousand acres of land at

Horseshoe Falls from the Stony Indians and had arranged the lease of water rights from the federal government. A site had been chosen near Seebe, fifty-five miles from Calgary. The company also secured a five-thousand horsepower contract with Canada Cement for their plant at Exshaw and a three-thousand horsepower agreement with the city, and arranged to supply a small amount of power to the village of Cochrane.

A new company, Calgary Power Company Limited, was created in 1909, and work began immediately to meet the April 1, 1911, deadline. The first upstream plant on the Bow River was the first major hydro-power development in Alberta. Two hundred men using only picks, shovels, and wheelbarrows laboured for two years, and the amazing feat was completed only one month and twenty-one days after the target date. The Horseshoe plant had a capacity of fourteen thousand horsepower, but was soon stepped up to twenty thousand horsepower. The day it began operation truly marked the start of a new age in Calgary. An enthusiastic *Herald* article on May 25, 1911 read:

The turning on of Calgary's hydro electric power was an event of immense importance to the city. It marked the beginning of a new era in its industrial development. Today, Calgary is released from coal-made power. She has stepped into the ranks of those fortunate cities to which the streams and waterfalls pay tribute.

Below: The same view thirty years later shows the impact electricity had on the town. Besides its sandstone buildings and paved sidewalks, the street now boasts streetlights, tramcars, and lighted signs.

CALGARY WATERWORKS PUMPING STATION

Nevertheless, cautious engineers kept the fires burning at the city steam plant just in case the new hydro source should fail. But hydro proved more abundant and reliable than steam, and was also less expensive. In 1905, when the municipal steam plant began operating, rates were fourteen cents for light and ten cents for power. By 1911, when hydro power was introduced, the lighting rate had been decreased to nine cents and the power rate to two and one cents per kilowatt hour, depending on the amount of consumption.

Although the pioneer power project was successful, it did have difficulties. Built before there was any accurate way to measure stream flow, it was soon found that the normal winter flow was lower than had been expected. Also, ice jams were frequent in severe weather, and the plant output had to be cut to twenty-five hundred horsepower or less. Obviously, upstream storage was necessary, and in 1912 a reservoir with a capacity of 44,000 acre feet was built at Lake Minnewanka to correct this oversight.

Under the 1911 contract the company had agreed to provide the city with three thousand horsepower, but by the end of 1912 the city was receiving and consuming five thousand horsepower. The steam plant, intended as a standby for emergencies or hydro interruption, was operating twenty-four hours a day. The city was growing rapidly, factories were springing up, industrial and domestic demand was increasing, and the situation was serious.

A new facility was planned. This was the Kananaskis Falls plant, two and one-half miles above Horseshoe Falls. Completed in 1913, it added 12,000 horsepower to the company's capacity. These two plants, supplemented by the Calgary Water Power plant and the steam plants of the Eau Claire Company and the City of Calgary, supplied power to the Calgary area until 1929, when the Ghost plant was built. Its 37,500 horsepower more than doubled the capacity of the Calgary Power Company.

And so from a humble beginning water power became an invaluable asset to the city. In twenty years the Calgary Power Company had built three substantial power plants, and it continued to expand with the growing demand. Ample power at a reasonable cost has been a decided factor in the industrial and commercial development of Calgary.

314

Calgary - "clear running water". The name of their community must have seemed ironic to some early residents. Their taps often yielded a murky, heavily chlorinated liquid — that is, if they didn't just cough and sputter unproductively. Fish were even delivered through the mains to two surprised Calgary households in 1912! The city's early waterworks system unquestionably did have problems — problems invariably aggravated and complicated by a steadily growing and constantly demanding population.

But in time each difficulty was successfully overcome, and today's citizen can expect to obtain a plentiful supply of clear water. Perhaps a backward glance to the beginnings of the waterworks system will make us a little more appreciative of the convenience many of us take for granted.

The first settlers drew their water from springs and wells drilled at various locations around the city. But a handy new service was introduced to Calgary in the 1880's — water distribution. It was an uncomplicated procedure and one man handled the whole operation single-handedly. John Brennan filled a galvanized iron tank with water drawn from his well opposite today's city hall. Then he hauled the tank around town on a horse-drawn cart and stopped off at kitchen doors to fill the empty barrels for twenty-five cents apiece.

Wooden frame buildings dried out by the sun and heated by coal- and wood-burning stoves were extremely inflammable. An outbreak of serious fires and an increase in population made a more abundant and efficient water supply necessary. Six large tanks were sunk at strategic points in the city. Four held 12,000 gallons, one held 20,000 gallons, and a 36,000 gallon tank apparently provided most of the water for the bucket fire brigade. It took four men to work the large wooden-handled pump at each well.

The new arrangement proved satisfactory for a time, but Calgary was growing and a better distribution system was needed. In those days waterworks were still an urban status symbol, the concrete evidence of a sophisticated municipality. And for a progressive centre like Calgary, it was time to get started on the project. In 1889 the city's first waterworks system was constructed by a private company, the Alexander Brothers. The water was taken from the Bow River at the headrace of the Eau Claire Lumber Company, not too far from the present Louise Bridge. It was pumped by steam-driven water pumps housed in a nearby building. The first water main was laid along Fourth Avenue W. to First

Waterworks

Opposite: The old sandstone pumping station. *Above:* The wooden flumes used to transport the water in early Calgary's first waterworks system were flimsy and easily damaged. Here men repair damage to the flume after an Elbow River flood, 1910.

Street W., south on First Street to Eighth Avenue, and then east on Eighth Avenue to the NWMP barracks.

"Cappy" Smart recalled that the services consisted of four hydrants, two drinking fountains, which he described as "more ornamental than useful," and several watering troughs. The system was tested in late June, 1891. Firemen poured streams over flagpoles and houses to show the height that the water could be forced. However, things came to an abrupt halt. Due to a misunderstanding, the water was turned off at the powerhouse right in the middle of the experiment!

The waterworks system may have been a hallmark of progress, but the service was constantly criticized. And for good reason. Commissioner A. G. Graves, a man who played a major role in securing a satisfactory waterworks system for the city, reported on the precarious condition of the original network in 1899: "At that time the plant and the whole system was in a demoralized condition. The mains were nearly all four-inch pipe and when a fire occurred and a good pressure was required it invariably happened that the pumps would break down." Some improvement in fire protection was imperative, and concerned citizens pressed for municipal ownership and control of the waterworks system. In 1900 the system was purchased from the Calgary Gas and Waterworks Company for ninety thousand dollars. Thus it became the first utility to belong to the City of Calgary.

The city now had a deteriorated system on its hands and was faced with the headache of trying to supply an expanding population. Money for badly needed repairs was scarce, however, and the original steam pump laboured along for five more years. In 1905 it was finally retired and replaced by an electrically driven two-and-one-half million gallon-per-day pump.

However, there was no reservoir for storage should the pump fail or need repair, so the new pump didn't improve matters to any great extent, and the situation remained critical. The year 1905-06 saw a large addition to the Bow Valley population which had grown from five hundred in 1881 to about ten thousand. Demand for water extensions became a live issue. Old mains had to be replaced by larger ones, and some system of filtration during high water periods was essential. The debate centred around whether to extend the existing pumping system or construct a gravity line. There seemed to be several advantages to building the latter. Financially, a gravity line would be much cheaper, since the costs of fuel, attendants, and supplies could

A group of enthusiastic fishermen try their luck off the Waterworks' water intake and screen on the Elbow River. The couples are Mr. and Mrs. G. Park, and Mr. and Mrs. H. Young.

be eliminated. Nor was there any machinery to keep in constant operation. All things considered, it seemed like the most sensible solution to the problem.

In 1907 the sum of 340,000 dollars was budgeted to construct a gravity system on the Elbow River. The new line, proposed by engineer J. T. Childs, was designed to supply the city with eight million gallons of water a day. During the summer of 1908 men began the work of laying eleven miles of thirty-inch wooden stave pipe. The intake was about five miles west of Twin Bridges, and was situated three hundred feet above the level of the street at the Calgary post office.

The new system proved inadequate within a very short time. In four years Calgary underwent another boom. There were now fifty thousand residents, many of them living on surrounding hills. The gravity pressure was not always sufficient to ensure the supply to the southwest districts of the city. So in 1913 a steel water tower and tank were erected at Thirtieth Avenue and Twenty-fourth Street S.W., and an auxilliary pump was installed at the reservoir to supply the affected area. Other alterations were also made. The original pumping station was abandoned and a new one constructed at Ninth Avenue and Twenty-first Street - a building that is now used as the Pumphouse Theatre. The new station had two 7,500,000 gallon pumps, but taps would still run dry during times of heavy use. And still the demand for water increased, severely taxing the system.

Right: Laying the flume. *Below:* The pipeline, seen here snaking along the Elbow, in many sections lay exposed to the elements. Besides damage from floods and storms it was also vulnerable to pollution when the river was low.

WOOD STAVE
PIPELINE FROM
INTAKE
- JUNE 9/32 -

318

The problem, quite simply, was that the system just couldn't supply the amount of water that had been anticipated. A 1913 study revealed that the gravity pipeline was often lined with two to three inches of ice during the winter. Repairs and modifications to the system helped somewhat, but there were still frequent and well justified complaints about turbidity. An attempt to improve the situation was made in 1917 with the excavation of a reservoir of twenty million gallons intended to serve as an additional settling basin. Calgarians then received relatively clear water except during spring breakup, when for two to four weeks "an odor due to vegetable matter is detected." Similarly, spring flooding and summer storms made both rivers exceptionally turbid for days at a time.

And so for twenty years Calgarians depended on the unpredictable gravity line on the Elbow and the pumps on the Bow for their water supply. No major renovations were made until after the disastrous fall of 1928, when both rivers were simultaneously blocked with floating ice. This difficult and dangerous situation hastened the construction of a new intake on the north side of the Bow River west of Twenty-fourth Street W. It was hoped that this addition would help meet the exigencies of the growing population and provide the necessary fire protection.

But even with the additional pumping capacity of eight million gallons a day, the system couldn't handle the demand. Clearly, stop-gap measures were not enough. The three intakes were hopelessly inadequate and the time had come to take drastic action to improve the situation. Not only were the volume and pressure unsatisfactory, but there was still no treatment plant to treat and filter the water and provide an acceptable year-round water quality.

In 1929 a major survey of the city's waterworks was completed. The consulting engineers were amazed that the existing systems had been as successful as they were. In fact, their conclusion was that only luck had averted a major disaster. By that time a system designed for thirty thousand people was being forced to supply about ninety thousand. Renovations to the gravity line were ruled out of the question - it was suggested that the line be abandoned altogether.

The study disclosed the many difficulties officials had faced in trying to maintain a water flow. Mr. Graves at one time referred to the problem of keeping the gravity line operational as a "continuous nightmare".

What was the reason for the dilemma? To begin

Dear Sir,

Replying to yours asking me to make a report to the Commissioners as to opinion and view of the purity of the water supply of the City coming from the Bow River.

It is quite true as mentioned in your letter that garbage and dead animals have been dumped into the river beyond the western limit of the City. Further, manure and refuse have been dumped on properties just beyond the City limits. Attempts have been made and are still being made to try and control this for there is no doubt that eventually this will lead to contamination of water from which we draw our supply.

We have at present a good supply of pure and wholesome water. Although the water at the intake is at present free from all suspicion of contamination, yet the time is fast approaching when there will almost of a certainty be contamination of the water above the present intake. As the property west of the pumping station becomes built up there will be an increase of waste and refuse etc. polluting the soil with a practical certainty of raising trouble in our household water supply from that neighborhood. To protect the water supply before there is any suspicion of taint is a question of extreme moment, a question to be thought out carefully, as well in the interests of the future needs of this growing community as in those of the present.

Report of Geo Macdonald,
Medical Health Officer, to
H. E. Gillis, City Clerk.
February 3, 1906

with, both the Elbow and Bow are shallow, rapid-flowing rivers. During some winters this results in the running water being filled with ice which chokes intakes and screens. Nor did things improve much in the spring. As banks and beds eroded, the rivers carried a lot of sediment, and as a result tap water became extremely turbid. The rapid-flowing water also caused gravel bars to shift, and sometimes the Elbow River would be diverted and the intake left high and dry. As if this weren't enough, the raw river waters frequently showed signs of contamination, necessitating the use of excessive amounts of chlorine for sterilization. Of course this led to many understandable complaints about the disagreeable taste of drinking water.

Another alarming problem was the high proportion of wasted water. The gravity main traversed the Elbow flood plain for a long distance, and was often undermined by floods and left partially broken. Besides causing leakage, the breaks were expensive to repair. Decay had also set in to the wood stave pipe, and the thin steel service mains had also begun to corrode. At one time it was estimated that 75,000 gallons a day were lost through a leak at First Street W. An almost complete absence of meters compounded the difficulty of checking the flow.

In addition, all the pumps had to operate at full capacity. Many were old, inefficient, and near the end of their effective service. If the electric supply was interrupted, or if any pump failed, water supply to many parts of the city would be cut off for long periods. More storage tanks were needed in higher areas. Although lower sections of the city had sufficient water reserves, the two reservoirs urgently needed repair. The twenty-million-gallon reservoir especially needed lining, since its soft banks were continually eroding and adding to turbidity.

The report made it clear that something had to be done with Calgary's waterworks system. Eleven plans for new projects were submitted. The most favourable under all conditions involved the construction of the Glenmore reservoir. Besides providing for storage and a modern waterworks system, the scheme also included the incorporation of the city's first water-purification plant. From the time the Glenmore complex was completed in 1933 it became the city's sole water source, and the Bow was not tapped again until the Bearspaw Dam went into operation in 1972.

Opposite above: No. Two Pumping Station on the Bow River. *Below:* Another view of the flume after flood damage.

CALGARY WATER SUPPLY
SCREEN HOUSE AT NO. 2
PUMP STN. ON BOW RIVER.
— JUNE 5/32. —

There She Blows

Previous page: Spectators view the first flare from the Bow Island pipe line, turned on in Calgary July 17, 1912. *Above:* Flare at the Calgary Brewing and Malting Company. The Company Brewery was run on gas from Colonel Walker's well. *Opposite above:* The Calgary Gas Company staff and artificial gas plant. They were bought out in 1912 by Canadian Western Natural Gas Company. *Below:* The Drilling crew that brought in Bow Island No. One, February, 1909. Left to right: "Frosty" Martin; G. Gloyd; Eugene Coste; G. W. Green; and "Tiny" Phillips.

That night around 9 o'clock, just after it got dark, there was at least ten thousand or twelve thousand people, I would estimate, gathered around the standpipe in East Calgary.

Eugene Coste and his wife were there, and Whitey Foster was in charge of the valve control. At a signal from Mr. Coste, Whitey turned on the valve and he turned it on plenty, because coming out of this standpipe there was first a tremendous amount of dust, then stones and great big boulders, two or three pairs of overalls, pieces of skids - almost everything came out.

There was a tremendous roar and the people started to back up. And there was almost a panic.

Well finally Mrs. Coste was standing by with Roman Candles and she was shooting these candles at the standpipe trying to light the gas. And away she finally went - with a terrible bang.

Then Mr. Coste signalled to turn it down. Whitey thought he meant to turn her on more. Whitey opened her up again and this almost caused another panic. People were backing into each other and yelling at this terrible flare going into the air.

And that was the commencement of the initial installation of natural gas in the City of Calgary fifty years ago.

P. O. Mellon, as reported in the Calgary *Herald*

It all began on July 17, 1912 with the first flare-lighting ceremony in Calgary. More than 12,000 Calgarians watched the spectacle which signified the arrival of natural gas to their community. The introduction of natural gas to Calgary was largely to the credit of one man - Eugene Coste, who is generally considered to be the father of Canada's natural gas industry.

Eugene Coste was born in Amherstburg, Ontario, the son of a French engineer who had assisted in the construction of the Suez Canal. He received an excellent education in France and graduated from Les Lycees de Grenoble et de St. Louis at Paris. He later received his science degree from the Faculte de la Sorbonne, then studied geology and mining engineering at l'Ecole Nationale Superieure des Mines de Paris.

In 1883 Coste returned to Canada to commence his life work. He was engaged for the next six years as a geologist and engineer with the geological survey of the Dominion government. In 1889 he brought in the first commercial natural gas well near Windsor Ontario. He

then entered private practice, living in Toronto, Buffalo, Marietta Ohio, and Toronto again.

Coste was a member of the Canadian Mining Institute and its president in 1903 and 1904. He was a member of the Institute of Mining and Metallurgy of England, of the American Institute of Mining Engineers, and of the Geological Society of America. He was the author of numerous papers on the origin of petroleum which attracted wide attention.

Coste was first employed by the Canadian Pacific Railway in about 1906 to investigate the presence of natural gas in southern Alberta and Saskatchewan and report on the use which might be made of any commercial supplies. As a result of his studies, the railway company drilled several exploratory wells in southeastern Alberta, one of them being located near the town of Bow Island on the south bank of the South Saskatchewan River. This well, which commenced in 1908 and was completed in February 1909 was called "Old Glory". According to the head driller, "Frosty" Martin, it was nearly abandoned before it began producing. Martin had been sending progress reports to Mr. Coste and at the 1,700 foot level, his money ran out. "I was ordered by wire to abandon the well," he said. "After waiting a day or two I wrote a lot of alibis instead of wiring — that way gaining precious time. A few days later we were at the 1,909 foot level and the well was producing about 8,000,000 cubic feet a day."

Six more wells were drilled in the area that produced at a promising rate. In 1911 Coste obtained a lease from the CPR for the development of the Bow Island reserves and founded the Canadian Western Natural Gas, Light, Heat, and Power Co. Ltd. Floating a stock and bond issue, principally in Great Britain, the company commenced the gas transmittal service that was eventually to encompass all of southern Alberta.

They started with Calgary. Up till that time the town had been receiving minimal service from two small Gas companies: the Calgary Gas Company, which supplied artificial gas to about 2,250 customers; and the Calgary Natural Gas Company, which supplied the Calgary Brewing and Malting Company and about fifty other customers from a well on Colonel Walker's Estate in East Calgary. Coste bought out both these operations and their franchises. He then built a sixteen-inch transmission line from Bow Island to Calgary. The line was 170 miles long and was completed in just 86 days, a remarkable undertaking in an era when work was done by hand and by crude ditching machines. At the time it was one of the longest gas lines in the world.

With the introduction of gas to Calgary the Canadian Western Natural Gas Company began an operation that was to last to the present day, servicing not only the residents of southern Alberta but commercial and industrial establishments as well. It was to provide gas for a multitude of purposes: for converting sugar beets into sugar; for cooking vegetables in canneries and food packaging plants; for poultry and meat packing operations; and for making livestock feeds such as alfalfa pellets.

Below: Tom Cavanaugh and "Joe" with an early gas meter rig, 1912. This horse drawn cart had all the necessary tools and fittings.

OLD GLORY

Some historic pictures of the first pipeline. The trenches for the pipe were dug with machines of the type shown above. A coal fired boiler provided the steam for the engine. The pipe for the line was shipped by train as close as possible to the location, then hauled by wagon the rest of the way. *Opposite below:* Maltman Shaw, son of pioneer Sam Shaw hauls away twelve wagonloads from the railway at Claresholm. *Opposite above:* A reconstructed photograph of "Old Glory".

Chapter 11 Natives

Our land is more valuable than your money. It will last forever. It will not perish as long as the sun shines and the water flows, and through all the years it will give life to men and beasts. It was put there by the Great Spirit and we cannot sell it because it does not belong to us.

Crowfoot

The Blackfoot

Bear Shield, Blackfoot warrior, 1878.

The largest and most dominant group of Indians at the signing of Treaty No. Seven was the Blackfoot Nation, which was composed of three distinct tribes, the Bloods, the Peigan, and the Blackfoot. By signing the treaty, the Blackfoot hoped to preserve their territory against the encroachment of the settlers slowly filtering into the area. They did not expect at that time that their life style would change greatly: the railroad was not yet in sight, and the buffalo were still plentiful. They assumed — as why shouldn't they — that they would still have free range of the prairies to hunt buffalo as always. Even the government had assured them that the great herds were in no immediate danger, would last another ten years at least.

But by the spring of 1880, only three years later, scarcely a buffalo was left in Canada, and the Blackfoot were faced with starvation and the total annihilation of their way of life. The Blackfoot depended entirely on the buffalo for every aspect of their existence, including food, shelter, clothing, and utensils. Not even the "buffalo chips" were wasted, but were used to fuel the cooking fires. Consequently the buffalo was regarded as a holy animal, a gift from the Sun. Its disappearance from the plains was so rapid and of such dire consequence for the Indians that many of them looked on it as a divine punishment. The Sun spirit, they said, was angry with the white people for destroying the buffalo so indiscriminately and wastefully. And he was angry with the Indian for allowing the whites to do so. Therefore he had taken his gift back; he had opened a huge hole in the ground and driven all the buffalo into it.

By 1880 the proud nomadic Blackfoot Nation found themselves confined to the Reserves they had chosen, living on the inadequate government rations of beef and flour, trying to cope with the mysteries and frustrations of an unfamiliar economy based on agriculture. The Blood Reserve was located south of Fort Macleod between the St. Mary and Belly rivers. The Peigans settled on the Oldman River close to Fort Macleod. The Blackfoot band went to Blackfoot Crossing just sixty miles southeast of Calgary and thus were to become the most familiar to Calgarians. Like the Bloods and Peigans, they found farming a distasteful and confusing pursuit. The railway, when it came in 1883, passed along the edge of the Reserve, and only added to their troubles. Their grazing lands were fired by sparks from smokestacks and many of their horses were killed by passing trains. But slowly, painstakingly, they adapted to the new and alien way of life.

As the years went by they built up a workable and fairly sound economy. While they were probably best known in Calgary for their prowess in racing and horse trading, at home on the Reserve they practised farming, ranching, and coal mining. However, disease and poor living conditions continued to assail them, and by 1910 their numbers had so decreased that they relinquished half their Reserve to be auctioned off to settlers. The sales that took place over the next ten years amassed about two million dollars for the Blackfoot band, and brought them a period of prosperity that lasted till the Second World War.

Left: This view of Blackfoot Crossing on the Bow River, 1900, shows a Blackfoot camp during the Sun Dance. *Below left:* Another photograph of a camp during Sun Dance. In the foreground is a sweat lodge decorated with a painted buffalo skull. *Right:* A Blackfoot and his wives, late 1870's. A nomadic people such as the Blackfoot left little permanent evidence of their culture, and it is often only in rare photographs like this that we can glimpse the flair they had for design and style.

"AS IT WAS"—SUN DANCE, BLACKFEET INDIANS.

Probably the most renowned and revered Indian of the western plains was the Blackfoot leader Crowfoot. The peaceable quality of Albertan history is probably due as much to him as to anyone, including the NWMP. Crowfoot welcomed the arrival of the Police. His people, already decimated by smallpox and other diseases, were no match for the whisky traders and their violent panacea, firewater. When the other chiefs of his own and neighbouring tribes voiced their reluctance to make any kind of agreement with the whites, Crowfoot cited the good record of the NWMP in establishing order and providing protection to the Indians: "If the Police had not come to the country, where would we all be now. Bad men and whisky were killing us so fast that very few of us indeed would have been left today. The Police have protected us as the feathers of the bird protect it from the frosts of winter."

Crowfoot knew that the advance of the whites upon the West was inevitable, that the power of the once-great Blackfoot Nation was a thing of the past, and that the best that could be hoped for was peaceful co-existence. It was largely due to his persuasion that the other chiefs signed the treaty.

The Blackfoot set great store by their dreams and visions, believing that they were a source of information and great power to the dreamer. The dreams of a young man were especially important, as they often revealed the direction his life was to take. Crowfoot had such a dream when he was a youth. A "buffalo man" appeared to him and foretold that he would lead the Blackfoot in the paths of peace. This was an unusual dream for a warlike Blackfoot, but Crowfoot remained true to his vision. There were many instances retold of his diplomatic and peacekeeping efforts. Once during battle with the Cree he ordered the release of all prisoners and allowed his men to take no scalps. Another time he returned horses that had been stolen without his knowledge. During the Riel Rebellion he protected and fed many refugee Cree, the Blackfoot's ancient enemy.

Crowfoot sympathised with the rebels and felt that the white man's handling of the rebellion was less than honourable. He expressed the general feeling of the Blackfoot when he said: "Though our enemies be as strong as the sun or as numerous as the stars, we will defend our lodges." However, he was well aware of the strength of the government forces, and knew that resistance would meet certain defeat. He persuaded his fellow tribesmen that peace was their only choice and thus averted what would certainly have been a bloody chapter in Alberta's history.

In his eloquence Crowfoot was extraordinary; few if any of the great statesmen of history could surpass his poetic sensitivity of speech. His last message to his followers, spoken just before his death in 1890, indicates not only the power (and yet

Crowfoot

Above: This sensitive portrait of Crowfoot was made by Alexander Ross, Calgary, 1887. *Opposite below:* The woman standing in the headdress in this picture is Stealing Woman. She and her companions are obliging a "Kodaker" at Shaganappi Point on the occasion of the Royal visit, 1901. The white settlers liked to see the Indians in ceremonial dress. It added festivity and colour to their celebrations. However, Indian ceremony was another matter. Rites such as the Sun Dance *(above)* were considered pagan and undesirable, and the whites did all they could to discourage and eliminate them.

the delicacy) of his expression, but the tragic nature of his vision:

A little while and I will be gone from among you. Whither I cannot tell. From nowhere we came; into nowhere we go. What is life? it is the flash of a firefly in the night. It is the breath of a buffalo in the wintertime. It is the little shadow that runs across the grass and loses itself in the sunset.

Among the Blackfoot to whom dreams and other visionary experiences were of such particular importance, it was only natural that the best dreamers, the shamen, should be just as greatly honoured as the bravest warriors. It was through them that the forces of nature could be tapped. In their dreams were shaped the symbols that held significance and power for the whole tribe. When the missionaries first encountered the Blackfoot, they tended to dismiss the shamen as childish tricksters. Some of them no doubt were, but many of them were truly visionary men with remarkable intuitive gifts and a rapport with spiritual and psychological forces. Modern man is only now beginning to realize — and regret — the absence of these qualities in his own culture.

Wolf Collar was a shaman whom even the missionaries respected. He agreed to be bapitized and even handed over some of his totems as a token of his conversion, but he never gave up his belief in his own mystical powers or in the potency of his dreams.

It was necessary to every Blackfoot that he acquire a magical power or "medicine", something that would be specifically identified with him and would protect and guide

Wolf Collar

Left: This extraordinary portrait of the widow of Bull Head, Sarcee Chief, is one of Wolf Collar's photographic studies. Made in 1915, it has an inscription on the back reading: *photographed, developed, printed, and mounted by Silas Wolf Collar Blackfoot M.C. and Catechist . . . so that the Sarcees may see their old Mother. Above:* Another example of Wolf Collar's photography - White Headed Chief and an unknown friend.

him. This 'medicine' usually appeared to him in a dream and was represented symbolically as an animal, a bird, or a spirit of nature. Once it had appeared to him in this way he was the sole proprietor of this symbol. Usually the design on his teepee would refer to this power and no-one else could use it or the symbol embodying it unless it was handed over by the owner in an elaborate transfer ritual.

Wolf Collar's particular medicine was derived from the Thunder Spirits who had appeared to him in dreams in his youth and given him the right to use their symbols on his teepee — the Blue Thunder Lodge and the Yellow Thunder Lodge. Moreover, they gave him specific powers: songs and rituals to cure people struck by lightning, and a drum and songs that would influence the rain. Iron Voice, the son of the Thunder Spirits, also came to him in a dream, promised to help him become a medicine man, and bestowed on him an impenetrable shield and two magical songs.

The Reverend Harry Stocken, a close friend of Wolf Collar's, noted in his memoirs the shaman's remarkable ability to do anything he set his hand to, whether it was playing the autoharp, mastering photography, or translating the scriptures into Blackfoot. It was Wolf Collar's claim that he was taught how to do these things by a small white man named Left Hand who appeared to him in his dreams. Left Hand instructed him in other arts as well; some of his friends called Wolf Collar the Barrel Maker because once after one of these dreams he made wooden barrels for them to carry their water in.

For his Blackfoot friends Wolf Collar's medicine was considerable, and remained so till his death in 1927. His sons claimed that when he died there was a raging blizzard with blue and yellow lightning in the sky.

Above: A Blackfoot woman stands before her teepee. A medicine bundle hangs above the entrance. The symbols painted on these teepees were typical of the Blackfoot dwellings and held specific meaning and power for the inhabitant. *Right:* Silas Wolf Collar is standing second from the left in this picture of an Anglican synod meeting in Calgary, 1914. Seated in front of him is his friend Canon Harry Stocken.

There were many Medicine Pipes among the Blackfoot at one time, which conferred great powers and social distinction on the owner. Many have been sold to collectors.

The legend of the origin is that the Medicine Pipe was given in a vision to the Blackfoot ages ago by the Thunder God, who required that it be wrapped in a grizzly bear skin along with the skins of many other birds and animals. With proper ceremonies and feasts it was thought to have the power to restore the sick to health. When a transfer was made the owner had to approach the one selected to take over the pipe, chanting a song and making the sound of a bear charging. When a man is "caught" the pipe is offered to him and he would not dare to refuse to smoke, which would be considered sure death, because no-one dares to turn away from a grizzly bear. Having smoked, he was forced to accept the transfer of the Medicine Pipe with all its obligations and taboos and to pay the fee that went with the transfer, which was very high. The pipe was brought out at the first thunder in the spring as a token of respect to the giver. In the ceremony that accom-

Medicine Pipe Transfer

Above: The Keg, a Blackfoot Indian, stands before his teepee with his medicine pipe bundle, 1900. Such bundles were usually wrapped in several layers with a piece of bearskin outermost. The contents consisted of the pipe, richly decorated with beads, weasel skin, and eagle feathers; and a varied assortment of articles that might include bird skins, tobacco and paint bags, bracelets, head bands and implements of bone and rawhide. *Overleaf:* Rare photographs of a Blackfoot transfer ritual taken in 1924 by Philip Godsell. In this instance the object being transferred is a medicine pipe bundle. In the lower picture the men making the transfer are from left to right: Stabbed Last; The Calf, a famous medicine man; Raw Eater; and Bull Bear.

panies the transfer, the precious skins from the sacred bundle are opened with proper ritual. Drummers and the giver and the receiver chant special songs accompanying each article or skin in the bundle, and the ritual may continue for four successive mornings, ending with a good luck song to the new owner. There were numerous rules and taboos to be followed and the burden of ownership was not always welcomed; the cost and ritual were often oppressive and wearying, but to the old, superstitious Indian there was no alternative.

The Stonies are the foothill and mountain-dwelling Indians of Alberta. The main body of the tribe now occupies the Reserve at Morley about forty miles upriver from Calgary, but when Robert T. Rundle, the first missionary, came into the area in the 1840's, they ranged along the entire eastern side of the Rockies, from the Athabasca to Montana.

It is generally accepted that the Stony Indians are a branch of the Assiniboine Nation. Like the Assiniboine in Saskatchewan and Montana, they speak the Sioux language, differing slightly in their pronunciation of certain sounds. Just when they broke away from the main body of the Assiniboine, however, is a matter of argument, not only with scholars but with the Indians themselves. Among the Assiniboine the Stonies are sometimes referred to as the "Lost Tribe". It is believed that they are the descendents of a band of people that fled the main tribe in the early nineteenth century to escape a smallpox epidemic. Chief Carry the Kettle of the Assiniboines, who died in 1923 at the age of 107, could remember both the epidemic and the resultant division of the tribe.

The Stonies, however, do not consider themselves to be this lost tribe at all. They claim they have dwelt in the foothills and mountains for generations. A reference in Anthony Henday's accounts seems to back up this claim. Henday records having met and traded with wood-dwelling Assiniboine Indians in the general vicinity of Red Deer in 1754. This was much earlier than the smallpox epidemic.

Robert Rundle encountered three distinct bands of Stonies: the Wesleys, who were the northernmost band and the most easily Christianized; the Chiniki, who occupied the territory from the Saskatchewan to the Bow; and the Bearspaws, who ranged south of the Bow and were the most warlike. These divisions remained up to the signing of Treaty No. Seven. The chiefs of each band (Bearspaw, Chiniki, and Jacob Goodstoney) all signed the treaty as head chiefs, and were assigned the area around Morleyville as their common Reserve — an area they had already mutually agreed upon as their central gathering place when they requested the McDougalls to build a mission there in 1873.

After the signing of the treaty the Stonies were able to ward off for some years the general disaster and famine that struck the Plains tribes. Game was plentiful, and they adapted easily and efficiently to farming and cattle raising. But with the rapid influx of settlers game soon became a scarce commodity, one they had to range farther and farther from the Reserve to find. Moreover, after the surveys of 1879 and 1888 that established and defined the boundaries of the Reserve, it soon became evident that there was not enough land to support the tribe. The Stonies that the early Calgarians knew

The Lost Tribe

A Stony Indian at Morley in the '90's, clad in a Hudson's Bay blanket coat. Note his braided rawhide halter and intricately beaded holster.

were peaceful, friendly, and eager to progress, but already sinking under the massive social and economic difficulties that were the Indians' common lot.

Chief White Cloud Remembers

In 1923, White Cloud, a Stony chief, was Alberta's oldest man. He recalled some of his experiences at that time for the *Herald*:

In the early days before the white man came the Indians made fire with two pieces of white flint. They would take a piece of touchwood (tree canker) from a birch tree and light it from the spark of the flints. This piece of touchwood would then glow for a whole day and a fire could be lit from it by placing dry grass against the coals and blowing upon it. When the Stonies moved from place to place they carried their fire with them in a small hollow log. This was the profession or business of Two Feathers in the Head [White Cloud's father]. He was the tribal fire man who kept this fire smouldering inside a log and sold it to the rest of the camp. The coming of the white man's steel put him out of business. It was much easier to make fire by striking the steel against flint. The Indians made a little striker that could be carried in their "fire bag" along with a pipe and tobacco.

The Stonies never had stone pipes before the white man came with his file. They had not learned to file down pipestones with other harder stones. We made bowls out of wood and the stems out of Indian rhubarb. I used to smoke the earth as a pipe. I would cut off a little tree very close to the ground and hollow out the little stump with a bone chisel and I would fill this little bowl with kinnikinic; we also smoked the thin inner bark of the red willow. Then I would drill a small hole in the stump close to the ground and stick in a rhubarb stem and lie down on my stomach and have a smoke. I had these stump pipes all over the country; wherever we camped I knew where to go and find my pipe sticking out of the ground. I used to call this "smoking the earth".

It was hard times in those days. We had to make our spear and arrow heads out of bone, and when we could find no feathers, we had to use fur in the other end of the shaft to guide it through the air. Sometimes the bone arrow head would break when it struck the animal and we would lose our game. We made our knives out of the ribs of animals. We polished them with stones and made them nearly as sharp as those we have today.

One animal, the grizzly, we could never kill with an arrow. We could not kill them with the shotgun either; they were too dangerous when wounded. But bullets are all

Left: Stony winter camp on the Bar U ranch, circa 1890. *Below:* Two Stonies in winter dress. *Right:* This much damaged picture is of Bearspaw, famous Stony Chief who signed the Treaty No. Seven.

right for the grizzly. Chief White Head here and Jacob Soldier once killed a big grizzly with the knife. They drove it into the Bow River near Morley and then swam after it. They caught hold of its hind legs and kept driving their knives into its back and stomach until its stomach went 'puff' and the blood began to spurt out of it. The way we hunted mountain sheep and goat, we went up the mountains and made our dogs drive them to us. The sheep and goats were the same to us as the buffalo was to the Blackfoot. It was our best food supply.

Looking at Tunnel Mountain almost mades me cry for a meal of sheep meat. That was our meat in the old days, and I spent most of my time hunting sheep on that mountain.

Their familiarity with the mountains and the forests made the Stonies invaluable guides. Everyone made use of their services, from CPR surveyors looking for suitable passes through the Rockies, to hunters looking for a good catch. Paul Amos had all the Stony knowledge of forest lore. *Below:* He stands proudly behind a winter catch of furs from the Kananaskis area, 1908. George Pocaterra is on his left and another Stony on the right. *Opposite:* Amos and his family in 1911, in a lovely mountain meadow.

My First White Man

George McLean was a Stony who achieved world fame through his activities with the Moral Rearmament Movement. Though he had many occupations in his lifetime his true vocation was philosopher, and it was his chief wish to express and communicate his philosophy to others. Like most Indians he was acutely aware of the destruction and waste the whites were causing in their use of natural resources. And he was appalled by the lack of respect for nature shown by the destroyers. *Opposite above:* A Stony camp at the mouth of Whiskey Creek in the beautiful Highwood valley; and a quote by George McLean. *Below:* A survey camp at Ghost dam, 1907. George McLean is third from the right.

One day when I was a young man I met a white man for the first time and at that time I smelled him — he smelt different; just like cattle. From that time on all the grub that we eat today I didn't like. I could not swallow it and when I did get some down in my stomach it would come up again. All the new food tasted just like that white man smelled and the smell of it always made my stomach feel queer.

But after a few years I could hold it down; now I like it. But I am sure that on account of that grub the Indians are not increasing. Before we ate that grub the Indians never died till they were very old — way over a hundred. Since we began eating the white man's grub we are just like bones and sick all the time. We keep getting worse and it will kill us all. We get sores on our necks — we never had that medicine in the old days. The young people's teeth are bad, just like the white man's. We old people, our teeth are still good, because when we were young we ate the food that the Great Spirit provided — no bread — no sweets.

That day at Rocky Mountain House the Indians brought many clothes from the Hudson's Bay. As soon as the Indians smelled those clothes they all got colds and coughed and became sick. We never knew anything about these coughs before.

They kept on working, working, trying to make us all white people. But you see that us old Indians do not act like white people.

All those Indians who cut their hair try to be like white people but they are not. When I travel through the country I have to camp on the road allowance. The white never tries to please me. He took all we had but never allows me to camp on the field once. All the white man thinks of the Indian is that he is useless — he thinks they should all die. They know that if the Indian cannot get anything from the white people he will die. The white people are making a living off the land and are happy — and the Indian instead of happy has to say "Please" for everything he gets.

And we Indians should make our living, the Great Spirit said, by hunting game, muskrats, lynx, coyotes, fox, wolves, bear, mountain lion, sheep and goats. Now this has all been taken away — just like white man grabbing grub off Indian's plate. If the Indian do that would the white man be satisfied? If Indian say that gold worth everything and chickens, cattle, sheep, worth nothing, what would white man think? He would think just the same as I am. The white man wants Indians to die so he can have the land.

The outdoors of the Great Spirit's making has been like a Bible to me - not one written by human hands but by the Great Spirit. Too bad the White Man doesn't know more about it. He's a smart fellow in some ways, this White Man, but he can't boss or bully Nature. He took the country that did not belong to him and pushed the Indian into some small corners he didn't want. He killed off the buffalo and then turned to other game animals and forests and grass and soil with the idea of selling them for money. Now he's digging into the heart of the earth to find something else he can sell for money - and he thinks he can teach the Indian how to live. He's a smart fellow but he should not lose his sanity about money and he should not allow himself to become a stranger in Nature's Community. The Indian can still teach him a few things about living. But the white man will not listen.

The Earth People

Above: Setukkomuccon, Sarcee Indian, arrayed for the Sun Dance, 1889. *Opposite above:* Astokumi and his wife at their encampment, 1887. The horse drawn travois shown here was common to all Natives in the area and was the chief means of transporting goods and possessions. *Below left:* Two Sarcee Indian girls, Siupakio and Sikunacio. *Right:* A tree burial at Dead Man's Bush on the Sarcee reserve, circa 1890. *Overleaf:* A Sarcee Indian camp, in the 1890's, with Calgary in the background.

In their own language, the Sarcees refer to themselves as *tsotli'na*, which means "earth people", because they were once as numerous as the grains of the earth. But when they gathered to sign Treaty No. Seven, they had been so reduced by smallpox, measles, and other adversities, that only a scant 255 people put their names to the treaty list. So small had their numbers become that the Sarcees themselves believed that extinction was their inevitable fate.

The Sarcees were not originally a plains tribe but were an offshoot of the Beaver tribe of the woods of northern Alberta, and drifted south in the seventeenth century. The Sarcees have a Pandora-like tale to explain their separation from the Beavers. The Beavers, as the legend goes, were crossing a large lake in midwinter. As they neared the centre of the frozen lake one of the women noticed something sticking out of the ice. It was a huge animal horn. Unable to resist her curiosity she pulled on it. There was immediately an unearthly groaning sound, and a great crack opened out east and west from the horn dividing the lake in two, and the tribe with it. Those who could, fled north non-stop till they reached their hunting grounds. Those stranded on the opposite part of the lake, fled to the south. They never rejoined their tribe but continued to the plains, where they became known as the Sarcees.

They became the most warlike of the prairie tribes, and clung to their individuality fiercely and proudly. Although they were allied with the Blackfoot for almost a century and became culturally almost indistinguishable from them, they preserved their own identity and never gave up their own Athabaskan language.

When the disappearance of the buffalo finally forced them, like their allies, to settle on the Reserve, the Sarcees demanded a Reserve of their own. The government had felt a corner of the Blackfoot Reserve was sufficient for the needs of the little band, and was reluctant to make any changes in its original allocation of territories. In this case they were especially reluctant, as the location the Sarcees wanted for their Reserve was on the outskirts of Calgary and was surrounded by cattle ranches. The possibilities for trouble or even alleged trouble were limitless. However, the Sarcees' insistence on having this location outlasted the government's interest in refusing, and they were granted 108 square miles on the western outskirts of the town.

Once confined to the Reserve the Sarcees were exposed to agriculture and Christianity, neither of which had much appeal for them. After ten years of devoted work the missionaries could count only three converts in the entire band. These were bad years for the Sarcees. Tuberculosis was added to the maladies that troubled them, and at one time all but four children in the tribe suffered from this disease. But the

145 SARCEE INDIAN ENCAMPMENT.

Sarcees still clung jealously to their individuality, and to the present day they have clung just as assiduously to their land. In spite of the pressures of city expansion they are determined to keep their property and develop its resources for their own benefit.

Making the transition to the new culture was even more difficult for the Sarcees than their neighbours. Besides the problems of disease and poverty they also had to cope with fear of extinction; at the signing of Treaty No. Seven there were only some 250 members of their band. Nevertheless some did adapt themselves to the new lifestyle. *Right:* David Big Plume and his family before their new log home in the 1890's. *Below:* Branding cattle near the Sarcee agency. *Below left:* Yellow Lodge, 1887. *Opposite:* Bull Head, truculent Head Chief of the Sarcees.

353

Bull Head

Probably the Indian personality best known to early Calgarians was Bull Head, chief of the Sarcees. A fierce, cantankerous individual, he was considered a troublemaker by the whites who had to deal with him. He was constantly in and out of the lockup, usually on charges of drunkenness, and his ferocious appearance and belligerent manner were cause for no little uneasiness among the townspeople. He reinforced their belief that the Sarcees were a warlike and dangerous people and were situated much too close to the town for security and comfort.

Troublemaker or not, Bull Head was ruled by an integrity that seldom wavered. A twofold purpose underlay everything he did — to better the welfare of his people, and to disrupt the complacency of the whites who, he felt, had wronged his tribe.

It was due to Bull Head that the Sarcee Reserve was located where it was — on the western limits of the town. The year 1880 had been a devastating one for the Sarcees. Suffering from the shock of the disappearance of the buffalo, starving on the inadequate Government rations and facing a winter of even greater starvation, and finally being forced to share a Reserve with the Blackfoot with whom at this time they had only an uneasy alliance, the Sarcees were ready to hand out ultimatums. Rejecting an invitation to come to Fort Macleod for the winter where they would be fed on Government beef, they struck camp at Blackfoot Crossing and angrily descended upon Fort Calgary.

Bull Head's demands were short and to the point. He wanted adequate winter provisions for his band and a Reserve on their old traditional hunting grounds west of the fort. If these demands were not met he would burn down the fort and the nearby trading posts. Fort Calgary, having been reduced to a detachment post the year before, was manned by only two men. Justly alarmed by Bull Head's threats, they conferred with G. C. King and Angus Fraser, the managers of the two trading posts. Help was definitely needed and was duly sent for. Within four days eight men and two wagonloads of food under the charge of Cecil Denny and John Lauder arrived from Fort Macleod. After three more tense and volatile days, Bull Head eventually agreed to winter with his band at Fort Macleod. But he did not give up his demands, and in 1883 a new treaty was drawn up assigning his band five thousand acres on the Elbow River.

177. OMUXISTOAN, SARCEE INDIAN

If Bull Head was truculent he had good reason. In his lifetime he had seen the glory of his people vanish. Struggling simply to stay alive, the Natives could only watch helplessly as the things that were vital in their culture slipped rapidly away from them. In 1887, when Big Knife *(right)* posed for the camera of Boorne and May, his splendour was unmistakable. The Sarcees were already in execrable circumstances but their culture was still well defined. By the time Arnold Lupson took the photograph below, of a Sarcee medicine dance in 1915, their self confidence is no longer visible. Big Knife is the man on the right in the centre of this picture.

The use of the sweat-bath was common to practically all Indians on the North American continent. Among the plains Indians it was closely associated with the Sun Dance, being used as a purification ritual. Usually the construction of a sweat lodge was accompanied by a special ceremony, with a buffalo skull sometimes placed on top of the lodge or before it on a mound of earth.

SWEAT LODGE

This series of photographs by Godsell show a Sarcee sweat-house under construction. They were probably taken in July, the "berry-ripe-month", at the time of the Sun Dance. It appears that a Sun Dance camp is being formed in the vicinity. There seem to have been three separate purposes for the use of the sweat-bath: as a religious rite for purification of the body; as a ritual for warriors about to leave on a war-party; and as a preparation for a serious or hazardous undertaking. Occasionally it was used to invigorate tired bodies after the hunt.

In these pictures we see a willow framework constructed and covered with blankets. Heated stones were placed inside in a hole in the centre. Those undergoing the ceremony crouched inside while water was poured on the stones to raise steam. Afterwards the bather usually plunged into a nearby stream.

Next to the NWMP the Natives' most important means of liason with the white culture was the church. Father Albert Lacombe and Rev. John McDougall were two churchmen whose success in their relationships with the Indians gave them patriarchal importance to the whites. On this page we see Father Lacombe with the Blackfoot Confederacy Chiefs and Interpreter Jean L'Heureux in Ottawa 1886; a page from Lacombe's Blackfoot Reader; and Lacombe in his study as a very old but still indomitable man. On the opposite page we see McDougall's Methodist Church built at Morley, 1875; McDougall and his associate the Rev. R. B. Steinhauer with Cree and Stony Chiefs on a visit to Toronto, 1886 (Left to right: McDougall; Samson, *Cree;* Pakan, *Cree;* Steinhauer; Jonas Goodstoney, *Stony*); and the McDougall family, 1900.

4. The cars are full of people.

MISSIONARIES

Chapter 12   The Gracious City

The first walk I took the morning after I arrived at Calgary will not soon be forgotten. The day was overcast but clear. I wandered over the prairies carpeted with lovely flowers for a couple of miles; mounted the highest hill I could find; took my first look at the Rocky Mountains rising like a rampart in the distance and glistening in some reflected light that did not catch the valley below. I know I sat down on a grassy mound, and lost all record of time till I was roused from my dreams by the sun coming out and beating on my head with a power and intensity peculiar to the West, which soon warned me homewards with hands filled with red lilies, hare bells and giant roman flowers.

From A Stranger's View of Calgary
by Ernest Smith, 1886

In the centrifugal, rapidly sprawling Calgary of today, there is scarcely a hint of the gracious city that was developing around the turn of the century. Elegant sandstone buildings were springing up everywhere, giving Calgary a character and credibility unique among prairie cities noted chiefly for their impermanent hastily erected frame structures. Large areas of undeveloped river frontage still existed whose possibilities as park and recreation areas had already come to the notice of such eminent and influential conservationists as William Pearce.

As early as 1911 Calgary formed a Planning Commission. The members concerned themselves with such things as street lighting, cheap housing, planting trees, and amendments to the city's building code. But they were also interested in the city's development as a whole. They were instrumental, for instance, in developing the Town Planning Act of Alberta. The shape that Calgary was to take was important to them, and in 1913 they commissioned Thomas Mawson to design their future city. The result was a modern and far-reaching plan beyond anything they had imagined. But the city that had been envisioned was not to be. The Great War terminated the Mawson Plan. The sudden exhaustion of sandstone put an end to the fanciful structures of the early days, and Calgary thus developed in a different fashion to become the city we know today — beautiful and impressive to be sure, but nevertheless totally different from the way it might have been.

Right: In 1892 the "Prairie Diamond" glittered in a virtually unspoiled setting.

The City That Might Have Been

CALGARY FROM N- 1892.

COPYRIGHT. ERNEST BROWN.

Stately sandstone dwellings and verdant walks characterized the early Calgary.

RESIDENCE OF HUGH McCLELLAND.

Calgary —
A Poem in Sandstone

The arrival of the Canadian Pacific Railway marked the beginning of a completely new stage in the architectural development of Calgary. The little western outpost was now accessible to anyone with the price of a train ticket. Heretofore the pioneer seeking fame and fortune in the new West travelled by Red River cart, by wagon, on horseback, or on foot; it was now possible to complete the journey from Winnipeg in a matter of days. The result was an unprecedented influx of new settlers whose most urgent need would be some form of permanent accommodation. The Mounted Police Post called Fort Calgary mushroomed first into a tent town, to be replaced by buildings of log and milled lumber. But a wooden town had a precarious existence on the fire-prone prairie, and the great fire of 1886 pointed up the necessity of using more substantial building material. Sandstone provided the answer.

The first sandstone quarry was opened in 1886 by Wesley Orr. In the spring of that year, Joseph Butland followed suit, advertising his sandstone as "equal to any in North America and within two miles of town." The quarry located on his farm on the Elbow River is described in Burns and Elliott's *Calgary, Alberta,* "for a distance of 300 yards on the exposed bank a seam of splendid freestone about six feet in depth crops out — Mr. Butland as owner of this valuable quarry is certainly to be congratulated on possessing a real 'bonanza'. The distance to the CPR line is only two miles and as the quarry is to be worked by enterprising capitalists a spur line can easily be constructed." Butland, by the way, arrived in Calgary with the NWMP in 1875, and left the Force in 1880 to start ranching.

Over the years the term "Sandstone City" became synonomous with Calgary. Sandstone structures gave the town the appearance of being successful and confident. Everybody wanted one. To meet the demand, Thomas Edworthy opened a quarry at Shaganappi, west of town; Colonel Barwis had a quarry on his ranch on the north side of the Bow River, close to the ferry near Prince's Island; John Quinlan and W. Carter operated the Glenbow quarry; another quarry was operated in the Cochrane area by the Shelby Quarry Company of Canada; and Blane and LeBlanc started a stone quarry west of Shaganappi in 1908. South of Calgary, the Sandstone Brick and Sewer Pipe Company and the Burnvale Brick Company operated quarries at a small settlement called Sandstone, near Okotoks.

John McCallum was so proud of his product — sandstone — that he shipped a sample to the Chicago World's Fair in 1896 for which he received a medallion. The exhibit — a sandstone bassinette — was so large it took a railway flatcar to haul it.

The Oliver Brothers opened a quarry in 1902, in the large gulley which ran north and south in the vicinity of Summit

Overleaf: Stephen Avenue at the corner of Scarth Street (Eighth Avenue and First Street S.W.). By the time this picture was taken in the 1890's, the business section of Stephen Avenue had been converted almost completely to sandstone. On the pages following this view we can see the same block between Scarth Street W. and Centre Street as it made its transition from wood to sandstone.

A STREET
IN TRANSITION

1888

Happy New Year,

Geo. C. Marsh, Real Estate,

Calgary Canada.

1889

1890

1912

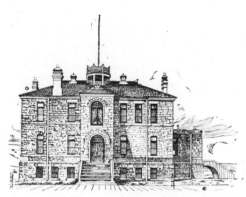

THE NEW CALGARY GENERAL HOSPITAL.

Above: Two examples of Calgary's sandstone architecture. *Opposite:* Brickyards at Cochrane *(above)* and Brickburn *(below).*

Street S.W. west of Richmond Road. Nearly all the Paskapoo-type sandstone for the old Land Titles Building and the former Carnegie Library in Remembrance (Central) Park, and for City Hall came from the Oliver quarry. In the City Hall, some of the stone blocks are fifteen feet long. The columns at the entrance to the Land Titles Building are made of individual circular blocks of stone three feet high.

Prior to closing down in 1915, William Oliver was employing forty men to operate equipment, which consisted of two steam shovels, two derricks with steam hoists, two horse-operated derricks, three steam drills, one electric gang saw, and a piece of equipment called an "orange peel stripper." Hourly wages at that time were forty-five cents for steam drillers, forty cents for quarry men, sixty-five cents for stone cutters, and thirty-five cents for labourers.

Sandstone cut and shaped at the quarry site sold for about twenty dollars a cord (128 cubic feet); rubble sold for seven dollars per cord. A sandstone block could be smooth-faced or rough cut. Rubble, the bits and pieces left over after a block of stone had been shaped, was used in the foundation walls of buildings.

From the late 1800's to the early 1900's, stone masons were paid a dollar and a half to two dollars for a ten-hour day. Carpenters worked for a dollar fifty per day; construction workers were paid thirty dollars per month. All put in a six-and-a-half-day week.

On September 2, 1907, the workers in the Calgary area united to stage a huge parade through the city streets. Represented were groups from the various trades and industries, including the stone masons and stone cutters, who were out in full force. An article in a newspaper of the day relates that "a monstrous stone measuring several yards long, the work of quarry men, received a cheer from the crowds. This received third prize and was well won. Six horses were required to drag it along".

The *Weekly Herald* of January 31, 1907, published an article written by Mrs. W. E. Hall. In part:

The Calgary Sandstone quarries within walking distance of the city are of inestimable value to her resources, furnishing residents with superior stone at minimum rates. This asset has contributed greatly towards the city's much-admired solidarity in appearance and has attracted a high-class of architects and contractors. The large Eastern Houses (wholesale) have unanimously selected Calgary as the most natural distributing point, have erected commodious handsome brick and stone buildings and have come to stay.

Calgary's business section began to take shape as Canada's

Sandstone City. It was estimated that half of the tradesmen were engaged in the sandstone industry.

It would be impossible to mention all the sandstone buildings, each with their individual charm and distinctive character: the business blocks in the downtown core, the churches, the schools, the government buildings, the homes. Like the old-timers of the foothills and prairies, the buildings that remain are now weatherbeaten and lack the lustre and glint of a modern generation. But they are distinctive in their old age, no two buildings being alike.

Various types and qualities of sandstone are to be found in Alberta, some being more useful for building purposes than others. Paskapoo type was the most suitable, because it was soft and was easily carved when quarried, and it then hardened with age and exposure. Ranging in colour from yellow in the Calgary area to greyish yellow in the Glenbow district, Paskapoo is the type prevalent in the Bow River Valley. If one is interested in seeing sandstone in its raw state, the cliffs of sandstone as formed by nature many, many years ago can be seen in Edworthy Park, close to the Sarcee Trail-Banff Coach Road intersection in southwest Calgary.

"CASTEL-AUX- PRES,"
RESIDENCE OF MR. JUSTICE ROULEAU

Some of the best people lived in sandstone. *Above: Castle Aux Pres,* the residence of Justice Charles Rouleau, the judge who replaced the controversial Judge Travis. *Left:* The home of Colonel Macleod for the four months prior to his death in 1894. *Right:* The famous *Beaulieu,* home of the Lougheeds, still stands on Thirteenth Avenue S.W. *Above right:* The Burns Block, 1906, headquarters for P. Burns and Co.

372

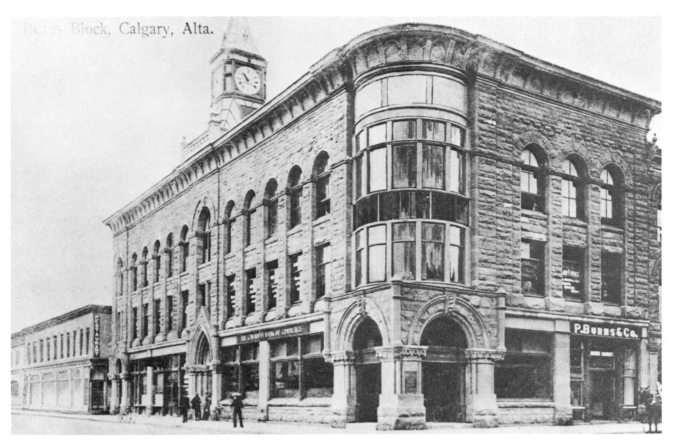

Burns Block, Calgary, Alta.

The Glenbow Stone Quarry

Above: Men working at the sandstone quarry on the Elbow River. *Opposite above:* A winter view of the same quarry. *Far right:* A stone planer at work. *Below:* Construction of the Anglican Cathedral, 1908.

One of the most interesting of the turn-of-the-century sandstone operations was the Glenbow Sandstone Quarry, located about five miles east of Cochrane on the north side of the Bow River.

A Mr. Carter, a man of considerable political influence, and a Mr. Quinlan, a short, rotund, blasphemous Irishman who owned a marbleworks in Montreal, obtained a contract to operate the quarry. Dave Kirkup, son-in-law of Mr. Quinlan, was master mechanic; and Mr. Carter's son was timekeeper. Two toolmakers from Kirnoostie, Scotland, both expert craftsmen, made the tools for the machines and tempered the steel in a small shed on site.

While the equipment was being set up, the CPR built a spur line to transport the stone. A Mr. Duncan supervised the installation of two bandsaws, a diamond saw, two cornice planers, and two flat planers. This equipment was supported by concrete bases with very heavy timbers. A railway extended up the hill from a CPR siding to where the stone was taken from the hill. An overhead track carried stone blocks of ten, twenty, thirty, or forty tons from the flat cars to the saw or planer and back again before being taken downhill for loading for shipment by CPR flatcar. A turntable derek at the top loaded stone on the flatcars, and another at the bottom performed the same function. The derek at the bottom was also used to unload coal for fuel into bunkers built near the track for storage.

A number of amusing incidents occurred during the construction stage. Mr. L. A. Duncan, the foreman responsible for building the foundations on which the equipment was placed, experienced difficulty in finding gravel. Locating a pit beside the CPR line west of the quarry, ingenious labourers pushed one of the flatcars along the track, an upgrade, and loaded it with gravel. When they started down, they lost control as they had no brakes, and jumped off. The flatcar collided with a freight train travelling west. The front of the engine and the cow catcher were wrecked, and gravel flew in all directions. In the resulting court case the CPR was awarded damages.

Despite such minor setbacks, however, progress was rapid. A powerplant was built into the base of the hill about fourteen feet from the saws. High-and-low-pressure boilers furnished steam power to operate the five-hundred-horsepower two-cylinder engine. The drive belt from engine to main shaft was made of eight three-and-one-half-inch ropes. To maintain tension, two boys were employed to brush the ropes with water.

Drills powered by Westinghouse high-and-low pressure air compressors drove holes in the stone in the form of a Maltese cross. Using a watering can, the blasting specialists

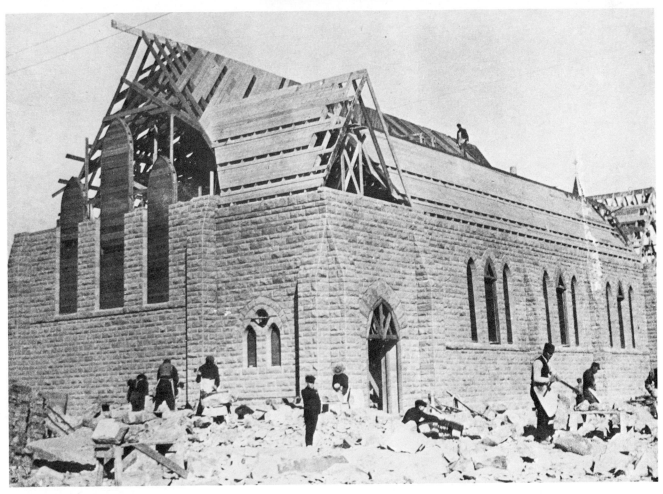

375

would partially fill the hole with blasting powder, insert the fuses and caps, and add more powder. The fuses were fastened together and led to a box. When the plunger was slammed down, the explosion would loosen as much as twenty or thirty tons of stone with one perfect crack all around, and set it out about one inch.

Once the sandstone had been blasted from the rockface, it was necessary to cut it into blocks. The stone was first wedged firmly into place, and enormous twelve-foot-high bandsaws were prepared to cut it into smaller pieces. Strips of steel were set in the stone to guide the cutting to the desired size. Water was pumped from the Bow River to spray the stone surface during the sawing. Silicon carbide was the abrasive — a ton was used each working day. Two diamond saws each six feet across cost eight thousand five hundred dollars apiece, and contained four thousand dollars worth of diamonds, each the size of the end of a lead pencil.

The cornice planer cut the fancy curved strips used at the base and top of buildings and around doors and windows. Each tool was cut to specifications by the toolmakers. The planer working in both directions would flip over at the end of one sweep and plane back. This relatively new procedure saved a lot of time and motion. Each sweep could be set to cut to tolerances of one sixty-fourth or one ninety-sixth of an inch. The flat planer, ten feet wide and twelve feet long, shaved off the rough saw marks. Removing a fine bit each sweep, it worked the stone until it was as smooth as paper. Then boards were placed in layers between the stone to prevent breakage during shipping.

The living quarters for the workmen consisted of a shack eighty feet long and two stories high. The lower floor was used as a cook house and storage area, and upstairs were three rows of cots, ninety in all, with only knee room between them. One man slept in a bed at night and when he arose another man climbed in. About 180 men were employed at peak production, double-shifted six to six. By 1912, however, the sandstone supply was almost finished. After two short years of operation the machinery was removed and taken to Calgary where it was stored in an old warehouse on the south bank of the Bow River. It was a depressing end to an ambitious business.

William Pearce

This is the story of a man whose profession was surveying — a pioneer who traversed a land described by Sir William Butler as like "no other portion of the globe in which travel is possible, where loneliness can be said to dwell so thoroughly, where one may wander 500 miles without seeing a human being or an animal larger than a wolf."

William Pearce was a natural pioneer, a man of powerful physique and great endurance. He also had a tremendous imagination; not only did great projects such as building a railway across an unknown continent or the settlement and development of vast territories hold an overpowering appeal for him, he could also envision the need to preserve the beauties and the natural resources of these territories.

The son of an Ontario farmer, William Pearce was educated as a civil engineer and land surveyor at the University of Toronto, and followed his profession in eastern Canada before moving to Winnipeg in 1874. As Dominion Land Surveyor he was in charge of the initial survey work for the Federal Government in Manitoba and the North-West Territories until the early eighties.

In 1882, at the age of thirty-two, he was appointed a member of the Dominion Land Board — a most important position and one which required not only optimism and initiative, but outstanding ability, as the policy for the administration of this vast country had yet to be formulated. A few years later, in 1884, he was appointed Superintendent of Mines — a title which failed to convey the great responsibilities of its holder, and the magnitude of his jurisdiction.

Early settlers regarded William Pearce, with his office in Calgary, as the ruling power in the West. He was undoubtedly a Czar in all western affairs which came under the jurisdiction of the Department of the Interior. It was his duty to investigate personally all claims of half-breeds and other settlers, and submit recommendations accordingly. As ranches grew in number and increased their grazing-lease holdings, and as the homesteaders and those others who acquired land by purchase or scrip began encroaching on the water rights of ranches and squatters, problems became alarmingly prevalent and increasingly difficult to solve.

Pearce's jurisdiction extended from Winnipeg in the east to the Rocky Mountains in the west, and from the International Boundary (the forty-ninth parallel, which, incidentally, he surveyed) on the south, to the fifty-sixth parallel on the north. Much of his travelling was done by Red River cart and by dog sled, and in later years by buck-board or democrat. He was noted as an indefatigable walker and snowshoer. He was also well known for his amazing memory. He never met with anyone without striking up a conversation, and invariably he could recall the complete incident and the details of what had been discussed.

Above: William Pearce in the 1880's.　*Opposite:* Boating at Bowness Park.

While he was Superintendent of Mines, Pearce had to rule upon many important and controversial questions in connection with railway development, such as land grants, townsites, and the adjustment of the ever-present squatter problems. There is so much one can write about the activities of this man during the early days of settlement outside Calgary and its environs, that it is difficult to confine his operations to Calgary.

Pearce first came to Calgary in 1884, but the office of Superintendent of Mines, which had been operated from Winnipeg, did not open in Calgary until July, 1887. From his first visit to this section of western Canada, he was very impressed with Calgary as the location for expanding settlement. He was convinced of its strategic position as an eventual commercial centre for the vast territory east of the Rocky Mountains.

But Pearce was not only concerned with the commercial possibilities of Calgary. He was also anxious that the beauty of its location be preserved and that conservation programs be initiated to ensure recreational facilities for the burgeoning population. He had already had experience in such programs; as the man who advised the Crown Minister, Pearce had exerted more than passing influence in the selection of the Canadian National Park at Banff, which was established in 1886 and was the first park reserve of its kind in Canada.

Thanks to Pearce and his vision of the future, citizens of Calgary enjoy the benefits of the group of islands known as St. George's Island. He was also largely responsible for Mewata Park (Mewata being a Cree word meaning "To Be Happy"). The land owned by the government had already been subdivided into lots when Pearce stepped in and arranged its reservation for park facilities.

It was also William Pearce who prevented the lands adjacent to the north side of the Bow River being acquired by squatters. Similarly, he ordered the reservation of river-access for the area known as Memorial Drive. Another contribution was to establish flood controls to prevent damage by mountain streams during periods of unusually high water level; this was accomplished by the construction of large reservoirs. Pearce's surveys and reports were the basis of a long-range plan which saved enormous amounts of money as well as damage to important natural resources. He was also a great believer in providing attractive sight-seeing driveways throughout Calgary and Banff, and thence to Jasper. And as a quite different example of his foresight, the General Hospital is located on land that Pearce had reserved for hospital purposes in 1891.

Pearce's home, "Bow Bend Shack", was one of the showpieces of the West. The "shack", described as the "finest house west of Winnipeg," had running water, three fireplaces,

Above: Bow Bend Shack, residence of William Pearce. *Opposite above:* Pearce not only advocated conservation of existing natural beauty spots, such as St. George's Island, he also believed in creating them through irrigation and tree planting. The spruce-lined drive of his estate was an inspiration to many similar-minded Calgarians. *Below:* Pearce's children enjoying a winter ride through the estate.

Above: William Pearce was one of the old-timers who never missed a Stampede parade. *Opposite:* His democrat, a familiar sight to Calgarians, as it appeared in the first parade in 1912. *Above:* A picnic on the Pearce estate, *circa* 1914.

steam heat, natural gas, a large refrigerator, and a billiard room in the basement. In 1889, the year the house was built, such features were rare in Canada's far West. The "architectural pride of Calgary" was built of local sandstone and the interior trimmings and panelling were of alder. The yard, featuring spruce trees that were nourished by Alberta's first irrigation project (originated by Mr. Pearce) was one of the sights of the vast prairie country; and during the eighteen nineties, and for many years thereafter, nearly every important visitor was driven to "Bow Bend Shack" to see the wonders Pearce had performed in developing this grove of trees, the shrubbery, and the general plantation.

Pearce's success with horticulture inspired other newcomers who longed for trees, flowers, and other foliage so often associated with their old home. At his own expense, he operated for many years the first irrigation experimental farm in Alberta. With great pride he would conduct those interested in the various kinds of trees, shrubs, vegetables, and flowers through his estate.

No man in western Canada was in closer touch with the chief planners of the CPR than William Pearce. It was Pearce who first directed the attention of government and the CPR to the possibility of irrigation east of the Rockies. Extensive surveys were made both by the Dominion government and the CPR before the huge irrigation scheme was undertaken. Pearce, as Chief Inspector of Surveys, accompanied all the preliminary survey parties, and practically day and night kept in closest touch with the creative planning side of the operation. It was said at the time that "he was the man to whom the people of Calgary owe an everlasting debt of gratitude for so successfully engineering this big enterprise which is a benefit to Calgary."

After thirty-two years continuous service with the Department of the Interior, Pearce resigned in 1904, and became an official of the CPR in an advisory capacity. In this position he was responsible for the administration of irrigation and other matters under the jurisdiction of the Department of Natural Resources.

Pearce was also one of the true pioneers in the search for oil in Alberta; it was due largely to his recommendations and persistence that drilling was started and continued in the face of much discouragement in the Turner Valley field. Pearce emphatically believed that the natural resources of the country should be held for the benefit of the people. The value of his work was acknowledged by Sir John A. Macdonald; in a letter to Pearce, the Prime Minister remarked, "Let me say now that I fully appreciate the strong interest you have taken in protecting the public and the revenue from land sharks and speculators."

Pearce was never idle. He was a man of very inquisitive disposition, and had an extraordinarily retentive and active memory. His determination and drive impressed everyone who worked with him. All in all, he was a remarkable man, to whom much is owed by modern Calgarians. Without the foresight, imagination, and integrity of William Pearce, the quality of life in this city could not have been as outstanding as it is.

William Pearce

The Mawson Report

Above: Mission Hill in the early 90's. *Opposite:*
The Mawson Plan.

In 1913 a qualified city planner, Professor Thomas Mawson of Liverpool University, England, was commissioned to develop a comprehensive plan of development for the fast-growing city of Calgary. The Mawson Plan, as the report was usually called, envisioned the best possible utilization of Calgary's natural beauty. The heart of the plan was to capitalize on the wonderful scenic vistas afforded by the Bow Valley, and in particular, to make the fullest use of Prince's Island, which was to be the focus of the new downtown area. There would be a great open square facing the Island, where the artistry of obelisks, statues, civic buildings, auditoriums, and spacious walkways would combine with the glorious view of the mountains and the river. As an intrinsic part of the concept, Mawson designed a mall with an arch over it that would connect the river square to the business section to provide a ten-minute walking access to this beauty spot. The river would be channelled around the square to give a lovely water setting. There would also be access to the square from the north part of the city by means of a bridge, which would connect with a road similar to the present Memorial Drive.

The Planning Commission that engaged Mawson was made up of forty citizens, including Alderman Costello, Mayor Sinnot, P. Turner Bone, William Pearce, A.G. Graves, Mrs. Harold Riley, Dr. Scott, Dr. Kerby, Dr. Alex Calhoun, and others. That they were pleased with Mawson's proposal is evident from the following report prepared for the City Council:

To the Mayor and Council of the City of Calgary:

Your City Planning Commission herewith submit their report of its workings since its inauguration in December, 1911. Its history and constitution are briefly these:

To obtain data and information on the subject of Town Planning and to prepare and recommend a comprehensive scheme of City Planning which will meet the requirements of this City for its future development, and in accordance with the above resolution has been prepared a comprehensive scheme of Town Planning, which is now submitted for your consideration.

This scheme, as you are aware, has been prepared by Professor T. H. Mawson, Hon. A.R.I., B.A., working in conjunction with your Commission, and consists of about thirty drawings together with a Report in book form, copies of which you have each received.

We believe that this scheme is one of the most complete that has ever been prepared and bearing in mind the fact that the majority of cities throughout the world have or are having prepared similar schemes, we believe that this report will have the fullest and most careful consideration from your honourable body.

Before any work could actually begin, however, World War One broke out, and virtually all public expenditure not connected with the war effort was frozen. With the return of peace, the pre-war real-estate boom failed to return with it. The Mawson Plan was first postponed, then postponed again, and finally shelved altogether — and thus died an intriguing alternative course of development in Calgary's history. It is indeed fascinating to speculate as to the appearance of the present-day city had Mawson's great vision been implemented.

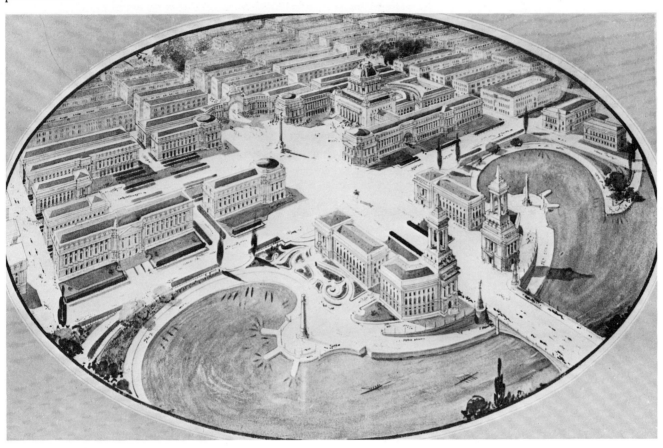

CHURCHES

First Baptist Church, 1900.

St. Mary's Church, 1905.

Laying foundation stone, Anglican Pro-Cathedral, 1904.

KNOX PRESBYTERIAN CHURCH, CALGARY

Central Methodist, under construction, 1907.

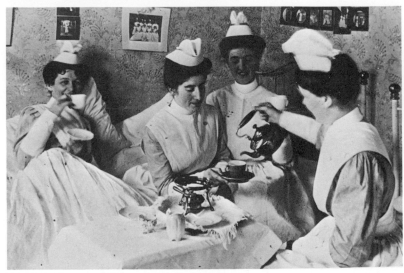

HOSPITALS

Miss Mary Dangerfield, lady superintendent, Calgary General, 1906.

Tea time for nurses, General Hospital, 1904.

General Hospital, Calgary.

Holy Cross Hospital, Calgary.

Miss Marion E. Moodie, the first nurse to graduate from Calgary General Hospital Training School for nurses.

Graduates of Holy Cross Hospital.

Chapter 13 Between Vacations

Looking into the dim future when Calgary shall possess colleges, when degrees shall adorn the names of its citizens, when this town of the far West shall furnish statesmen, educated here, to administer the laws of our Province, it will be a pleasant reminiscence to these children to remember their little rough schoolhouse and this first examination within its walls.

From The Calgary Herald on the occasion of the first examinations given in Calgary, 1884

Public Classrooms

The first schools in the Calgary area were Indian missionary schools founded by the various churches to educate their parishioners. In 1875 John McDougall imported Andrew Sibbald to instruct at his mission in Morley. In 1884 Father Lacombe instituted vocational instruction for his pupils: something that would not be available to white students for quite some time.

Calgary was almost ten years old before its first public school opened. On January 24th, 1884, the Lieutenant-Governor of the North-West Territories, the Honourable Edgar Dewdney, visited Calgary. Dewdney advised concerned parents that in communities where ten or more children between the ages of five and twenty lived, the North-West Territories Council would create school districts. Not only that, the Council promised to pay one-half the teacher's annual salary, provided it did not exceed six hundred dollars.

A public meeting was held at the Opera House on February 6, 1884, to find a building, raise three hundred dollars in donations, and, last but not least, hire a teacher. Three men interested in the development of the community were chosen to head the project. They were H. Douglas, operator of the stagecoach line between Fort Macleod and Edmonton; A. McNeil, the government fruit inspector; and W. M. Costello, a local lawyer. The holiday was over for Calgary youngsters!

On February 18, 1884, a bitterly cold morning, twelve children tramped through the snow across the open prairie to Boynton Hall, a log building on Stephen Avenue east of Drinkwater Street. There they were welcomed by Calgary's first teacher, Mr. J. W. Costello, who valiantly faced his class with no books and few supplies. The classroom furniture had all been made in Calgary expressly for the new school. Nobody had a desk to himself — students sat on long benches in front of long tables. The drafty building was heated by a box stove stoked with wood and coal, and instead of heading for a drinking fountain, thirsty students lined up for a dipper of water from the bucket at the back of the room. If such "primitive" facilities made it a little difficult to concentrate, it took only a glance at the leather strap hanging on the wall to remind everyone to behave.

By April all the money that had been collected was spent, and school closed for the summer. Among the pupils of that class of '84 were L. Meikle; H. Moulter; Kate Douglas; Mabel, Honey, and Louise McNeill; and Samuel, Thomas, Michael, and W. Costello. The latter four pupils were the children of the teacher; Michael Costello was later to become a prominent doctor and also a mayor of Calgary.

In the fall, classes resumed under a new teacher, J. Spencer Douglass. They were held in a more conveniently

Above left: The Dunbow Indian Industrial School at the junction of the Bow and Highwood rivers. *Right:* An interior shot of Dunbow, showing the girls' sewing room. *Left:* A group from Calgary's Industrial School. Parents in Calgary were envious of the Indian Industrial Schools, initiated by Father Lacombe in 1884, and would have liked similar instruction for their own children. The natives on the other hand felt the schools were a mixed blessing, for their children had to board away from home. Furthermore the children's separation from their culture was reinforced by rejection in the schools of their own language and traditions.

located frame building at Atlantic Avenue and Irvine Street, which was rented for thirty dollars a month. The school flourished and there were soon fifty pupils attending. As promised, the Calgary Protestant School District No. 19 was formally organized on March 2, 1885. (The following year the word "Protestant" was dropped from the name of public school district, but it continued as the official Calgary title until 1914).

With the establishment of the district, the school changed from a private undertaking dependent on uncertain contributions to a public institution financed through property taxes and government grants. The firm backing of public support meant schools in Calgary were here to stay. The responsibility for arranging operating expenses fell to the new trustees: Stephen N. Jarrett, James Lougheed, and Charles W. Peterson.

Yet so many newcomers filled the crowded classroom, that by the fall of 1885 a second room was rented on the top floor of 234 Stephen Avenue E. In the winter youngsters had to watch their step on the slippery outside stairway, the only access to the room. Mr. Douglass must have been grateful to relinquish the primary grades to two fellow teachers, the first women to teach in Calgary, Miss Grier and Miss Rose Watson. Whether Miss Grier ever actually taught here is open to some doubt, however, since some reports indicate that she was the victim of a housing crisis in the boom town. She was apparently living in Morley, and had accepted a teaching position here, only to have to turn it down when she couldn't find a place to stay. The story does illustrate just how quickly the town was growing at that time.

Reverend J. McLean, first school inspector for the North-West Territories, paid his first visit to the school in 1886. He gave a glowing report of the progress and attitudes of the sixty pupils: "A healthy atmosphere pervades the school, the pupils trying eagerly to excel." The students and teachers (Joseph Boag, who had become the new principal, and Miss Watson), were congratulated, but the building they were using received his strong criticism as being "in poor condition, lacking proper arrangement, suitable location and the necessary warmth in cold weather."

This hastened plans for constructing a more comfortable structure, and in 1887 the pupils were more satisfactorily accommodated when Calgary's first proper school building opened. Made of brick veneer, the four-room schoolhouse at Scarth Street and Reinach Avenue was named Central School. Everyone hoped that the new school would be adequate for the foreseeable future.

But the 177-pupil enrollment the following year was the second largest of any school in the North-West Territories. So

First
1884

The first school instruction in Calgary was given in Boynton Hall *(left),* alias Calgary Theatre Hall. The first official school was the building above on Atlantic Avenue. It was rented for thirty dollars a month and housed fifty students. It soon became overcrowded and the overflow attended classes upstairs in a building rented from I. S. Freeze. This picture *(opposite)* shows how it looked in 1924.

many students were arriving in the middle of a population boom, that by 1889 one heroic woman teacher had a class of 113! By November, Central was ridiculously overcrowded, so a new teacher was hired and fifty-three of the youngest students moved into temporary quarters in the dark cold basement of the Presbyterian Church. Nobody was very comfortable because for the first few weeks there were no desks to work at — the only furniture in the room was chairs.

The tremendous expansion of the school system put a great strain on the caretaking staff of one. According to the faithfully recorded School Board minutes of 1888, the solitary caretaker was responsible for "scrubbing the occupied rooms and hallways once a quarter, sweeping the same each evening and dusting every morning, kindling fires at all times when required, carrying in the fuel, keeping the seats of the water-closets in order, locking the school gates every evening and opening them every morning." All for two dollars a week!

At the end of 1889 Calgary schools had been open for five years, and although the system had been expanded to five classrooms, already there was pressure to provide additional services. A group of parents wanted their daughters to be taught fine arts and sewing. Their request was turned down, but a second demand was accommodated.

Some students were already working at a high-school level without the necessary provisions for their courses such as books or even teachers. The students' cause was taken up by "a short, slight man with a moustache and Van Dyke beard, a twinkle in his eye, and a ready smile." It was largely through the efforts of James Short that a high school was finally organized. A pioneer of Calgary education, Short succeeded Joseph Boag as principal of Central School, and by fall of 1889 had organized one of only two high-school departments in the entire North-West Territories! The senior department was further bolstered when 178 dollars were spent on the books that formed the first school library in the city.

Expansion continued at a fantastic rate throughout the 1890's. In 1890 the primary class moved out of the Presbyterian Church to the hot stuffy rooms in the Town Hall, just above the jail. E. A. Lucas recalled how recess periods were occasionally enlivened by the presence in jail of a well known early-day citizen, Mrs. Fullham. "Her roaring profanity, ascending to heights of blasphemy and descending to depths of obscenity, would have us boys jumping up and down in wild glee; the girls grinning sideways at each other, their hands over their mouths."

Even with the addition of these entertaining surroundings as well as other rooms in the Methodist Church, space was still limited; and the waiting room at the curling rink was converted into a classroom. But these temporary quarters were

Above: Central School after it was enlarged in 1892. In all the views of this old school the belfry is empty. *Opposite above:* Ladies' Basketball Team, Normal School, 1906. Misses Burnett, Christie, Ross, Munro, McLean, Sinclair, and Emery. *Below:* Teacher and pupils of South Ward School, the first school to be made of sandstone. This picture was taken in 1902 eight years after it was built.

Right: Children at Victoria School 1907. *Below:* The class of '06 jubilantly adorns the fence in this picture of Sleepy Hollow High School. Located on the corner of Seventh Avenue and Second Street E., one of the twin structures was later hauled away to be used as the public market.

barely adequate. Calgarians had to start planning more permanent schoolrooms. Residents east of the Elbow helped out by donating six building lots, and in January 1892 twenty-seven pupils began classes in a new one-room school. Called East Ward, it was situated on Pacific Avenue. The same year four rooms were added to Central, and the school was modernized with the installation of water and electric lights.

Now all the pupils were in regular classrooms, and supervised by seven teachers. And Calgary students got their first music teacher when Professor Fenwick, choirmaster and organist at Knox Presbyterian Church, convinced the School Board to hire him. For 300 dollars a year he promised to conduct regular classes and organize two music festivals a year, sharing the proceeds with the Board. Objections about the ill effects of late nights on younger pupils, and indeed the effect of public appearances on all students, were over-ruled, and music entered the classrooms to offer a stimulating change from the regular academic subjects. Something that might have delighted children less, however, was the new resolution "that monthly reports be sent to parents showing attendance, conduct and progress of each child by all teachers, to be signed by the parents and returned."

As the school program developed, Calgary itself was undergoing a transformation from a small, isolated town to an important transportation and industrial centre. The increase in population brought an increase in students, up from 60 in 1885 to 402 in 1894 — an increase of well over 500 per cent! In May and June of 1894, students had to attend primary school on a shift system. By August the third school was finished — a two-room bungalow named South Ward, it was the first school to be made of sandstone, and still stands on Thirteenth Avenue and Second Street W.

A growing school system demands qualified staff, and in 1894 a room above Jacques' Jewellery Store became a Normal School, the first teacher-training centre in Alberta. At the end of the year the Calgary School Board could boast eleven classrooms in three buildings — quite a change from the one rented hall of ten years earlier. The rooms were filled with three hundred and fifty students supervised by ten teachers, two of whom taught high school. The phenomenal growth of the system during the first decade of the schools' existence is perhaps more obvious when we consider salaries. In 1885, nine hundred dollars was paid; in 1895 the cost had risen to seven thousand and twenty dollars.

After a few years' fluctuation the school population skyrocketed again, accompanied by radical shifts in the concept of education. One of the most striking examples of the changing philosophy was made possible through the generosity of an eastern tobacco magnate. Mr. Macdonald sunk some of the

What
Do
You
Know
About
Calgary

?

READ

PONDER

BE CONVINCED

fortune he had made from the manufacture of cigarettes into what was known as the Macdonald-Lloyd Training Fund. The idea had been suggested by Dr. J. Robertson, then Canada's Commissioner of Agriculture. Under the scheme, Mr. Macdonald not only provided a fund for those schools that would set up a manual training class, but he also offered to import trained teachers from England. The idea was closely in keeping with the changing times. Throughout Canada the shift from rural to urban living was unmistakable — Calgary, for example, had grown to 4,091 by 1901 — and people were needed who were trained in the skills necessary for building cities and helping them run.

Under this program, a Mr. Snell came to Calgary in 1901 and began a three-year trial program in a room in South Ward School. The classes in elementary handwork, wood and metalwork were so popular that they were soon extended to include the girls. Lest they neglect a lady's traditional role, four female staff members offered to teach the girls sewing while the boys were occupied in the shop. Finally, students were learning "motor skills" — activities that would prove not only interesting but practical.

Meanwhile, more students were crowding into the schools than ever before. In 1902 a contract was signed for the first four-room section of Victoria School. Two single-room buildings, including one for manual training, were also begun; one was placed on the South Ward schoolgrounds, and the other was located next to Central. Both opened early in 1903. That fall the younger children were separated from teenagers for the first time when high-school students moved into City Hall School, Calgary's first distinct high-school building. A two-room frame building on the south side of Seventh Avenue between Second and Third Street E., it was nicknamed Sleepy Hollow school, and later became the Calgary Produce Market.

Despite the added space, crowding was still acute, and the first large school was planned. This was to be the ten-room Central School, which was renamed James Short School in 1938. The building on Fifth Avenue and First Street S.W. was a new departure in schools, the first in a series of modern designs constructed to last a lifetime. Inspector Bryan hailed the school as "superior to any other school building in the territory, and compares very favourably with structures of the same kind in Eastern Provinces."

Beneath the cornerstone bearing the inscription "Victoria Day, 1904," was buried a sealed container with samples of coins and stamps, issues of the local newspapers, a list of the names of the Board of Trustees and the teachers, and the autographs of all the pupils attending the ceremony. These items were retrieved recently when the school was demolished.

Above: Alexandra School, East Calgary. *Opposite below:* The new Central School in 1905. It was renamed James Short School almost immediately after it was built. The old Central School can be seen to the right. *Above:* Mount Royal School, built 1909.

Central School, Calgary

Visitors to Prince's Island can still see the cupola that gave old-world elegance to the castle-like building.

When Central opened in 1905 it was overcrowded almost immediately. The school population had more than doubled in five years to 1,571 students. Room had to be found somewhere, so classes were held in First Baptist Church, Scarth Avenue Mission, and the Swedish Church. Manual training classes had been suspended in the fall of 1904 so that the classrooms could be used for regular schoolwork. More schools were needed.

Two similar ten-room schools were planned. A new South Ward (renamed Haultain in 1910) was begun just east of the original bungalow school. A new East Ward was also built, and it too was later renamed, to Alexandra School. These schools featured spacious, well lighted rooms and large assembly halls, and were attended by Calgary youngsters for sixty years.

But even the addition of two new large schools couldn't handle the population boom in the early years of this century. Expansion of the teacher-training relieved some of the pressure; when the new Normal School opened in 1908, eight rooms were used for practice teaching.

Not surprisingly, administrative work was becoming increasingly complicated, and in 1906, soon after Alberta became a province, a superintendent of schools was appointed. It was the first such position in the province, and the office was assumed by Dr. A. Melville Scott, who had been the dean of Physics and Electrical Engineering at the University of New Brunswick. Scott took charge of twenty-five grade-school classes and three high-school rooms, and in his twenty-five years with the board introduced pre-vocational training, a commercial high school, and special classes for the handicapped.

Within ten years the school attendance increased almost five-fold from 1,571 in 1905 to 7,461 to 1914. The overcrowding was aggravated by extensions of the city boundaries to include the outlying areas. The number of teachers had grown to 198, and a full-time secretary-treasurer and a superintendent of buildings had joined Dr. Scott in the first School Board offices, in City Hall, in 1911.

Of course, the building program that accompanied the increased enrollment was fantastic. Several cottage schools, intended as temporary accommodation to keep pace with serious overcrowding, were built. So were several stone buildings. One of these was a new high school, the eight-room Central Collegiate Institute on Twelfth Avenue and Eighth Street W. Opened in 1908, it was the only school in Calgary at the time to have a modern heating plant and indoor plumbing.

The large sandstone buildings were planned to last a long

Above: Dr. Arthur Melville Scott. *Opposite above:* Pupils of Haultain School, 1914; and Central's hockey team, 1912. *Below:* A group of aldermen and school trustees 1912. Left to right: H. A. Sinnot; F. W. Mapson; R. J. Hutchings; ——; Frank Riley; Magnus Brown; James Walker; A. C. McDougall; and James Short.

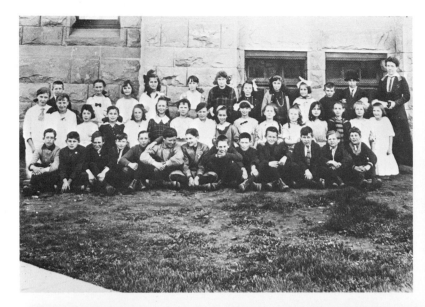

401

time. Modern structures, they were built with the aid of all the technical knowledge of the day. They were the first buildings in the city with slate roofing, a material effective in reducing fire hazard. A *Herald* article of 1913 echoes the community's pride in their schools:

The heating and ventilation in all the schools is of the modern type, each room being provided with a constant supply of fresh, tempered air at all times when the room is occupied. All air supply is taken fresh from the outside atmosphere: in no case is it used the second time. Sanitary drinking fountains are provided on every flat, and the other conveniences are of equally modern conception.

Most of Central's team is in the scrimmage at the right in this wonderful action shot of Central Collegiate versus Alberta Varsity, 1913. But, in spite of the fierce opposition, one of Central's men gets off a magnificent kick. To the right is a lineup of the team that year. Below that is a picture of Calgary Collegiate.

These sandstone schools included Riverside (1909), later renamed Langevin after one of the Fathers of Confederation; Mount Royal (1909), Hillhurst (1911), Earl Grey (1911), King George (1912), King Edward (1912), Stanley Jones (1913), Colonel Walker (1911), Balmoral (1913), Connaught (1910), Ramsay (1912), and Sunalta (1912).

Besides the phenomenal building that was going on, other programs were being introduced into the school system during this period. More specialists were appointed to head the increasingly diversified courses. In 1909 Mr. E. C. Brooker was made Supervisor of Drawing, the first art specialist on staff. A Director of Technical Education, Mr. T. B. Kidner, was hired, indicating the increasing importance of this field of study. The first domestic science classes began in 1910.

In 1912 the medical services were organized under Dr. T. G. MacDonald, who was responsible for inspecting pupils twice a year, examining the sanitary condition of the schools, and caring for the general health of all members of the school system. High school and normal students came under his jurisdiction the following year, and in 1915, in conjunction with the municipal government, clinics were organized for dental care and treatment of eye, ear, nose, and throat problems.

Cadets at a rifle range in East Calgary.

Of the many outstanding School Board employees at this time, three deserve special mention. F. G. Buchanan, who would succeed Dr. Scott as Superintendent of Schools, became assistant principal at Victoria School in 1908. Sergeant-Major Ferguson was appointed Drill and Physical Training Instructor in 1910, and remained in that capacity for thirty years. The same year Alexandra had a new principal, William Aberhart — who remained a school administrator until becoming Alberta's first Social Credit premier in 1935.

The period also saw the introduction of two regulations: monthly fire drills were instituted in 1907, and also the policy of opening classes with the recitation of the Lord's Prayer. Students during this period received all their school supplies free, and could skate on rinks provided on school grounds and vacant lots owned by the Board. One major change was the revision of the program of studies in 1912, with the public-school course divided into eight grades instead of five standards.

A review of a 1907 program of studies for public schools shows the emphasis on academic subjects: history, geography, reading and literature, spelling, composition, grammar, nature study, agriculture, arithmetic, drawing, and some unusual topics — stimulants and narcotics, and manners and morals — which were discontinued when the curriculum was revised. There was no instruction in "manipulative skills" or physical training, although cadet training was offered at various times, and boys learned military manoeuvres and the use and care of firearms (in fact, Sergeant Bagley of the NWMP had taught such a course to Calgary schoolboys as early as 1895). A 1906 purchase of two .22-calibre rifles and one thousand rounds of ammunition is recorded in the minutes, and stands as a grim reminder of what was stressed in physical exercise.

The revised program of 1912 gave recognition to the physical development of children by setting up a mandatory physical-culture course. Manual training, begun in Calgary in 1901, was also added to the provincial curriculum. As early as 1905 a local School Board publication read:

It is quite evident that the subject of manual arts is doing more for our pupils than any other subject, and in many cases, than all the subjects on the curriculum towards reviving and developing in them those features characteristic of truly successful and desirable citizens, viz., self-respect, interest, perseverance, ingenuity, originality, adaptability, etc.

Below: William Aberhart was one of the more controversial figures to rule the classrooms of Calgary. Here he poses with his pupils on the steps of King Edward School.

High-school studies had also remained primarily academic, and no departmental recognition was given commercial or technical courses until after the significant revision of the senior curriculum in 1916. Under the new and broadened program, manual training and household arts became compulsory subjects for grades nine and ten, with facilities provided at Crescent Heights Collegiate.

In order to prepare students for entering the business world, Mr. E. B. W. Dykes had begun commercial classes at Central in 1908. With no departmental recognition of the courses, however, enrollment was limited. The revised curriculum of 1916 included a two-year commercial program, and this attracted more interest. It had been set up to try to stop the increasing of dropouts.

So throughout its early history, the Calgary School Board attempted to remain flexible and adapt the educational system to changes in the social and industrial climate of the time. It was a difficult task in a city continually undergoing the rapid and extensive growth characteristic of Calgary, but the measure of its success was undeniably impressive.

The Separate Schools

St. Mary's Separate School, 1911.

Refugees from the Riel Rebellion in Saskatchewan founded the first Separate School in Calgary. Sisters of the Faithful Companions of Jesus were invited to safety in the town, and travelling by wagon and construction train, reached Calgary on July 26, 1885. A log cabin was enlarged to hold a chapel, a waiting room, a dining room, and two classrooms on the ground floor. By September, the day school was opened under the supervision of Mother Greene, a dedicated teacher, administrator, and the first superintendent of the Separate School. She also overlooked the construction of the Sacred Heart Convent, and the building, consecrated by Bishop Grandin on October 3, 1885, provided boarding accommodation for pupils of all denominations.

The same year, steps were taken to incorporate the first separate school district in Alberta. Called Lacombe Roman Catholic School District No. 1, Calgary was substituted for Lacombe in 1911 after confusion arose with the town of that name. Mr. J. W. Costello, the first public-school teacher, sat on the first Roman Catholic School Board, and also served as school inspector. Other early board members included Dr. E. H. Rouleau, Father Lacombe, J. R. Miquelon, and Patrick and John Burns.

Although initially only the junior levels were taught, enrollment rose steadily to 112 in 1889. That year fifteen students passed the high-school entrance examination, and regular high-school classes were begun at Sacred Heart Convent. It wasn't until 1918, however, that grade twelve subjects were included in the curriculum. Up to that time, the senior students attended the public schools for the nominal fee of $1.50 per month.

Indeed, there was close co-operation between the two boards, and there were many instances of combined efforts. For example, the public and separate systems shared the same truant officer, Robert Barker, who was appointed in 1905. In his *Anecdotal History of Calgary Separate Schools*, W. Barry recalls how "Mr. Barker arrived at each school once each week by horse and buggy. He tethered the horse and then consulted with the principal. He departed in search of the offenders and occasionally returned with one or more in tow. More often, however, transportation being what it was, the culprits had ample time to be 'Across the border and awa'."

As the population expanded, more space was needed in the separate schools, and a new sandstone Sacred Heart Convent was begun in 1893. More teachers were required to handle the extra load, and in 1901 Miss Theresa Thomas became the first lay teacher in the system. Plans were made to establish a boys' school, and in 1904 the boys were moved into St. Mary's Hall, which later served as a CNR station. Despite Sister Greene's preference for women teachers, the first man to be employed as an instructor, Mr. William Ryder, took over the boys' class in 1906.

It wasn't until 1909 that work began on the construction of the first building to be used exclusively as a school. Called St. Mary's, it was located on the corner of Nineteenth Avenue and Second Street W., and later became St. Mary's Girls' School.

As the city grew and spread, schools were needed in other locations. In 1912 two four-room brick schools opened — St. Anne's for students in East Calgary, and the Sacred Heart School at the corner of Thirteenth Avenue and Fifteenth Street W.

St. Mary's Hockey Team.

Although the separate school system was continually hampered by a smaller enrollment and less financial support than the public system, during the early days of Calgary no effort was spared to provide the best of educational opportunities. Arrangements were made with the public school board for students to take commercial subjects at James Short before a program was set up in the separate schools. Domestic science was introduced in 1920, taught by Sister Nancy M. Nolan. A music supervisor was appointed in 1928. And in 1938 manual arts were included in the curriculum under the supervision of Thomas Barry.

SCHOOL DAYS

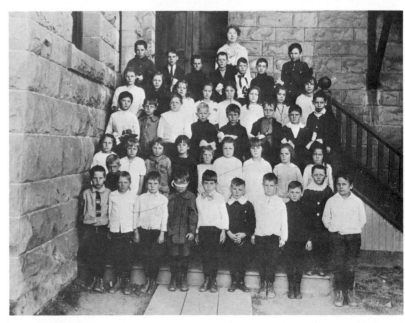

Chapter 14 Sports

I remember the first hockey or "shinny game" that was ever played in Calgary. It was held on the Elbow River on New Year's Day, 1888. A wooden block was used in lieu of a regulation puck, and in addition to hockey sticks, old brooms and clubs of every kind were used. We played ten men a side. The playing surface was a hundred yards long and we played for exactly one hour and a half. As usual in those days the game wound up in a fight. As I recollect, some of them who took part in this game were Billy Kinnister, "Nap" Perry, Charlie Gallion, Spencer Douglas, Jack McKelvie, Jimmy Linton, Pat McNeill, "Skinny" McNeill, Tom McNeill, C. McNeill, L.H. Doll, Sr., S. Ferland and myself. It was some contest and was the fore-runner of many an exciting contest.

Cappy Smart, in The Calgary Herald

Deerfoot

As is not surprising in a rugged frontier town such as early Calgary, sports of all kinds ranked high as a form of popular entertainment. Probably the first sport to be formally organized in the young community was running. Calgary boasted one of the swiftest runners of the day, an Indian named Deerfoot, who emerged victorious in many of the races held in the area. One of his rivals was an overly confident fellow named Stokes. The following account is of one of their matches:

The ten-mile race at the Star Rink attracted a large crowd of spectators. Deerfoot started favourite and, as was obvious to the meanest capacity, obtained a good lead early in the race and kept it to the finish.

However, the gentlemanly manipulators of the tally boards brought out quite a different result, according to their count Stokes winning by one lap. The judges came to the conclusion that there was something in this which they did not understand and declared the race and all bets off. We should suggest to the proprietor of the Star Rink that some totally different method of scoring be adapted at the next race. With regard to the real result we must say that we would not care to be in Stokes's running shoes if Deerfoot ever got after him to cut his hair. At the conclusion a purse was made up to console Deerfoot for the loss of his well earned prize.

The rematch between Stokes and Deerfoot was reported in the *Herald* on November 13th, 1886:

The ten-mile race for the medal between Stokes and Deerfoot attracted a considerable number to the Star Rink on Saturday night. The first hour and one-half was spent in persuading Deerfoot to run. The condition was that each man was to draw half of the gate money, expenses deducted. After a mournful calculation of the number of dead heads assembled on the premises, Mr. Claxton stated that twelve and one-half dollars would be each man's share. This amount Deerfoot demanded should be placed in the hand of some person whom he could trust. This was done. Then he wanted it raised to twenty-five dollars. The hat was sent around and the required collateral collected. Then he wanted fifty dollars cash down, two lots in Section 15, and a free pass on the CPR for the remainder of his natural existence. Then he said there was glass on the track and it wasn't a good night for running anyway. Finally at ten o'clock Stokes demanded a start, which the judges granted, the Indian meanwhile sitting in the far corner

Above: An Indian race at Cochrane, 1900. *Opposite:* Deerfoot, famous Blackfoot runner, *circa* 1887. Scars from the Sun Dance ritual can be seen on his chest.

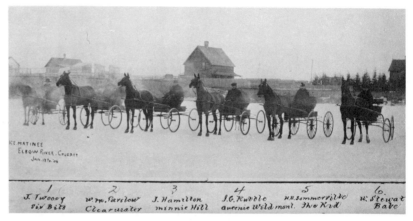

ICE MATINEE
ELBOW RIVER - CALGRY
Jan 13th 06

1	2	3	4	5	6
J. Twoody	W. W. Barslow	J. Hamilton	J. G. Ruddle	H.B. Sommerville	W. Stewat
Six Bits	Clearwater	Minnie Hill	Queenie Wildmont.	Two Kid	Babe

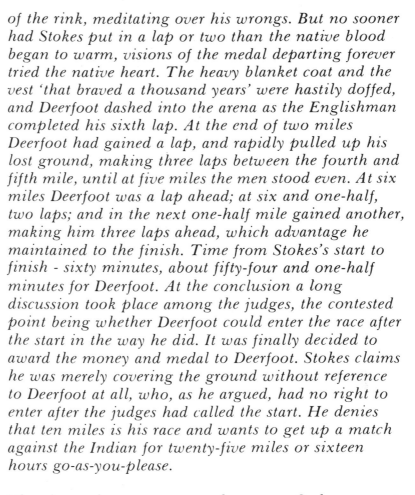

of the rink, meditating over his wrongs. But no sooner had Stokes put in a lap or two than the native blood began to warm, visions of the medal departing forever tried the native heart. The heavy blanket coat and the vest 'that braved a thousand years' were hastily doffed, and Deerfoot dashed into the arena as the Englishman completed his sixth lap. At the end of two miles Deerfoot had gained a lap, and rapidly pulled up his lost ground, making three laps between the fourth and fifth mile, until at five miles the men stood even. At six miles Deerfoot was a lap ahead; at six and one-half, two laps; and in the next one-half mile gained another, making him three laps ahead, which advantage he maintained to the finish. Time from Stokes's start to finish - sixty minutes, about fifty-four and one-half minutes for Deerfoot. At the conclusion a long discussion took place among the judges, the contested point being whether Deerfoot could enter the race after the start in the way he did. It was finally decided to award the money and medal to Deerfoot. Stokes claims he was merely covering the ground without reference to Deerfoot at all, who, as he argued, had no right to enter after the judges had called the start. He denies that ten miles is his race and wants to get up a match against the Indian for twenty-five miles or sixteen hours go-as-you-please.

The sixteen-hour go-as-you-please race Stokes requested was run at the Roller Rink on November 26th, 1886, "in the presence of a good crowd of spectators." Deerfoot was the victor.

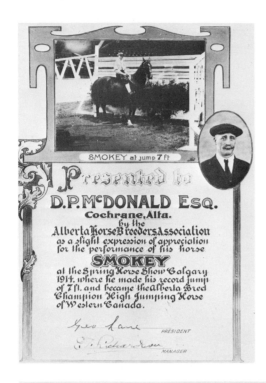

SMOKEY at jump 7 ft

Presented to

D.P. M^cDONALD Esq.
Cochrane, Alta.
by the
Alberta Horse Breeders Association
as a slight expression of appreciation
for the performance of his horse
SMOKEY
at the Spring Horse Show Calgary
1914, where he made his record jump
of 7 ft. and became the Alberta Bred
Champion High Jumping Horse
of Western Canada.

Geo. Lane _____ PRESIDENT

T. Richardson _____ MANAGER

W. E. WING, PHOTO

THE HORSY SET

Opposite above: Calgary polo team, 1894; and a scroll in honour of "Smokey", Champion High Jumping Horse of Western Canada. *Opposite below:* Brandy and Soda Race at a gymkhana in Calgary, 1895. *Below:* The annual coyote hunt of the Sons of England Benevolent Society, Calgary. This view was taken in the North Hill district.

Roller Rink

The first formal gathering place for sports in Calgary was Fraser's Rink, which belonged to G. L. Fraser, a fruit seller on Stephen Avenue. This venture was so successful that Fraser decided to try for the summer skating business as well. Carpenters were hired to lay down a maple floor on the rink. The necessary accoutrements were then ordered from Chicago. And on September 2, 1885, an announcement appeared in the *Herald:*

A hundred pair of roller skates for Fraser's rink have arrived. The rink itself is beginning to present a remarkably handsome appearance, and when finished, will be ahead of anything of the kind west of Winnipeg. Mr. Fraser expects it will be finished some day this week. There will be no season tickets. Tickets (each costing One Dollar) representing six admissions, will be issued instead.

Above: Roller skating hockey team, 1908. *Opposite:* Calgary Curling Rink; roller skating polo team, 1886; and a Calgary curling group of the 1890's. That's Colonel Walker, fourth from the left.

The rink was an attraction to the public not only for the recreation it provided, but for the competitive events that were held. On October 6th, 1885, G. L. Fraser staged a one mile race on roller skates. "B. Pugh easily outdistanced the only other competitor R. McFarlane. There was a good attendance at the rink to witness the competition."

A number of curious roller-skating sports developed, such as the Calgary Roller Skating Polo Team. There were also roller-skating entertainments such as the one reported in the Calgary *Herald* on April 24, 1886:

The exhibition given in Roller Skating on the rink last night by Messrs. Steele and Smith was a revelation to the large number of spectators present on how roller skating can be perfected. The skating feats of these gentlemen were simply wonderful and drew forth round after round of applause. Acrobatic feats on roller skates are not the kind of thing many men would care to go in for without an accident insurance policy in their pockets. Several new features will be introduced tonight and we advise all who can do so to go and see what is, in its line, an unrivalled exhibition.

THE PRAIRIE

CALGARY CURLING RINK

—1886

Cricket

Sport stories, written in the style of the day, capture for posterity a record of the lives of Calgarians during the 1880's. For instance, in an article appearing in the Calgary *Herald* dated March 26th, 1884, we read:

Although everything around us indicates press of business, yet we think there are times when a little judicious recreation would be not only acceptable but beneficial. It has occurred to us that the formation of a cricket or baseball club, or even both, would give us the opportunity to indulge our tastes in this respect.

Within the week Frank Hardisty, son of the Hudson's Bay factor, sent to Winnipeg for a complete cricket outfit and called a meeting of "those who wish to form a club." Notice was given that:

The first match of the season will be played on Saturday afternoon, between the Mounted Police and Calgary Cricket Clubs. We hope the players will be honoured by the attendance of the citizens generally and the ladies particularly. It is cheering to the players to have a good turnout, and it will all be the better of varying the

Below: The Calgary Cricket Club, 1908. *Opposite:* Ladies' Cricket Club, 1922

monotony of every day life. Now ladies, don't be "wicket", but attend, and we go "bail" that some of the lads will make a good "strike" that will do your heart good. You will see some fine "round arms", a few capital "sky rockets", some very delightful "muffs", some lovely "slips" and pretty "byes" as well as learn some "short cuts", "long stops" and other things equally interesting to the female mind. Wickets pitched at 2 o'clock.

Calgary enjoyed bragging weather over the Victoria Day weekend 1884. The sports editor in the May 28th paper wrote "The day was fine and the ground in good condition, but rather lively for the bowlers." A respectable number of citizens turned out to witness the game. The match resulted in a win for the Mounties with one inning and twenty runs to spare. The reporter observed "From the score it will seem that our boys require considerably more practice before they can cope successfully with their antagonists." After the game dinner was served in the Royal Hotel. A return match played on June 16th, 1884, was won by the Citizen's Team with nine wickets to spare.

Respecting the need for practice the Calgary Cricket Club arranged a match between players over twenty-five years of age and a team picked from players under twenty-five. Despite the brilliant batting of J. C. Gordon for the "Veterans", who went to bat first, the youngsters won. Regarding the return match that was scheduled, the *Herald* encouraged the ladies "to put in an appearance as the cricketers say they will feel capable of 'much greater effort' if the 'beauties' of Calgary will come to encourage them with their 'fascinating' presence."

The Calgary Cricket Club went to Fort Macleod to play "the first match that has been played between outside teams in Alberta" on August 15th, 1884. Meeting on the grounds at eleven o'clock, Wright for Calgary won the toss and sent the host Club to bat in the drizzling rain. In the words of the reporter, "To Calgary belong the 'evergreen' honours of the first victory. The local players speak in the highest terms of their treatment by the Macleod Cricketers and will try to use them correspondingly well on their return."

In the last week of July, 1885, the Calgary Cricket Club won a match with the High River eleven by a score of one inning and thirteen runs; and a game with the "Mounted Rifles" in a single inning by over forty runs.

Members of the Calgary Ladies Cricket Club. 1922.

On September 16th, 1885, however, the *Herald* was moved to observe "What has become of the Cricket Club? Last summer a fellow could get his legs and ribs pretty well banged up, but this summer, not even a bruise."

Nevertheless, the local side managed a respectable showing against a touring team from England. A press release dated July 3rd, 1886, tells "The Cricket match between England and All-Comers resulted in a victory for the English Team by one inning and a run. The most remarkable performance was a very neatly put-together twenty-eight by Mr. E. Moore."

The 1888 cricket season opened on May 17th with a match between the Alberta Club and the NWMP. "At 1:30 p.m. the Mounties took the field, Messrs. Dundas and Byers going in to open the Alberta defence. The Police fielded well and Currier sent down some rattling good balls. The Alberta innings closed for sixty-nine runs. Mr. May showed good form for his total and was unfortunate in playing on. Mr. Cornish also played well. At 3 p.m. Ellerton and Slater came to the wickets to commence the Police innings, but the bowling of Mr. Wright was so good that the innings were concluded for forty-eight runs only."

The game of cricket was played on the old Barracks Park adjoining the site of the CNR freight sheds on Ninth Avenue east of Fifth Street; on the grounds occupied by Victoria School on Twelfth Avenue and Third Street E.; and, in the years 1909-10, on the Colonel Walker School site at Ninth Avenue at Nineteenth Street E. Riley Park, the scene of the majority of games in recent years, was first used in 1914, when games were played between the soldiers and the Calgary Club.

An interesting story is told about the Western Canada Tournament staged in Calgary in 1912, when a very strong Alberta team under the leadership of William H. Napper from Fort Mcleod "Swept away their opposition in most convincing style." In that tournament no team scored more than 150 runs against Alberta and the batsmen from the Foothills scored no less than 250 runs in each innings and were never all out. The story is told of Napper's phenomenal luck in winning the toss on every occasion during that week. He used a French coin loaned to him by an old friend, Jim Coll of Calgary; on the last day of the tournament, Coll being somewhat late in turning up, Napper hid himself until Coll arrived, in order that he would not have to toss without his lucky coin.

Right: Sometimes winter sports in Calgary took an unusual turn. A chinook on January 23, 1892, brought the players onto the tennis court beside Hull's Terrace. The players are left to right: Mr. Turnock; Mr. Lay; Mr. Lafferty and Jerry Jessup. On the fence are left to right: Geo Kirkpatrick; Mr. Almon; Mr. Day; Mr. Wilson; Mr. Bernard (with dog); Mr. Thomas; Mr. Braden; Paddy Nolan; and Mr. Frank.

LAWN TENNIS MATCH, PLAYED AT CALGARY, JANY 23RD 1892.

Below: Group at Calgary Golf Club, Calgary, Oct. 7, 1899. Clubhouse was situated on south side of 14th Ave. between Centre and 1st Streets West. *Left to right, back row:* Mrs. Barker, stewardess (with horse); William Toole; Mrs. Richards; Miss Macfarlane; Chief Justice Harvey; Col. Williams; Mrs. W. Pearce (standing in front of Col. Williams); Mrs. Williams; Mrs. P. Turner Bone; Miss Tannis Marsh (later Mrs. Allison); Guy Toller; Miss de Sousa; J. J. Young; Rev. Langford; George Sharpe; Ed Vincent; Edmond Taylor; Larry Toole; Judge David L. Scott; M. J. S. Springer; John Anderson. *Middle Row:* Miss Phena Pearce; Mrs. Forbes (nee Grace Stuart); Mrs. Harris; Miss Louise Meyer; Mrs. D. L. Scott; Mrs. J. P. Sutherland; Mrs. Tom Christie; Miss S. Harris; Miss Helen Harris; Miss Templeton; Mrs. William Toole; Mrs. Mackid; Miss Bruce; Mrs. Templeton; Miss McCarthy. *Bottom Row:* Noel Winter; Jeremy Jephson; Miss Marjorie Sutherland; Miss A. Perley; Miss E. Harris; Miss C. Saunders; Miss C. Rhodes.

THAT OLD TEAM SPIRIT

YMCA Basketball Team, 1910.

Calgary Caledonians (Callies), 1908. They held the Dominion Championship for three years.

Maple Leaf Basketball Team, champions 1911-12.

Above: Football Team, Calgary, 1911.   *Below:* Rugby Team, Canucks Athletic Club, 1915.

In the Ring

PHOTO, THE CHER[...] ST[...]

From the early days of 1883, no boxing match was properly patronized at which "Cappy" was not the referee. He enjoyed the tough sports as well as the spectators and participants. If it was a special event, he would honour the occasion by appearing in evening dress. Invariably he referred to these bouts as "boots" which always brought shouts and hurrahs from the crowd.

A professional boxer from Butte, Montana, on arrival in Calgary wrote a letter to the papers announcing how good he was, and invited anyone to meet him for a side bet of one thousand dollars. A few days later a letter was received from an unknown middleweight, saying he was good enough to accept the bet. A week later he arrived in Calgary and arrangements for the fight were underway.

The two men had apparently never met before. There was no suspicion that there might be anything wrong. Followers of the manly sport knew it would be on the level - it was announced "Cappy" Smart would referee. The old Hull Opera House was crowded to see the visiting pugs knock each other's block off. It was a rough crowd composed of cowboys, ranchers, and men from the mountains and railroad camps. Chief of Police English was there with a show of force to keep order.

These men knew the Marquis of Queensbury Rules. "Cappy" the referee held up his hand and announced, "this ruckus is going to the finish. I can't say personally that I know these lads, or what they can do, but I know this fight is going to be on the level or you get your money back." In the first round the fighters landed no blows. There was a little more action in the second - the crowd became restless. In the third it became obvious that the men were pulling their punches. By the time the fight had gone to the sixth the crowd were standing and roaring, "Make 'em fight, 'Cappy', make 'em fight." The fire chief walked to the centre of the ring, held up his hand to say, "Don't worry, you're going to see a fight, men." Then turning to the fighters, "You mutts might as well make up your minds that you're going to fight. These people paid five dollars to see a fight and they're going to see it! You fight each other or I'll step aside and let you fight the crowd. Take your choice!"

Evidently the men were fakers, and like all crooks, scared in the presence of the crowd they expected to dupe. They could fight. The next round opened one of the bloodiest exhibitions of prizefighting ever witnessed in Calgary. Amid the wild yells of the crowd, they slugged each other until each was beaten to a pulp. At the end of the round they weakly appealed to "Cappy" for approval. When the blonde Mike Casey was knocked down it was obviously no fake. Before his opponent could reach his corner he also collapsed. Amidst roars of approval "Cappy" promptly counted them both out.

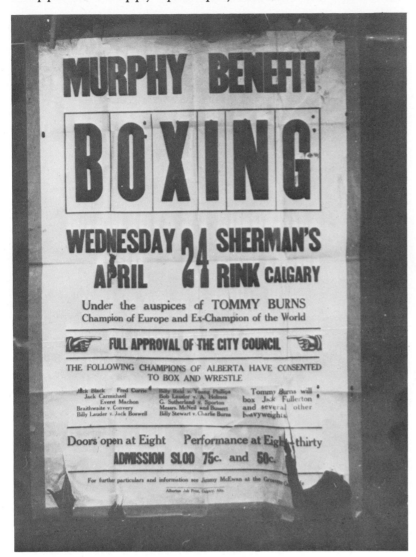

Above: Tommy Burns, onetime Heavyweight Boxing Champion, also known as Noah Brusso. He promoted boxing events in Calgary.   *Left:* One of Burns's posters.   *Opposite:* Freddie Wells, who boxed professionally in Calgary.

Chapter 15 Entertainment

At an early hour, crowds were noticed winding their way in the direction of the theatre hall, all anxious to secure a good seat.

At the appointed time, the curtain rose and the farce, 'Turn Him Out', was presented, all parts well sustained and in consequence well received by the audience. The second part of the program consisted of songs by popular and well known vocalists of Calgary and a clog dance by Constance Belair.

The farce, 'Mrs. Green's Snug Little Business', was then placed on the boards, to conclude the entertainment and the acting in this was fully in keeping with the former part of the program.

We must congratulate Douglas White, the scenic artist, on the effect produced by his artistic skill.

From The Calgary Herald, January 9, 1884

How did people living in early Calgary spend their leisure time? From the mundane to the eccentric, there was usually some diversion in town guaranteed to banish boredom or the blues.

The first residents *obviously* couldn't sit in front of a television, listen to a radio program, or take in a movie, but there was still plenty to keep them busy. Chilly evenings were perfect for drawing closer to the fire to relax with the family and read or write letters. Neighbours would drop in for a chat, someone would bring out the cards, and long hours passed quickly in pleasant companionship, for the isolated pioneers deeply appreciated company. Mutual trust and friendship were essential for survival in the harsh land, and many a stranger was given a warm welcome.

For anyone fortunate enough to have some spare time during the day, there was nothing nicer than a stroll by the Bow or a ride across the prairie. The rivers were ideal for fishing, cowboys busting broncs always put on a good show, and there were shops to visit downtown. But most people put in twelve-hour days, and it wasn't common practice to automatically have weekends free. So a holiday was something special to look forward to - "a leaven to the toilsome year of the world" - a day to celebrate!

In the summertime a favourite way to mark the occasion was with a picnic. You didn't just sit on the grass, share hampers of food, and soak up the sun. A picnic meant foot races for lively children, bucking-horse contests and obstacle horse races for indefatigable youths, and horseshoe pitching and ball games for the elders. Somebody might sing a comic song, someone else would stand up and make a speech, and darkness would always fall much too quickly.

These affairs were cherished by lonely pioneers, far away from their homelands and the families they had left behind. There were opportunities to gather socially and enjoy each others' company. Gradually a number of clubs were organized, and regular activities were planned - everything from sports days, sewing circles, debates and political campaigns, to church-sponsored fairs and suppers. But perhaps the favourite pastimes of all were those accompanied by music, which always helped to ease the tensions of trying days on the frontier.

Without radios, much of the music heard in Calgary was made by the townspeople themselves. When they got together there would invariably be an impromptu boisterous singsong of familiar tunes - minstrel songs,

Left: A card game at the Beam ranch, in the 1890's.   *Right:* The Rutherford family are off for a picnic in an Alberta Hotel carriage, summertime, 1897.   *Below:* A holiday gathering in Calgary, 1887. The location is somewhere near present day Ninth Avenue and Twelth Street E.

Gilbert and Sullivan choruses, and the always popular western ballads. Anyone who could handle a mouth organ or fiddle joined in enthusiastically, and everyone would have such a great time a concert would be planned. The whole town turned up for these evenings to listen to the others perform, to join in the choruses, or to step out on the dance floor. These occasional evenings of entertainment were not the only source of music on the frontier, however; music entered into the whole life of the town, with the formation of local bands, church choirs, and choral societies.

In the decade after 1875 most large gatherings of Calgary residents were held in the NWMP barracks. The Mounties' annual ball was a night of enchantment'', the highlight of the social whirl of the 1880's, and the traditional lavish banquet was talked about for weeks before and after the feast.

By 1884 the town needed a community centre to accommodate the blossoming social calendar, and so Boynton Hall was built on Stephen Avenue and Osler Street. The hall was named after an ex-naval officer, later a baron, who himself was not above appearing on the stage — as H. Frank Lawrence wrote, "Boynton in deer stalker cap, a lengthy Newmarket coat and a hunting crop tucked into a side pocket and appearing under his arm, on the grand opening night of his theatre giving us the old hunting song "Drink Puppy Drink", was quite worthy of the occasion." As Calgary's first "theatre", Boynton Hall was home for all kinds of activities: theatricals, concerts, balls, musical recitals, political meetings, church services, and school classes.

Variety was usually the keynote of the entertainment programs presented those days, for an effort was made to include something for everyone. For example, on Christmas Eve 1883 a concert was held "which was a great success and creditable to all that took part. The programme consisted of instrumental music, dialogues, songs, both comic and sentimental, two hours being pleasantly spent by those present . . . A dance was given after the concert was over . . . The proceeds amounted to seventy-four dollars which were contributed to charitable purposes."

There wasn't much diversity at a peculiar masquerade ball that "Cappy" Smart attended at Boynton Hall, however. Aside from fifty who turned up as Indians, everyone else was wearing kilts! Nor was there a hint of gravity in the January, 1884 program of hilarity that promised fun-lovers a night of chuckles:

Captain John Stewart of Rocky Mountain Ranger fame at a fancy dress ball.

THE GRAND
CONCERT!

IN AID OF

KNOX CHURCH,

Will be given in the

N.W.M. POLICE BARRACKS,

ON

TUESDAY, JANUARY 22ND, '89.

PROGRAMME:

INSTRUMENTAL DUETT, ...
Mrs. Neale and Miss Ground.
SOLO, ... "Michael Roy," . . . .
Mr. J. W. Curry.
RECITATION, (by request) "Cuddle Doon," . . . .
Miss Netta Duff.
SOLO, ... "Jessie's Dream," . . . .
Mrs. White-Fraser.
Dramatic Selection from Sir Walter Scott's "Lady of the Lake,"
(Combat Scene)
FITZ JAMES,   -   -   -   Mr. W. B. Higinbotham.
RHODERICK DHU,   -   -   -   Mr. J. D. Higinbotham.

HIGHLAND FLING, (In Costume) . . . .
Mr. J. M. Harper.

INTERMISSION.

SOLO, ... "Robin Adair," . . . .
Mrs. Godwin.
RECITATION, ..."The Polish Boy," . . . .
Miss Jardine.
SOLO, ..."The Shamrock of Ireland," . . . .
Mr. King.
To conclude with a Pantomime,

"The Cannibal Islanders at Home."

CHARACTERS:

KAME-HA-HA, King of the Cannibal Islands . . . .
OKEE-POKEE, His Son . . . .
REV. MR. SLEEK, A Missionary, short, fat and juicy . . . .
RATZ, An Infant Fegee . . . .

Doors open at 19:30; Concert commences at 20.

Admission 50 cts.; Reserved Seats 75 cts.

Tickets may be had at J. D. Higinbotham's Drug Store, where plan
of Hall may be seen.

"Cappy" Smart in his kilt.

Part I The laughable farce "Turn Him Out"
Part II Songs, sketches, etc., etc.,
Part III The screaming farce, "Mrs. Green's Smug Little Business"

Sounds like just the thing to crack any enamelled faces in the crowd.

But nothing could match the contagious excitement generated by the news that a dance was upcoming. People thought nothing of riding twenty miles at twenty below zero if they could rollick until dawn. Laughter and foot-stomping fiddle tunes echoed through the night. The ladies prepared a meal — nothing pretentious or fancy, just a snack served from a clothes basket. To rejuvenate the frenzied dancers, drinking water was dipped from an "ordinary washing jug", although no doubt other elixirs also soothed parched throats. Merry-making was the rule and it was a time for revelry. But there was one restriction: placards adorning the walls proclaimed "Gentlemen are requested not to spit on the floor." Other than that, anything went, and before the dance was over everyone was looking forward to the next one.

There were amateur drama enthusiasts in the small town too, and they banded together to put on some delightful performances. A *Herald* article of March 12, 1884 reads:

On Monday evening last, the Calgary Amateur Dramatic Club presented to the public the laughable farce entitled "Chopsticks and Spickens". The characters were all well sustained. Mr. Mortimer sang a song "Peer Relations" and was deservedly encored. Mr. Couzner's comic songs were highly appreciated and that gentleman was encored again and again . . . . The house was full and the audience went away highly satisfied.

George Murdoch recorded having attended "the Burlesque of Fra Diavola by the Calgary Club" in June 1884, and "Dunn's variety entertainment" at Boynton Hall in September. So there was plenty of action on-stage that year. From these first amateur performers who got together and amused their neighbours came the increasingly diversified and sophisticated entertainers and entertainments that have appeared in Calgary since.

An important meeting place in early days was the local barbershop, and even it once offered a "musical troupe of fiddlers, banjos and guitars." Hot and cold baths were another barbershop specialty - Tuesdays and Fridays thoughtfully reserved for the ladies.

Auctions of every article imaginable were very popular and drew large crowds. The pool halls did a booming business; an 1884 billiard tournament lured competitors with such prizes as "a first class Revolver" and "a very fine fishing rod with reel and line." Debates were also widely attended and you could hear wits argue such topics as "That a man gains more by travel than by study."

All opportunities for fellowship were welcomed. The Bow River Lodge of Masons gathered on January 26, 1884, and George Murdoch wrote: "we were there by the invitation of Mrs. Reilly entertained at her house, this being the first Masonic Social in Calgary or this section of Alberta." Members had held organizational meetings in Murdoch's cabin the previous year, and it wasn't uncommon for the stalwart faithful to ride or even walk forty miles to the meetings. Murdoch also became the first vice president of the Evening Literary Society that year. Now readers had a chance to meet and discuss books and exchange reading material.

The milestone of 1884 was the incorporation of the "Town of Calgary". The first mayor, George Murdoch, was anxious to start a town band, but he had to wait until the following year before the brass instruments arrived. By recruiting a band, the town council had acquired a sure-fire tactic to arouse public attention and attract townspeople to civic functions on holidays and special occasions. Who could resist the festive air of stirring band music? Especially if it included a parade with important visitors receiving the traditional ceremonial escort. Calgarians were proud to have a town band to play on such momentous occasions.

With the support of local businessmen and the newly organized I.O.O.F. behind it, the Calgary band began to tune up. The six-piece band (three cornets, a trombone, a bass, and snare drums) immediately made the anticipated impact. In June 1885 the following appeared in the *Herald*:

The Calgary Brass Band is making noticeable progress. As they parade the streets these summer evenings under the able leadership of Mr. Millward and the enthusiastic attendance of notable Indian visitors and Spencer Douglass' disciples, no patriotic citizen refuses to put his loyal head out of the window and shake his fist approvingly.

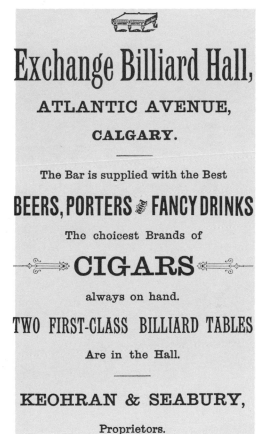

I LOVE
A PARADE

438

All the vehement practising was for the band's two official appearances that July. Their vigorous numbers so brightened the annual Dominion Day Sports celebration that they became its feature performers every year. The band's second public exhibition was to welcome home "Calgary's largest police force", the "Scouts", who had ridden out to assist at the Riel uprising. A July 22 1885 *Herald* article reads:

Mr. Millward's new band had got two new cornets and an armful of music and the rink resounded during hours of heat and cool to the soul-stirring strains of "The Girl Dressed up in Green" and "The Harm I Can't Explain."

But the limelight was stolen from the musicians the day of the Orangeman's parade in 1889. Ma Fullham was the major attraction on that occasion. Leishman McNeill recalled: She had gone into the Hudson's Bay Company store and obtained a wide silk paddy-green ribbon and draped it from her neck to her knees, topped with a huge green bow. As the parade passed she staged a one-woman show, shouting her caustic remarks, telling those Orangemen what she thought of them. The band may have been a calculated attention-getter, but Ma Fullham had her unique methods of beating anyone at that game!

The band also played for the July 21, 1890 visit by the Honourable E. Dewdney, Minister of the Interior, who was in town to turn the sod for the Calgary-Edmonton railroad. After the customary speeches were made and the first sod cut, the real festivities began. A whole ox had been roasted, and the tables groaned under loaves of bread by the hundred, cake, ice cream, lemonade, and ale. Fifteen hundred sat down to a hearty meal, and then headed for Boynton Hall for a dance to round out the day's activities. Guests were always extended a hearty welcome to Calgary!

The same year the town band was replaced by the Fire Brigade Band, directed by H. E. Stanhaft, who "contributed violin and clarinet solos to the first program." The new band was the pride of the citizens and played on all civic occasions. "Cappy" Smart was often in the crowd that gathered to hear their open-air concerts downtown. Many times they would play until dark, and then everyone would retire into the hotel for refreshments.

Among the clubs organized around this time was one for ranchers who came to town on business and needed

Opposite: The festive decorations on G. C. King's store are in honour of the visit of the Honourable Edgar Dewdney, and the commencement of construction of the Calgary and Edmonton Railway.

a place to stay. By 1891 they had established the Ranchman's Club for "gentlemen of similar and affiliated interest to gather and pursue social activities." For seventy-five cents the members could work on a forty-ounce bottle of whisky in rooms leased over Mariaggi's Restaurant on Stephen Avenue. They obtained their own quarters at the corner of McIntyre Avenue and Hamilton Street the following year, and today the club is thriving in the handsome building on Sixth Avenue and Thirteenth Street built in 1914, although it's been many years since anyone saw a big bottle for such a small price.

No one missed an excuse for merrymaking if they could help it. *Opposite:* Every vantage point on Stephen Avenue is crowded as the Dominion Day parade passes by. *Below:* The Salvation Army Band plays while the cornerstone of their new barracks is laid. *Left:* The celebration on its completion.

In 1895 the town welcomed another new band, the popular Salvation Army Citadel Band. Their numbers enlivened hospitals and homes, and rousing performances echoed in the streets and animated army meetings. The band also marched with the Fire Brigade Band in parades, and entertained at patriotic gatherings. In 1913, under C. W. Creighton, this band was considered one of the best brass bands in the West.

But there were hazards to street playing. Bill Gray, an early band member, recalled that when the mud on Stephen Avenue was too deep, the bandsmen walked on the plank sidewalk, and one member had the misfortune of walking into a fire hydrant and knocking out all his teeth! Another time the bass trombonist marching along the sidewalk was so absorbed in his music that he carried off the awning from Dickie Diamond's Liquor Store. But the biggest worry for the musicians was runaway horses startled by the strange hullabaloo. More than once the bandsmen had to put down their instruments, pick up their lariats, and round up the scattered critters before continuing with the concert. Horseless carriages never have whims like that!

Rollerskating and curling were big fads in the 1880's. In 1885, Claxton's Star Rink opened for these sports, and also ice skating, a favourite activity during the long winter months. Several evenings a week Calgary citizens could circle the covered arena to the music of the NWMP band. Many attended the masquerade carnival that year, an event that "went off well," and seems to have inspired more imaginative costumes than the earlier affair. Among the characters attending were a huntress, Grace Darling, the morning star, grandma, an Irish washerwoman, a fish wife, the queen of fairies, a Highland lassie and laddie, a sailor, and a bootblack.

The following year Claxton's Rink was the scene of the first local agricultural fair. There were competitions for draft horses, swine, poultry, home cooking, embroidery, knitting, buggies, carriages, plants, flowers, and even babies. The latter were the big winners. Only three proud mothers entered their little ones, and of course they all deserved a prize. Since nothing had been entered in the sheep contest, the resourceful judges transferred the money from that class to the children's, and each child went home a winner.

By 1890 the Calgary Opera House was built, complete with skating rink and concert hall. It was the scene for many famous - and infamous - local events. "Cappy" Smart was in the audience that night in 1893 when

Although Calgary boasted good indoor skating facilities almost from its inception, Calgarians continued to patronize the Elbow and Bow rivers. These Breugal-like scenes of Sunday skaters were taken in 1914.

THE LANCERS

"Georgia Wonder" made her notorious Calgary debut. A mere slip of a girl, hardly ninety-five pounds, she boasted she could support a platform loaded with five men whose total weight was about eight hundred pounds. The opera house was packed for the unprecedented occasion. The little miss lifted Dr. Mackid, one of the heaviest men in the town, "like a toy." The audience gasped - it had to be a trick. It wasn't until she'd left town with a pocketful of cash that it was revealed that yes, Calgarians had been duped. Her husband was the act's real strong man, and instead of pressing his weight on the chair Georgia balanced, it was he who gave the necessary boost to accomplish the "marvel".

A craze for "living pictures" hit town in 1895, and that January such a production was held at the Opera House. The first living picture was "Pygmalion and Galatea" performed by R. Newbolt and Miss Wainright. A song followed while the stage was set for the main feature, a series of living pictures depicting incidents in the Cinderella story. "Cinderella dressing her sisters for the ball" was ably performed by Misses M. Ryan, A. Perley, and J. Pinkham. While costumes were being changed for "Cinderella Meets the Fairy Prince at the Ball" with the above-mentioned ladies and Master Lucas and Clarence Lougheed, Mrs. Kerr gave her rendition of "When Mother Puts the Little Ones to Bed". The final scene, "Cinderella Trying on the Slipper", was "spoiled to some extent by the gas in the little reservoir escaping, reducing the light to a minimum glow and almost asphyxiating the actors."

The 1890's was also the era of the travelling shows that stopped in small towns to present what was currently popular in larger centres. Many commercial stock companies began to include Calgary on their routes. To accommodate the productions, the large brick Hull's Opera House replaced Claxton's Rink on the southeast corner of Angus Avenue and McTavish Street. Completed by 1893, it was a prestigious building, and during its heyday ladies dressed in gowns and long gloves and their escorts donned ties and tails for a night at the theatre.

Hull's Opera House was also the scene for amateur productions of melodramas. The local actors were often so polished that these shows could compete successfully against the imported productions. But the big rage was light opera, and the Calgary Amateur Opera Society, organized in the 1890's, staged such presentations as "The Pirates of Penzance" and "Erminie". Involved in

Opposite: Children in formal dress, dancing and playing the harp, 1899. *Above:* When these well dressed and well rigged citizens lined up outside Hull's Opera House they obviously had a formal portrait in mind. However a group of curious and grinning schoolboys got into the act and lend an air of candid charm to the scene. *Right:* An interior view of the Opera House.

Above: Crispin Smith, who figured prominently in Calgary theatricals, is here surrounded by the ladies of the Calgary Light Opera Company for the cast picture of "H.M.S. Pinafore", 1897. *Right:* A costumed production of 1900. *Opposite:* The chorus from an amateur musical production, 1900 — "Madame Butterfly" or "The Geisha".

the organization were Colonel Dennis, always very active in choral music; J. J. Young, an early Methodist church choir leader; George Tempest; violinist Fred Bolt; and the noted musician Johnny Augade, who conducted the orchestras. Musicians included Mrs. Parlow, the mother of world-famous Calgary violinist Kathleen Parlow; Miss J. Pinkham; and Laura Eschelman.

The Opera Society's productions received a big boost when Mrs. Roland Winter, an actress with considerable professional experience on the English stage, moved to town. She brought down the house in the leading role of O Mimosa San in "The Geisha", performed in 1899. It was the North American premiere and a resounding success. There wasn't one empty seat in the old opera house for the four-night engagement, and it is reported that many in the audience were ranchers who rode into town especially for the show and Mrs. Winter's performance, which reminded them nostalgically of the Old Country.

Displays of daredevil aerobatics were one of the forms of entertainment that rapidly gained popularity in the early years of the twentieth century in Calgary. As Hugh Dempsey wrote, "Barnstormers, amateur inventors, cranks, and mystery men flew, glided, and talked their way into the early history of aviation in Alberta. The first years were romantic, hair raising, and crazy. Pilots offered death-defying thrills, while the crowds waited below for the frail craft to crumble and plunge to earth. Watching also were wide-eyed boys who had devoured every magazine or newspaper article about the Wrights, the Curtisses and the Bleriots. Many of these boys were later destined to win their own wings when Europe was caught up in the Kaiser's great conflict." Above and below are two views of the Simmer Curtis pusher biplane, taken in Calgary about 1913.

The Calgary Operatic Society flourished until 1921, and Calgarians could enjoy such operettas as "Dorothy", "Floradora", "The Mikado", "Yeoman of the Guard", "H.M.S. Pinafore", and "Iolanthe". The latter, presented in 1897, inaugurated the latest in stage effects: "Another full house greeted the third and last performance of 'Iolanthe'. The colored light was introduced for the first time and lent a beautiful effect to the stage."

Mrs. Winter was active in most of the productions, and both she and her husband soon became leaders in the town's cultural life. The judge played his cello in the local orchestras that accompanied the amateur theatrical presentations. His wife was an enthusiastic participant, director, and critic; and for many years her advice on artistic matters was sought and respected. She attended every musical and dramatic gathering, and encouraged excellent productions in each field.

Indeed, many of the town's early musicians and actors gave themselves untiringly to all the artistic events, and their names appear again and again as they performed for the amusement of others. Among those busy with the opera society were lawyers Charlie Bernard, P. J. Nolan, and Crispin Smith.

The latter became the new leader of the Fire Brigade Band in 1901, under somewhat unusual circumstances. A popular character, Smith was jailed for refusing to submit certain evidence in a case he was defending. The court's decision didn't go over well with the townspeople. When Smith was released, he was saluted with fanfare, and given a noble and noisy hero's escort through town by the Fire Brigade Band. Within a short time he was its director. He made a dashing sight, too, for "when conducting, he always wore a bushy bearskin hat and long Prince Albert coat with white belt and sash."

The fire department sponsored an exciting annual holiday event that year - the May 24th Sports Day. A highlight of the season, it signalled the end of winter and the promise of spring, something to celebrate in itself after a long cold spell. The festivities began with a grand parade of bands sent from the nearby towns, and contestants and spectators from all over arrived in Calgary in special trains hired expressly for the gala occasion. There were running and jumping games, tugs of war, horse races, Indian pony races, ball games, and other contests. The big event of the day was the fire drill - the crowd cheered as the city's beautiful black horses, hitched to the red fire engine, went galloping down the street. The fire department was especially proud

Costumed entertainments were not confined to the stage in early Calgary. This resplendent pair are the Duke of Cornwall and his brother-in-law Prince Alexander of Teck. The occasion was the presentation of medals to South African war veterans. Some of the recipients can be seen in the crowd of onlookers, sporting stetsons and the lately bestowed medals. Alexander is reasonably alert but the Duke looks a little bored with it all. *Above:* A Calgary theatrical group, early 1900's.

Just what the occasion is is not known, but just about everyone in town has turned out for this celebration in Central Park, 1908, including the Mounted Police and the entire repertoire of the Fire Department.

450

of their thirty-five-member band that afternoon when it was announced that they had taken first place in the North-West band competition. Later in the year the band played for the visit of the Duke and Duchess of Cornwall and York, and a *Herald* article noted that "City fathers urged Calgarians to be particularly careful about fire hazards, so the civic firemen's band could play for the royal visitors without interference."

Visits by distinguished figures were big events in a small town, and this particular one was no exception. Storefronts were splendidly decorated, and the *Herald* hit the streets printed in royal purple. The royal couple first presented medals to South African veterans at a ceremony in Victoria Park, and then headed for Shaganappi Point, along with scores of townspeople who took advantage of the CPR excursion trains that set out for the point every few minutes. The feature attraction was, of course, a gathering of Indians arrayed in their colourful native finery. Indians were a distinctive part of Calgary life, and no visitor left without watching a display of their extraordinary dances and outstanding horsemanship.

Nor was a trip to Calgary complete without the entertaining spectacle of dexterous cowboys performing their stunts. Thus the royal party returned to Victoria Park for an exhibition of bronc busting and steer roping. This brought their visit to a close, a day brimful of the characteristic flavour of the West.

The year 1901 also saw the first bandstand erected in the CPR park. Crispin Smith encouraged the project, ably assisted by "Cappy" Smart, himself an enthusiastic amateur musician. Smart's Scottish Choir presented concerts each year on St. Andrew's Day and Burns's Anniversary, and he later organized the Tonic Solfa Choral Society. Thanks to the energies of these two men, the picturesque bandstand was set amidst the lawns and gardens, the scene of many successful open air summer concerts. When the Palliser Hotel was built on its site, the bandstand was moved to Mewata Park, remaining there until 1939 when it was demolished to make room for army huts.

Concerts were also given at Central Park, a favourite summer evening resort. The bandstand at the western end was designed after the one in Golden Gate Park, San Francisco; and on this stage the Fifteenth Light Horse Regimental Band gave several fund-raising performances. Following the gradual dissolution of the Fire Brigade Band, this band, under skilled musician and conductor Major Fred Bagley, was to put Calgary on the map. In 1907 it became the first Canadian regimental band to tour the British Isles. The highlight of the trip was a two-week appearance at the Dublin International Exhibition, a distinction every Calgarian could rightly take pride in. The band's forty-five members included several prominent citizens, among them Colonel Walker, Robert Mackay, superintendent of the electric light department, and Dr. Lymen, a local dentist. The band was later reorganized as the Calgary Citizens' Band, and continued to give performances until 1914.

Calgarians were less than enthusiastic about other musical offerings, however. Secular choral music, for example, had quite a struggle trying to gain a foothold in the young town. Colonel Dennis introduced the genre in the early 1890's by directing the production "The Holy City". In 1904 he presented "The Atonement", and immediately sparked a raging controversy. A Canadian premiere, the choral work was presented within six months of its first being heard in England. Everyone wondered why an unfamiliar work had been chosen to initiate choral productions in the city, and the *Herald* lead the attack: "It lacks nearly all the elements of popular music . . . to the average music lover, it is more or less obscure, fantastic and lacking in variety of treatment." To Bob Edwards it represented an unwelcome attempt to sophisticate the Calgary music scene that was neither necessary nor appreciated. He lamented "the irresponsible gaiety of an earlier period," and pleaded, "Why not give the public what it wants?"

Both productions failed. But if Calgary audiences weren't quite ready for the novel undertaking, it didn't dampen the enthusiasm of the choral performers. They banded together and formed the Calgary Philharmonic Society, with Colonel Dennis as president. Their first performance in the newly opened Lyric Theatre didn't fare much better. Sir Arthur Sullivan's "The Golden Legend", staged on February 28, 1905, was criticized as being beyond both the players and the audience. With two unsuccessful attempts behind them, the society finally decided to abandon long works in future performances and give more appealing miscellaneous selections.

The Calgary Philharmonic Society finally triumphed in 1908, however, when it formed the nucleus of a choral group that won nation-wide acclaim for the city. Sir Frederick Bridge, organist at Westminster Abbey, visited Calgary during a Canadian lecture tour on the history of English cathedral music. In each city visited, a mass choir was organized and rehearsed selections to

Left: Ceremony at Shagannappi Point for the decorating of South Africian war veterans. The Duke wasn't the only one dressed up that day in 1901. A mounted Blackfoot and his horse display their own version of military splendour. *Below:* The Calgary Citizen's Band, 1912. Conductor Fred Bagley is the one with the saxophones at his feet. He formed the first band in Calgary, the NWMP band. You will find a picture of him and that band in Chapter One.

Calgary Citizen's Band

accompany the speech. The Calgary singers were drawn from various church choirs; with 120 members it was the largest choir west of Winnipeg. When Calgary was awarded the "blue ribbon of western Canada comprising all the territory from Winnipeg west to Vancouver," Calgarians were elated to have defeated such rivals as Regina and Vancouver.

After the turn of the century, and particularly after the Lyric Theatre opened, there was a growing need for orchestras in the town. They were an essential part of road shows and vaudeville acts, and professional musicians were often part of the entourage. The theatre managers graciously consented to allow some of these musicians to accompany local operatic and choral productions. In time there were enough performers to form the "Calgary Symphony Orchestra" under violinist A. P. Howells.

But townspeople really got serious about symphonies when the Apollo Choir, a first-rate choral group under the direction of P. L. Newcombe, sponsored the St. Paul Symphony Orchestra at public concerts in 1911 and 1912. The audiences were so enthusiastic, in fact, that Calgary was able to lure their second violinist, Mr. Max Weil, to become the first permanent conductor of the Calgary Symphony Orchestra. The Apollo Choir helped to attract people to the introductory concert by offering a combined concert of choral and orchestral music at the Grand Theatre on January 27, 1913. The result was very effective, and the symphony was off to a good start. To reach as wide an audience as possible, convenient evening concerts and children's matinees were offered. At the time, Calgary was the only Canadian city besides Toronto that supported a professional symphony orchestra. That certainly was something to be proud of, and it excited enviable reviews in other cities. An article in the *Canadian Courier* read: "The progress of the Calgary Symphony Orchestra for one brief, almost giddy season of splendid programs, has been quite the most brilliant orchestral outburst in Canada."

From another source it was hailed as the apex of "social refinement and contentment." Its first season was its last, however; the outbreak of war and financial difficulties put an end to the organization, and fourteen years were to pass before another symphony orchestra was formed in the city.

The amateur entertainment scene was very active in Calgary's early years. But the simplicity and spontaneity of small town community theatrical and musical

Right: A musical evening at the Creighton's, 1914. *Below:* The Calgary Symphony Orchestra, 1913.

offerings was becoming a thing of the past as Calgary grew into a substantial urban centre. Mass entertainment was the sensible solution to keeping more people with more leisure time amused. Commercial amusements were on the uprise, and into this fertile scene came W. B. Sherman, early Calgary's most colourful theatre personality. In Leishman McNeill's words: "What I remember best about him was the tremendous diamond stick-pin and finger ring that he wore. It was as big as a searchlight."

Sherman took over Hull's Opera House, and on January 27, 1905, re-opened it as Sherman's Opera House. Two years later he bought the Calgary Auditorium Rink on the northwest corner of Centre Street and Seventeenth Avenue S.W. It had opened in December 1904 as Calgary's first indoor "ice palace" - a far cry from the bumpy skating on the frozen Elbow river. Lloyd Turner, later manager of the Stampede Corral, became the administrator of the so-called Sherman Rink in 1909.

Everything happened at the Sherman Rink. It held 2,200, and there was room for 400 more if chairs were placed on the ice. Hockey games were the main attraction in the winter, and roller-skaters invaded the arena during the summer. Leishman McNeill says "all large gatherings were held in the Sherman Rink: political meetings, concerts by noted artists, prize fights, and charity balls." Stars of the theatre and entertainment worlds performed on its large stage. Dame Nellie Melba, world-famous Australian soprano, was cheered by a record crowd; as Mr. McNeill wrote, "I remember top price was five dollars, an unheard-of price for Calgary, but the rink was packed." Late in the spring of 1915 the Sherman Rink burned to the ground and was not rebuilt.

In the meantime several theatres had gone up around town, catering to popular stock companies and vaudeville troupes. With improved transportation and communication facilities, they were coming to Calgary with increasing frequency, and these new buildings ensured them of adequate accommodation. Now Calgary was far from isolated - you could see the same things here as people right across the country were watching in their theatres.

Sir James Lougheed actively encouraged and supported entertainment by financing three theatres. The Lyric, on Eighth Avenue W., opened in 1905, and was the scene for such local productions as Mrs. Broder's "A Springtime Musicale" in 1907, and a series of band concerts presented on Sunday evenings to take some of the chill out of winter nights.

Below: The Sherman Rink Fire, 1915.

MADAME SARAH BERNHARDT
Who appears at the Sherman Grand next week under the direction of Martin Beck

The Sherman Grand, the biggest theatre in Canada, was able to attract the big name stars. *Above:* This promotional picture that appeared in the Calgary Standard, January 11, 1913, probably excited a great many theatre buffs. *Above left:* The Starland Theatre. *Right:* Florence McHugh, daughter of Calgary pioneer Felix Alexander McHugh, was one of the few Calgarians who made it to the big time. She became a noted actress of the British stage. The costume she appears in opposite is not for one of her many stage roles. It was the bridesmaid's dress she wore at her sister's wedding.

Lougheed's second theatre was primarily a vaudeville house, the Empire Theatre, which opened in December 1908 on Eighth Avenue near First Street W. Lougheed's most impressive contribution to Calgary's entertainment scene, however, was the Grand Theatre on Sixth Avenue and First Street S.W., better known as the Sherman Grand because that ubiquitous character held the original lease. For many years the Grand was one of the most famous legitimate theatres in North America. An advance in the *Herald* January 22, 1912 announced:

Without a doubt the opening night of Calgary's new theatre will be the highlight of the theatrical season in the city, and it will inaugurate a period of great improvement in the quality of touring companies. From February 5, Calgary will possess a theatre second to none in the Dominion, and one fully qualified from a mechanical standpoint to undertake the largest productions on the road.

The Grand boasted the largest stage in Canada, although some theatres exceeded its 1,504-seat capacity (812 in the pit, 692 in the gallery, and 6 persons in each of the 12 boxes). The half-million-dollar building was said to be absolutely fireproof, and included the latest in fire escapes, ventilation, heating, lighting, and dressing rooms, and the acoustics were second to none in North America — a feature every artist could appreciate.

On February 5, 1912, first-nighters, attired in their formal evening wear, pulled up to the entrance in horse-drawn cabs. They marvelled at the ornate carvings on the walls and ceilings, and admired the famous cantilevered balcony. When the lights went down, the audience settled back in the cushioned seats to enjoy "The Passing of the Third Floor Back", starring Forbes Robertson. The acclaimed actor seemed slightly taken aback by what he found in "cowtown", but not in any cultural sense:

I am surprised at your climate. I have always imagined it was cold here. It was our Mr. Kipling, I think, who put this beautiful country in bad by writing of Canada as Our Lady of the Snows. Instead of a bleak, frigid land, you seem to have sunshine and beautiful weather all the time. At any rate the sun has been shining on me ever since I arrived in Alberta, and I hope that is a good omen for Mr. Sherman's splendid undertaking in building one of the finest and most commodious theatres in all of western Canada.

The accent was on variety, and a review of some of the Grand's 1912 program shows what was awaiting Calgarians. The local Apollo Choir, one hundred and ten members and seven soloists, accompanied by the fifty-piece St. Paul's Symphony, chose the Grand for their three concerts. It was the year of Calgary's first Stampede, and appropriately, Cecil B. DeMille's "The Stampede" ran at the Grand. Sophie Tucker and Barney Bernard with a support cast of sixty were onstage in August, as were six Kentucky thoroughbreds appearing in "In Old Kentucky". The great vaudeville performance "California", with Fred and Adele Astaire in the cast, was presented that October, and the Grand began to bill the Orpheum shows, the reknowned vaudeville circuit that brought many world-famous performers to Calgary. So even in its first year, Calgarians were treated to spectacular sights at the Grand.

The early 1900's was the heyday of vaudeville, the "theatre of the people". And Calgarians had many chances to let their hair down and have a riotous time. Besides the productions at the Grand and small independent burlesque houses, the Pantages circuit played here, taking over the Lyric Theatre in 1910. Again Calgary could boast of attracting top-notch performers, and comic stars included Clifton Webb, Fibber McGee and Molly, Jack Benny, and Stan Laurel.

A ticket to a vaudeville house was an invitation for fun. Negro minstrel shows complete with a "cake walk", baggy-pant comedians and shabby straight men, jugglers, musicians, acrobats, animal acts, soft-shoe dancers, elocutionists, burlesque - it was always a rip-roaring good time.

But a novelty was being slipped in between vaudeville acts - "flickers" or "tapes". The forerunners of moving pictures, they made their commercial debut in 1904. They were anything but an overnight success. The film was run on a hand-cranked machine, and if it didn't break or the projector quit, the "flicker" might last about five minutes. Dimly lit, jerky, and silent, they were also plotless, as indicated by some titles showing at the Opera House and Lyric in 1904: "A Horse Eating Hay", "Children Swinging", and "Dramatic Scenes in a Western Lumber Mill". But by the next year the Lyric was proudly presenting the first motion picture with a plot, "The Great Train Robbery".

In 1907 a Calgary store was converted into the Edison Parlor Theatre. Straight-backed kitchen chairs were lined up facing the sheet which served as a screen. Before the picture began a slide was flashed showing a

461

lady wearing a very large hat, and peeking from behind, a man's face. Underneath was the caption "Just to remind you, there's a little man behind you, thank you!"

In 1908 the Arcade Picture Parlors advertised "Subjects That Cost Money to Get" and "The Count of Monte Cristo and Other Good Things - Illustrated Song". The Orpheum circuit featured Edison's talking movie on April 24, 1913: "the action and voice are as simultaneous as is possible even in flesh and blood." But patrons were assured this new-fangled curiosity would not detract from the regular vaudeville program.

Nevertheless movies promised a better and cheaper alternative to live entertainment. They quickly became real commercial attractions as they developed from the first crude attempts into the smooth professional works of the silver screen. Movie stars were becoming cult heroes, and Calgary audiences clamored to see more of them. It wasn't surprising that following Calgary's 1912 real estate boom, several theatres were built both for live productions and to show the popular new silents. In fact, several went through various stages, catering to live shows, then combinations of the two, and finally offering only movies.

By the end of 1915 there were at least ten show houses in Calgary. The Grand was still primarily a legitimate theatre. The Pantages (later the Regent) and the Princess were vaudeville houses, and the rest, including the Alberta, the Monarch (later the Liberty), the Bijou, the Globe, the Majestic, and the Allen, were regularly showing movies. Some of these buildings were large and elaborate, and their openings were major social events.

The Variety, Calgary's "newest and most luxurious" theatre, opened as the Princess Theatre during a howling snowstorm on St. Patrick's Day 1914. A *Herald* reporter enthused, "many were astounded at the beauty, comfort and size of this new house." Topping the opening night bill were a silent two-reeler, "The Big Horn Massacre", a biographic comedy, "Edwin's Badge of Honor", and the Princess Orchestra playing the Light Cavalry Overture. Local vocalists and performers were also featured.

The "Allen Theatre Beautiful", part of a Canadian theatre chain, opened November 14, 1913. Calgary's most luxurious movie house at the time, it had a lovely carved ceiling and — its crowning glory — a pipeorgan, the only one in any Calgary theatre. It was famous for the gimmicks and promotional stunts carried on by its irrepressible manager, Pete Egan. Passersby did a double-take when somebody dressed as Charlie Chaplin or Fatty Arbuckle passed them on a downtown street. But Calgarians soon got the hint - if the "star was in town", then he'd be at the Allen. Or, when "The Great Circus" was playing, Egan piled sawdust on the floor of the lobby. "Well it started to pour rain and everybody who came in went out with the sawdust sticking to them halfway up to their knees. When they walked around the streets everybody would stop them and ask where they'd been. We got a lot of free advertising that way."

But not all the stunts went off as planned. For instance, to tie in with the theme of a picture being promoted, Pete had an old car remodelled so that when going forward, it looked like it was being driven backwards. The spectacle scared so many Calgary drivers off the road that Pete was arrested. He paid a small fine, but it was well worth the publicity!

Despite the advent of the movies, the theatres didn't offer the only attractions in town:

No less than three carnival companies drawn by the assured big business which awaits any meritorious attraction in Calgary, have included "The Prairie Diamond" in their route, and soon voluble press agents and armies of bill posters will be heralding the local engagements of the "greatest shows on earth". Parker's shows, an old-time carnival friend, which left Calgary last fall richer by many thousands of freely spent dollars of the opulent westerners is coming with 18 sideshows. Herbert A. Kleine's 22 show carnival will be here as the big midway event at the fall exhibition and Patterson's 18 show carnival company will also visit the city.

The midway, Calgary Exhibition and Stampede, 1912.

The year was 1912. Not only were the carnivals in town, but the tents of five circuses, including the Ringling Brothers, were also set up in Victoria Park. According to a description written at the time:

The park was transformed into a veritable fairyland, thousands of electric lights, the beautiful gold and silver carved fronts of the massive wagons, music from half a dozen bands, the singing of the performers, the voices of the barkers, and the laughter of thousands of happy, old and young children, all served to create a scene of beauty and animation seldom, if ever, witnessed in Calgary . . . The Trained Wild Animal Show was visited by vast crowds who enjoyed to the fullest, the wonderful performance. When the tiger rode the horse, the man

*carried the huge lion on his shoulders, the lady fed
the leopards raw meat from her bare hands, the bears
shot the chutes, and the other various acts were given,
the audience burst into earnest appreciative laughter . . .*

The crowd went home happy after holding its breath as
Captain Charles Strahl shot through the air 135 feet
to the net below in the "Highest of Dives, the most
hazardous act of its kind in the world."

Formal entertainment was not the only means of
distraction in early Calgary. The parks were a big feature of the town. As the city pressed in around them,
Calgarians were grateful for the green open spaces,
and spent many sunny days in them. St. George's Park,
situated on three islands in the Bow joined by rustic
bridges, was a favourite spot for picnics. In 1918 the
Rotary Club sponsored what must rank as the biggest
cookout the city has ever seen. Fourteen thousand
people were invited, the families of men serving overseas. Six hundred cars transported everyone to the park
for a day of fun and games. While the sun shone and the
bands played, the crowd consumed 50 kegs of cider and
1,200 ice cream cones. Two thousand feet of movies
were taken to be sent to the troops.

Riley Park, twenty acres of land below the North
Hill, was established in 1913, and was nearly always a
hive of activity. A showpiece was a miniature lake
formed by a natural depression, complete with an island
in the centre. There was a cricket field, football was
played in the adjacent Hillhurst Athletic Park, and in
the winter a rink was flooded for skaters.

Another of the attractive parks established about
this time was Bowness. "When the rest of the country
is so brown and burned, it is delightful to visit Bowness
and see the wonderful green of the trees. It is restful and
refreshing," remarked an early Calgarian. For those who
wanted a little more action, there was music at the "pal-
latial" dancing pavillion - "cool and airy and the floor
is the very best."

Of course it is impossible for Calgarians not to feel
the attraction of the ramparts reaching up to the sky
on the western horizon. Banff may be an international
mountain playground, but the park's mountains, forests, and clear blue lakes and creeks are particularly
dear to Calgarians. In the 1880's a trip to Banff meant
a ride in a spring wagon over eighty miles of winding
road. A stop was made for the night, bedrolls laid out
under the stars, and the journey was completed the next
day. "Cappy" Smart used to camp at Morley the first

Surrounded as they were by so much natural
beauty, picnics and outings continued to be a
favourite pastime for Calgarians. *Above:*
Boaters at Bowness Park. *Opposite:* Better
transportation made the mountain areas accessible for family excursions. Here an alarming
number of tourists crowd blithely onto the little
steamer at Lake Minnewanka, 1907. *Above:*
Civic employees picnic with their families at
Bowness Park, 1912. *Below:* West Calgary
Methodist Sunday School Picnic at St. George's
Island, 1913.

evening, and carry on to Devil's Lake (now Lake Min-newanka) in the morning. He loved to take the peaceful moonlight excursion trips on the steamer "Minne-wanka" that plied the lake's waters on summer evenings.

Everyone who visited Banff stopped at the hot springs. The dimly lit cave and basin was entered through a small hole, and a climb down a rope ladder took you to the comforting waters. Leishman McNeill never forgot the pool's caretaker, D. D. Galletley, one of the unique characters of Banff before 1910. "Dressed in kilts he presided over his domain with all the dignity of a Scottish chieftain. To have him conduct a party through the cave was impressive, to say the least."

For many years the horse-drawn tally-ho was the only vehicle allowed in the park. McNeill writes:

As late as 1913, cars were barely tolerated, and it was the rule of the park that all automobiles entering the park go directly to their destination, to be parked until departure. Later, one-way traffic was introduced with a speed limit of 10 miles an hour, and ruling to stop when horse-drawn vehicles approached . . . I remember, about 1909, the newly formed AMA organized a caravan to make the trip. I have a photo that shows about a dozen cars (practically every car the city boasted) lined up on Seventh Ave. - ready to go. In the lead was the pilot car, and coming up at the rear was a trouble car loaded with extra gasoline, extra parts, tires, pumps and chains.

A trip along the highway to Banff today may not be as eventful or hazardous, but the beauty and silence that refresh the soul still await the visitor. There are many ways to be entertained in the city, but some of our favourite times will always be spent in the high country - "From the forest and wilderness come the tonics and barks which brace mankind . . ."

THE ROCKY ROAD TO BANFF

Chapter 16 Stampede

We rode down to the Indian encampment near the banks of the Elbow river, and while looking over the Indian horse herd, I experienced a burning desire to "break" a bucking bronco. In my youth and ignorance I had come to the conclusion that it was not hard to stay on a bronco for eight or ten jumps. The Indian led forward a crop-eared pinto cayuse . . . and I climbed aboard. The last thing I remembered was that as soon as my feet touched the stirrups, there was a violent upheaval. My chin hit the saddle horn, I lost both stirrups, my back seemed to break in about a dozen places, my neck snapped in two, and when I finally came to, the little birdies were chirping and I was rolling on my back on the bald-headed prairie. The Indians held up three fingers to signify that I had stayed three jumps. Right there and then I lost any desire I might have had of becoming a broncobuster. My body was black and blue for days, and even now, forty-seven years later, I shudder every time I see a bucking horse come out of the chutes at the Stampede.

"Cappy" Smart - The Calgary Herald

Like something out of fantasy, "The Greatest Outdoor Show on Earth", the Calgary Exhibition and Stampede, can trace its beginnings back to a broken collar bone and an argument.

Settlers in the newly incorporated town of Calgary, anxious to show their triumphs to their neighbours, decided to hold an Exhibition Fair to display the fruits of the harvest. Colonel James Walker shared these aspirations, and gave the matter a great deal of thought. Where could such a fair be held? The prospect of an annual Exhibition necessitated a permanent locale.

Then a horse played into Colonel Walker's hands. Unfortunately the horse is unwept and unsung, but certainly is not unhonoured. The horse had the foresight to toss the Honourable A. M. Burgess, then Minister of the Interior, who was visiting the government ranch at Fish Creek. The result — a broken collar bone. Burgess was taken to Colonel Walker's home for treatment, and while under the doctor's care, the Colonel discussed with him the possibility that the Dominion government might grant the Agricultural Society a parcel of land for exhibition purposes. The two men inspected the present site of Stampede Park, and before returning east, Mr. Burgess agreed to support the application.

The Calgary Agricultural Society purchased this land, ninety-four acres, at two dollars and fifty cents per acre, and title was issued July 11, 1889, on the condition that the land would never be subdivided for building purposes, but would always be maintained as an exhibition grounds.

The first Exhibition was held in 1886. Colonel Walker was president and J. G. Fitzgerald was secretary. Owing to the sparse settlement of the area, the directors experienced difficulty in financing the project. The Society minutes record resolutions to appoint a committee to negotiate a loan with the Society's bankers: first four hundred dollars, then for five hundred dollars, one thousand dollars, fifteen hundred dollars, two thousand dollars, and in 1914 the directors had to negotiate a loan of ten thousand dollars to meet expenses. In each case the directors had to sign notes personally to obtain the money. In March, 1900, the Calgary Agricultural Society was reorganized as the Inter-Western Pacific Exposition Company Limited, and in 1910 the name was changed to the Calgary Industrial Exhibition Company Limited.

Outstanding among the early exhibitions was the one and only Dominion Exhibition held in 1908, under federal government auspices. Opening day, July 1, attracted twenty-six thousand people, more than the population of Calgary. On the third day, "American Day", all attendance records were broken when thirty thousand people passed through the gates. The program featured performances by the Iowa State Band, Indian Races, pack-horse demonstrations, horse races, a polo

Above: The midway - Dominion Exhibition, 1908. *Opposite:* The front cover of the 1912 Stampede program featured the hero of western lore, the bronco-busting cowboy, surrounded by portraits of the Big Four, the benevolent fathers of the Stampede.

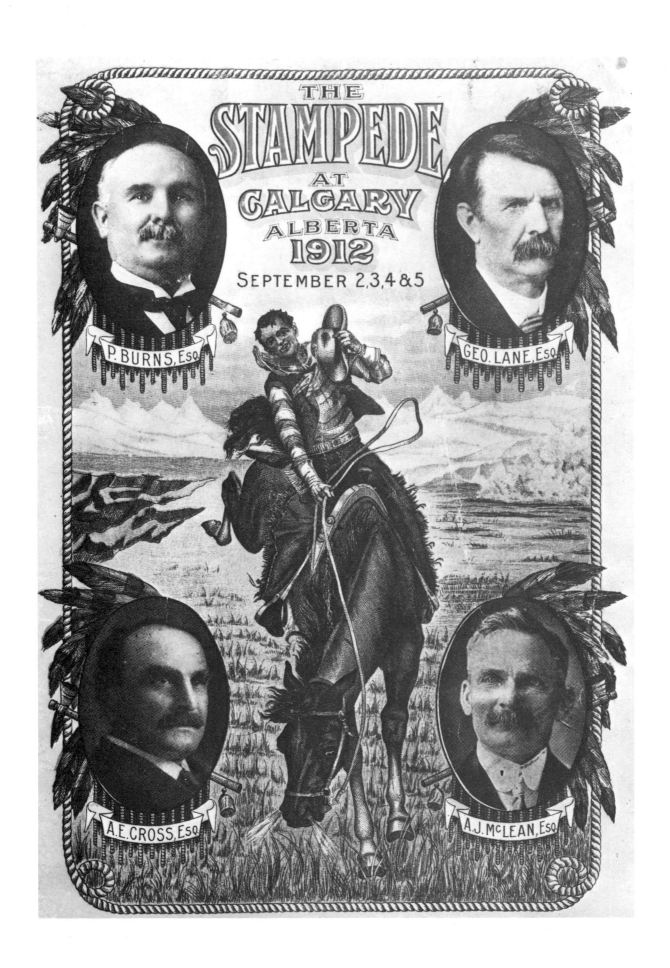

LAW AND ORDER

LITHOGRAPHED AND PRINTED BY THE HERALD WESTERN CO. LTD. CALGARY ALTA

game (polo was first played on the North American continent at Pincher Creek), vaudeville acts in front of the grandstand, and fireworks. Balloon flights, managed by Captain Dallas and Bert Hall, ended in disaster. A high wind blew the bag against the ropes; a pole falling crosswise burst the balloon, and the resulting friction caused an explosion which shot flames fifty feet high. The loss of the airship, covered by insurance, amounted to six thousand dollars plus an additional twenty-five thousand dollars in contracts. Total attendance for the six days was 89,435 — the fair was declared a success.

Opposite: Possibly an even more important romantic figure in the Canadian West was the Mountie. The back cover of the first Stampede program displayed a stern and heavily armed member of the Force, presiding over a peaceful view of placidly browsing cattle and playfully romping Indians. *Below:* Calgary's fair of 1886 began a tradition of annual exhibitions that culminated in the Stampede.

COME TO
THE FAIR

Above: This view of the Exhibition grounds at Victoria Park, taken in 1901, suggests that Calgary's annual fair still retained much of its rustic charm. By 1908 the event had become much more citified and sophisticated. The view below shows a family approaching the newly erected Industrial Building.

By 1908 Calgary had also entered the air age. One of the big features of the 1908 Exhibition was a hydrogen-filled airship, owned by American J. Strobel and operated by Jack Dallas. It made five spectacular flights over Calgary before its disastrous and equally spectacular explosion. *Above:* The ship ready to ascend. *Below:* Spectators examining the rubble of the burned out ship. *Overleaf:* Guy Weadick and preparations for the first Stampede.

Guy Weadick, a vaudeville cowboy, was riding with the Miller Brothers Wild West Show at the Dominion Exhibition. Already well known in the rodeo world, and more talkative than most, this long-geared itinerant cowboy interested H. C. McMullen in staging a big rodeo — one with historical as well as entertainment value. They agreed that Calgary would be a good place to stage a big annual cowboy field day at world-championship level.

Nothing came of the discussion at the time, but McMullen and Weadick kept in touch with each other until March of 1912, when Weadick returned to Calgary with his friend Tom Mix (later of movie fame) to promote a frontier classic. The success of the proposed rodeo would depend on financing. Business men were interested, but not to the point of risking their own money. But George Lane, the owner of the Bar U Ranch and himself a cowboy, was receptive, and he told McMullen as they sat in the Alberta Hotel that he would talk it over with a "couple of friends." The friends were A. E. Cross and Pat Burns, and the next day a request was made to the Calgary Exhibition for the use of Victoria Park. A. J. McLean came in with the three cattlemen and together the "Big Four" agreed to back Weadick's plan to the extent of one hundred thousand dollars, with the condition that contestants and patrons get a "square deal". It was settled: George Lane would be chairman and Guy Weadick manager.

Publicized as "The Greatest Show of the Age", the first Calgary Stampede was held from September 2 to 7, 1912. "The money is here, come and get it. The best man wins irrespective of where he comes from or what his colour is," blared the advertisements. The Rodeo prize list of twenty thousand dollars (unprecedented at that time) attracted the top North American cowboys and cowgirls. Even the "Mexican Bandit", Pancho Villa, sent his best rider. "Do you think the Stampede will make a good annual event?" Guy Weadick asked in the prize list. "If so, advise us. This is some country!"

Weadick's rodeo blueprint called for two hundred Mexican Longhorn cattle secured from a herd imported by Gordon, Ironside, and Fares, and grazing on the Blood Reserve. Three hundred of the wildest horses available were purchased from A. P. Day of Medicine Hat for fifteen thousand dollars. Day was appointed Arena Director. A replica of notorious Fort Whoop-Up was erected, with frontiersman Fred Kanouse in charge to make the old whisky traders feel more at home when they visited the Stampede. At the expense of the organization every member of the original North-West Mounted Police who could be located was invited to attend.

The first Stampede Parade has been described as a "Visit of Primitive Life brought before eighty thousand people by the

Whoop--e-e-e

STAMPEDE

Lay your plans now to visit Calgary for the Stampede, September 2 to 7, the greatest frontier day celebration that has ever been held anywhere and Calgary's most enthusiastic display of the spirit of the bounding west.

The Frontier Day Celebration
SIX DAYS, SEPTEMBER 2 TO 7

The World's Champion Cowboys, Ropers and Riders from the ranges of Alberta, the great ranches of Montana, Idaho, Wyoming, Colorado, California, and Mexico. The Vaquero riders from the Sierras of Chihuahua and Sonora—Untamed and Untamable Horses—Trained Horses—Trick and Fancy Riding Horses—Bucking Broncho—Horse Riding, Steer Roping and Bulldogging Contests. Complete programme of events each day.

All cattle used in both roping and bulldogging events will be from Old Mexico.

$30,000 in cash prizes, besides many troubles.

Visit Calgary. See the frontier day celebration. Do not miss the last and only pageant of the disappearing Wild West.

The Pageant of the Last Great West
LABOR DAY, SEPTEMBER 2nd

A vast and remarkable Historical Pageant that can never be reproduced again—the Indians of the old days—Hudson Bay traders and trappers—trains of Red River carts—the Mounted Police of 1874—Père Lacombe and the men of the missionary whisky traders of 1874 and their historic outfits—miners and prospectors with their packs—the troopers of the early boom days, headed by the veteran cowman, George Lane, Honorable Archie McLean, Pat Burns and A. E. Cross—the cowboys of the West, hundreds of them—the railway builders, and—lastly—the industrial pageant of Calgary of to-day, with 24,000 men in line.

The biggest and most realistic event of its kind ever staged anywhere on earth—passing in review before their Royal Highnesses, the Duke and Duchess of Connaught and Princess Patricia.

Stampede—Stampede to Calgary

Calgary, Sept. 2=3=4=5=6=7

Reference: Dominion Bank. Committee: Geo. Lane, Pat Burns, A. E. Cross, A. J. McLean, Guy Weadick, manager. E. L. Richardson, treasurer.

Some views from the first Stampede. *Above:* Indians parading in full ceremonial regalia. *Opposite above:* Clem Gardiner, the Canadian All-Round Champion of 1912 on a bucking bronco. *Far right:* Colonel James Walker leads NWMP veterans in the Stampede parade. *Below:* Another old-timer, Rev. John McDougall parades with the Stony Indians.

Grandest Pageant of all History." All Calgary turned out in mass, and in addition thousands of visitors had come to participate in Calgary's big carnival. Two hours before the parade was to start, crowds began to form along Eighth Avenue. Spectators lined seven and eight deep on both sides of the street along the parade route. Every roof, window, rafter — in fact, every elevated position of any kind that would support a human being — had its quota of eager faces. The steel girders of the new Hudson's Bay store and other buildings under construction were as black with people as telephone wires with swallows. The CPR viaduct over Second Street E., down which the procession passed, was jammed.

The parade route looked wonderfully gay. Long festoons of red, white, and blue bunting draped from pole to pole on Eighth Avenue, and streamers of small flags looped across the street joined with the decorations on private homes and business establishments to make Calgary's main street a perfect riot of patriotic colours. Wheat sheaves lashed to pillars and poles added the distinctive Western touch to the scene.

This was to be no circus parade of actors tricked out in tawdry and unauthentic trappings of a pseudo-picturesque nature, but an assemblage of genuine characters — real Indians, real cowboys and cowgirls, real old-timers, real Hudson's Bay traders, real veterans of the NWMP — in short, real Westerners of every historic type.

This is part of the Calgary *Daily Herald's* account of the parade:

Before nine o'clock the procession had begun to assemble on Sixth Avenue between Eighth and Seventh Streets W. As they were to lead the parade the Indians were first to take up their position. Fifteen hundred representatives of the six Tribes of Plains Indians were lined up by the Parade Marshalls, Glen Campbell, superintendent of Indian Affairs, the Reverend John McDougall, the veteran Western Missionary, and his brother Dave McDougall; pictures were taken and then they were arranged in parade order.

"It is the finest collection of Indians ever gotten together," said Glen Campbell to the Herald. "Buffalo Bill never had such a band. All these are the real thing and are wearing the actual old time costumes and war paint. It is a perfect historical reproduction of the Red Man as he was before the white man came."

Sixth Avenue was one mingled splash of glorious colour. The noble Red Man has a passion for bright colours and he did not suppress it on this occasion. Every Indian, brave, squaw, and papoose was rigged out in full war paint and

'THE STAMPEDE' CALGARY 1912
THE FAMOUS COWBOY
BAND

feathers and in costumes whose brilliant hues were never known in Tyre. "Wouldn't you like to have that for a dressing gown," remarked one spectator to his companion pointing to a portly squaw calmly smoking her pipe in the most wonderful blanket grab of daring yellows, reds, greens and purples.

There was some delay in starting the parade. The Indians were told to stand easy, and as they lounged around in comfortable attitudes, talking among themselves or smoking the pipe of patience, the kodakers were given a fine chance to snap the groups. The squaws with their bright-eyed papooses on their backs or folded in their blankets, won particular favour, and all showed an eagerness to be photographed that was gratifying to the camera men, even consenting to pose in fearsome attitudes.

Chief Yellow Horse of the Blackfoot evinced considerable pride in showing off his two medals, one presented by Queen Victoria the other by King George V when Duke of York. Another Chief, his almost naked body protected only by a coat of yellow paint seemed to feel the cold and wished the parade would start. The husky dogs prowled around restlessly and were sometimes held in with difficulty by the squaws. By request of the kodakers Rev. McDougall held a pow-wow with the group of old time Indians at the head of the parade and the latter seemed to enjoy being talked to in their native tongue."

About ten minutes after ten Mr. McMullen and Guy Weadick arrived, the Calgary Citizens Band struck up a marching air, and the great procession headed by Director-General McMullen, Manager Guy Weadick and Mrs. Weadick, Glen Campbell, Goldie Sinclair, and several other noted cowgirls started majestically down Sixth Avenue. The other units of the procession fell in behind the Indians as the different streets where they had assembled were reached.

At Eighth Street the procession was augmented by the Hudson's Bay men, the miners, the fur traders, and other old timers; at Seventh Street W. by the RNWMP, including the men of '74 led by Colonel Walker and Major Page. The old timers including Postmaster G. C. King, Inspector McDonald, W. Barker and H. McIlree presented a most soldierly appearance and seemed glad to be back in harness if only for one day. The police were followed by the buffalo and bull trains. At Sixth Street W. the Round-Up outfits of cowboys and cowgirls joined the parade; and at Fifth Street W. by the Labour section of the parade.

The big procession containing upwards of 3,000 people and over two miles in length then turned down Second Street W. to Eighth Avenue and proceeded between the packed lines of spectators to the heart of the city. All along the route they

Above: Rose Wentworth's team of trained buffalo were featured at the first Stampede. *Opposite above:* John McDougall and a number of Stony Indians wait patiently for the parade to begin. The vertical feathered headdress worn by the rider second from the right was common among Indians of the area. However the Sioux-style war bonnet of the person to his left was more popular with "kodakers", and before long had replaced the more traditional head-gear. *Below:* Some of the Stampede bands.

were greeted by cheers and the waving of hats. The Indians were the object of special applause, especially the squaws with their papooses and the Medicine-men in their tom-tom cart crooning an incantation. As the Mounted Police came into view someone cried "Three cheers for the Mounted Police" and a series of ringing hurrahs burst from the crowd. The cowboys and other units of the parade including the labour men also received their share of plaudits. The parade, moving at a fairly rapid gait, took approximately one hour to pass Centre Street.

The crowd were very orderly, the police had little difficulty in keeping the route clear, except when delays occurred, when people flocked out into the road. The first delay occurred when a westbound streetcar held up the procession for a minute or two. It was backed up to Fifth Street W. and out of the way. The cars caused another blockade lasting some ten minutes at First Street E., and the motorman became the embarrased object of impatient hoots and cries of "Get those cars out of the way."

Proceeding down Second Street E., the parade continued to the Stampede Ground where the Stampede units disbanded, the labour men turning west along Seventeenth Avenue. Near Seventeenth Avenue the cowboy contingent was received by Pat Burns, "Archie" McLean, George Lane, A. E. Cross and other old timers who received a great ovation and waving of hats from the cowmen and cowgirls.

Above: Estevan Clemento from Mexico demonstrates his steer roping technique. *Opposite above:* VIP's of the 1912 Stampede. *Left to right:* White Headed Chief; ——; Mr. Galbraith; Inspector James Spalding, R.C.M.P.; George Lane; ——; Mrs. Charlie Russell; Mr. Blackstock; Archie McLean; Alex Newton; Pat Burns; ——; Charlie Russell; A. E. Cross; ——; Edward Borein. *Below:* The old grandstand at Victoria Park.

Superb in all the beauty and wonders of primitive plain life, the greatest historical western pageant up to that time began to unfold itself in Calgary. Six months of unceasing preparation culminated in the most colossal and graphic portrayal of pioneer and range life ever to be staged in all the world. With the parade, the Stampede graduated from a promise into a reality, pulsating with excitement, and featured riding and roping that exceeded all expectations. Almost thirty thousand people passed through the turnstiles to see the opening performance.

Even though the parade of Indians was undoubtedly the outstanding feature of the day, the arena performance was also something to marvel at. The riders who stuck like tanglefoot to the backs of the bucking stock; the ropers who handled their lariats with incredible dexterity; the bull-doggers who dropped through space onto the horns of a running wild steer, and then coolly up-ended the steer and threw him to the ground — all the skilled and courageous performers sent admiring shivers fleeting up the spines of thirty thousand people. It was a vision of incredible excitement!

The afternoon performance opened with a parade of all the contestants — cowboys, cowgirls, and Mexican vaqueros.

THROWING A STEER IN "BULL DOGGING CONTEST"
STAMPEDE CALGARY CAN. OFFICIAL PHOTO #84
MARCELL CALGARY

A GRAND STAND PLAY—BULL DOGGING A STEER
STAMPEDE CALGARY ALTA CAN. 1912 PHOTO #65
MARCELL CALGARY

STEER ROPING AT THE "STAMPEDE" 1912 CALGARY ALTA CAN.
PHOTO #33 BY MARCELL OF CALGARY.

Headed by the famous Cowboys' Band from Pendleton, the skilled riders of the Plains, the greatest the world had ever seen and to whom the rodeo was only a pastime, paraded around the track to form a semi-circle where they were photographed by moving-picture men.

Three girls, Miss Dolly Mullins, Miss Bertha Blanchett, and Miss Arlene Palmer entered the first event — the world championship fancy and trick riding. The spectators cheered the contestants as they contorted themselves around and over their mounts. At break-neck speed they performed "the most spectacular evolutions" standing erect and swinging over the sides of their horses.

The next event, the world's championship for steer roping, proved to be one of the most exciting events of the day. Texas steers, the wildest of their kind, were released one by one from the chutes. A rider would dash after the steer, twirling his lariat, and with uncanny accuracy rope the animal. The horse would stop, set, and acting on instinct tighten the rope and tug away, almost dragging the long horn, while the other member of the team dismounted, ran up the rope and tied the steer. In one trial, so great was the impact when the horse braked, that a contestant's saddle was broken. John Douglas of Arizona won day-money with a time of forty-five seconds.

The cowgirls' relay race gave the people an opportunity to see how fast girls can ride. Each contestant was provided with two horses to ride two miles, a total of four times around the track. At each half mile she was required to stop, unsaddle, and resaddle a fresh mount, and ride another half mile (three changes in all). Being able to change horses in the shortest time, Mrs. Bertha Blanchett won with a time of five minutes six and one-half seconds.

O. K. Lawrence of Oklahoma won day money in the bareback bucking horse contest.

In the steer bull-dogging, the steer is released from the chute, the contestant "rides hell for leather" to an advantageous position alongside, reaches over, grabs the frightened animal by the horns, and, leaving his saddle by the mid-air route, wrestles the steer to the ground. Charley Tipton, throwing himself with such force from saddle onto his target that he broke one of the long horns, won the event with a time of eighteen seconds.

This event was followed by an exhibition of roping by Miss Lucille Mulhall, billed as the only woman in the world capable of roping, throwing, and tying a steer. The crowd applauded her time of fifty-two seconds.

Taking up positions on the track, Florence LaDue, Bertha Blanchett, and Lucille Mulhall then proceeded to thrill the audience with a display of fancy roping by lassoing riders from different angles and positions. At the same time in the arena,

Above: Ed Eckels, World Champion Steer Tier, 1912. *Opposite above:* "Buffalo" Vernon and Dell Blanchett demonstrate bulldogging — or are the steers bulldogging them? *Below:* Texan Alf Vivian has coped with his steer and has him firmly tied.

Señor Magdalena and Señor Randon showed the crowd how the Mexicans handle the lariat. "Tex" McLeod, a past master, demonstrated why he was in a class by himself by roping six horses and riders in a bunch.

A long list of contestants entered the cowboy relay race. It is reported they "gave a good sample of the real cowboy race." Jim Mitchell of Medicine Hat, with a great sprint, crossed under the tape first with a time of four minutes fifty-three seconds.

Miss Goldie St. Clair showed the audience why she was champion rider of the world in the next event, the lady's bucking horse contest. It was reported, "This was their first appearance before the public in bronco busting and they showed they are no mean factor in this event."

In the final event of the day, the boys' bronco busting contest, Johnnie Robertson of Calgary drew the notorious outlaw "Gavorote" and B. C. "Red" Parker of Ashcroft, B.C. tried to ride the one and only "Cyclone".

The displays featured in the store windows during the first Stampede also came in for favorable comment. The Calgary *Daily Herald* of Tuesday, September 3, 1912, described the display in Neilson's Furniture, 118 Eighth Avenue E. in the following terms:

The arrangement is very unique and presents a vivid panorama of Cowboy and Girl Riders in miniature, that is cleverly gotten up. Dummy riders on their mounts are to be seen in the act of roping wild steers. Indian riders dashing across the plains and trick riders in the act of executing various fancy stunts. The entire window is tastefully banked with bunting and flags, forming a pretty decoration and background. Standing space in front of the display is always at a premium, so firmly has it caught the fancy of the people as they pass down the thoroughfare.

The Indian encampment was one of the most picturesque ever seen in Calgary. Over three thousand Stonies, Crees, Peigans, Bloods, Blackfoot, and Sarcees moved their teepees to the Exhibition Grounds. Two months of preparation had reawakened all the innate love of pomp and primitive splendour in their souls, and they produced an unrivalled spectacle. Their teepees furnished with feathers, furs, beadwork, and the ancient symbols filled with religious significance, were the highlight of the Stampede. The leather work and beadwork on the costume worn by Weasel Calf, made Chief at the first Blackfoot Treaty thirty-six years before, attracted special attention.

The evening performances commenced with a general parade of the performers headed by H. C. McMullen and Guy

Right: Goldie St. Clair, Ladies World Champion Bucking Horse Rider, 1912. *Below:* Stampede views.

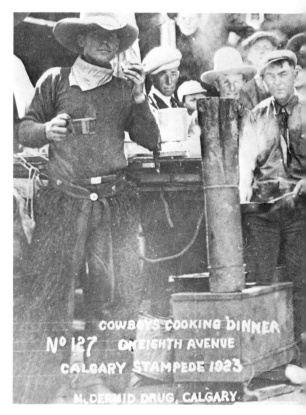

488

This resplendent welcome arch erected for the first Stampede was located on Centre Street between Eighth and Ninth Avenues. It was dismantled after the show. *Opposite:* Stampede favourites — bucking bronco events *(above)* and *(below)* Indian war dances, here performed by a group of Sarcees.

Weadick, and ended with a display of fireworks. Fifty of the finest riders in the world, each one an expert in several branches of range work, performed before the grandstand. Miss Arlene Palmer, careening around the ring on almost every place on the horse but the saddle, gave a display of Cossack riding. Otto King, one of the best trick riders on the North American continent, performed hair-raising stunts in the saddle by galloping with head to the ground, dismounting and mounting on the move, landing on the off-side of his mount. An exhibition of mail-carrying and express work completed his act. In his "drunk cowboy ride", Jason Stanley showed a suppleness and grace difficult to describe as he picked up handfuls of sawdust while careening around the ring. On foot, a Mexican vaquero lassooed a pony and dropped it with his rope tied to his leg. Ian Carr rode a buffalo. Bronco busters Miss Annie Shafer, Miss Hazel Walker, Tex McLeod, and Johnnie McMullen concluded the program with a display of riding "outlaws". When Red Parker went to mount his bronco, the horse reared and fell on its back. Parker jumped aside, mounted, and rode on, demonstrating to the crowd the risks the "buster" runs every day, and proving without doubt that no matter what risks the cowboy takes he is ever willing and able to do his part. Colonel Fells Warren gave a masterly display of horsemanship when he drove his stage coach and team of six horses at the gallop, "twisting and turning in a bewildering fashion." Twenty-four Indian chiefs and headmen in full regalia followed with a demonstration of native horsemanship. The arena presented a passable likeness to the Mexican bull-ring when several long-horn steers were let in, on which Estevan Clemento and his party of Mexican vaqueros demonstrated their skill with the lariat. Those who lingered on the grounds after the show were treated to a genuine pow-wow between the six tribes led by their chiefs.

The Rodeo stock, over nine hundred horses and steers brought in for the first Stampede, was valued at over two hundred thousand dollars. The bucking horses brought in from Montana and Colorado, including "Cyclone" and "Tornado", cost management two hundred dollars to five hundred dollars each. The two hundred steers were valued at sixty dollars each. The cowboy's saddle, worthy of his mount, was worth five hundred dollars.

There were many breath-taking moments in the days that followed. Probably the most hair-raising was the bucking horse event.

The events held on Saturday, September 7, 1912, produced the finest riding and bull-dogging ever witnessed in Calgary. Tom Three Persons, a Blood Indian from Macleod, was the last contestant to ride in the finals for the world championship in this event. When it was announced he would

Unbroken Bronchos
The Stampede" Calgary 1912

At "The Stampede" Calgary 1912. Marcell Pho- No 15

Indian War Dance
1912 "Stampede" Calgary Alta Canada.

Marcell Photo B
Calgary

TOM THREE PERSON
1912 WINNER

LET'ER BUCK
"THE STAMPEDE" CALGARY. ALTA 1912
OFFICIAL PHOTO No 41
MARCELL

HOLDING "CYCLONE" THE TERROR AT THE STAMPEDE"
CALGARY. ALTA 1912 OFFICIAL PHOTO. No 99.
MARCELL OF CALGARY.

attempt to ride "Cyclone" the crowd grew apprehensive; the famous bucking horse had never been ridden, and up to this event had thrown twelve riders during the Stampede. The Calgary *Daily Herald* of Monday, September 9, 1912, reports the ride as follows:

The horse thrown to the ground, Tom jumped across him, placed his feet in the stirrups and with a wild whoop the black demon was up and away with the Indian rider. Bucking, twisting, swapping ends, and resorting to every artifice of the outlaw, Cyclone swept across the field. The Indian was jarred from one side of his saddle to the other, but as the crowds cheered themselves hoarse, he settled himself each time in the saddle and waited for the next lurch or twist. His bucking unable to unseat the Redskin, "Cyclone" stood at rest and reared straight up. Once it looked as though Tom was to follow the fate of his predecessors. He recovered rapidly and from that time forward "Cyclone" bucked till he was tired. The Indian had mastered him. Tom Three Persons had won the world championship in the bucking horse event. Thousands of spectators created a pandemonium of applause that was not equalled all week. The Princess Patricia and the Duchess of Connaught, the Stampede's Royal Guests of honour leaned far out over the railing applauding vigorously, along with the native Canadians who had witnessed the ride in the enclosure to the north. It was a thrilling moment. Tom Three Persons had captured the championship of the world, the most coveted rodeo event for himself, for Calgary, and for Canada.

To commemorate the 1912 Stampede, management commissioned the Oklahoma cowboy artist Edward Borein to do a drawing typical of the range-land spirit exemplified by the Alberta cowboy. His etching of the famous bucking horse "I See You" hangs in the Administrative Offices on the Stampede Grounds.

When the first Stampede was over, the cowpunchers and riders congregated to express their keen appreciation of the treatment they had experienced from management and Calgary citizens. They were loud in their praise for the manner in which the events had been run and the impartial awarding of the prizes. Some of the contestants had travelled four thousand miles. Joe Bartles of Dewey, Oklahoma, an old timer and one of the biggest ranchers in the south, expressed himself, "Personally I did not win a cent in the contests, but it was a good square show throughout." Henry Gramnar of Kalls City, Okalhoma, who brought a number of leading cowboys with him, said, "In my opinion the show was one of the best I have ever attended: we have enjoyed ourselves immense-

Above: Tom Three Persons, famous Blood Indian bronco buster. *Opposite above:* Three Persons displays the tenacious style that won him the 1912 World Championship in the bucking horse event. *Below:* Cyclone, the horse he vanquished, was no minor adversary. He had thrown every contestant who tried to ride him and was generally considered to be unbreakable. Here, on the final day of the Stampede, Three Persons looks on while the dreaded Cyclone is saddled. The subsequent ride was a triumphant conclusion to the exciting event-filled week.

ly and cannot say too much of the fair manner in which we have been used by the Management of the Stampede. While I did not win a cent myself, I am just as happy as if I won all the money, and only hope to have the pleasure of attending another one of the same kind here again." Similar opinions were expressed by many of the other contestants. Al McLeod of Winnipeg was given the award for the best outfitted cowboy, Mrs. Guy Weadick got first prize as the best outfitted lady rider, and Miss Alberta McMullen won the Black Diamond ring for the best outfitted Canadian rider. The presentation of prizes brought the Rodeo — the first Calgary Stampede — to a close just before midnight.

Guy Weadick, the man who was responsible for putting the first Stampede together, resumed his travels. When the Calgary Exhibition decided to adopt the Stampede as a permanent feature of the summer show, Weadick returned to Calgary to manage what has developed into "The Greatest Outdoor Show on Earth".

Above: Two beauties of the first Stampede.
Right: The *Herald* ran a splashy advertisement for the show.

THE STAMPEDE

Sept. 2, 3, 4, 5, 6, 7th, 1912

A Reunion of Old Timers in the Great West "Off to the Wild Bunch"

Left: Guy Weadick - he conceived and produced Calgary's big show. *Centre:* Royal Guest Princess Patricia, daughter of the Duke and Duchess of Connaught, arrives for the grandstand show. *Below:* Sightseers crowd the streets and rooftops to view the parade.

Acknowledgements

For permission to adapt and abridge both published and unpublished materials in this book, I would like to thank the following:

The Alberta Historical Society, Chinook Country Chapter, for *Calgary - In Sandstone*, 1969, by Richard Cunniffe.

The *Albertan* for biographical articles on Felix McHugh, Senator Patrick Burns, and James "Cappy" Smart; and for the interview with Senator James Lougheed June 2, 1925.

The Calgary Chamber of Commerce for "The Founding and Naming of Calgary", by J. E. A. Macleod, from *The Story of Calgary*, Calgary Publishing Co., 1950, by E. C. Morrison and P. N. R. Morrison.

The Calgary *Herald* for biographical articles on G. C. King, Archie McLean, J. J. McHugh, John "Scotty" Ormiston, William Pearce and Edward Windsor; the *Herald* interview with Mrs. R. G. Robinson, 1926; for James "Cappy" Smart's memoirs "I Remember Calgary When", 1933; for reports on the first Stampede, 1912; and for innumerable quotes from early editions of the *Herald* illustrating the life and opinions of the first Calgarians.

Calgary Transit for materials on the electric street railway in Calgary.

Canadian Western Natural Gas Company for information and pictures on the Gas Company and Eugene Coste.

The City of Calgary Electric System and Calgary Power Ltd. for information and pictures on the history of electric power in Calgary.

The City of Calgary Public Information Department for historical records and information on the city of Calgary.

The City of Calgary Waterworks Division for historical information on the city's waterworks system.

P. B. Crosby-Jones for his research paper "CHOSEN TO SERVE - Policing Calgary; The First Twenty Years".

Mary Julia Dover for her article "Alfred Ernest Cross" from *The Story of Calgary*, Calgary Publishing Co., 1950, by E. C. Morrison and P. N. R. Morrison.

The Edmonton *Journal* for "Calgary and Edmonton Railway", by an Old-timer.

The Glenbow-Alberta Archives for materials and photographs on the Medicine Pipe Transfer Ritual and the Sarcee Sweat Bath from the Gooderham and Godsell collection; for "Jerry Potts", "The Sarcee Indians" and "The Blackfoot Tribe", all by Hugh A. Dempsey, and "The Stony Indians of Alberta", by John Laurie.

Mrs. Norman Kennedy for "The Growth and Development of Music in Calgary", by Norman Kennedy, unpublished thesis, 1952.

Grant McEwan for material on James Lougheed from *Calgary Cavalcade*, Western Producer Prairie Books, 1958; and on Bob Edwards from *Eye-Opener Bob*, Western Producer Prairie Books.

E. C. Morrison and P. N. R. Morrison for materials from *The Story of Calgary*, Calgary Publishing Co., 1950, including articles on Calgary booms, Bob Edwards, and R. C. Thomas.

Grace and Gordon Murdoch for excerpts from the diary and papers of George Murdoch.

And finally, I would like to thank the Commissioners of the City of Calgary for the opportunity of writing this book.

Nearly all the picture research for this book was done in the Glenbow-Alberta Institute Archives, and the author owes a great deal to Glenbow's archivists for their invaluable advice and assistance, and to the photographic department for their superb co-operation and help. With the exception of those listed below, all the photographs in this book are from the Glenbow Archives. I would like to thank:

Canadian Western Natural Gas Company for the pictures appearing on pages 322, 325 (bottom), 328, 329 (top and bottom).

The City of Calgary Electric System for pictures appearing on pages 309, 310 (bottom).

The City of Calgary Public Information Department for the pictures on pages 109, 110 (bottom), 196 (centre).

The A. G. Graves collection for pictures appearing on pages 238-9, 310 (top), 315 (bottom), 321 (top and bottom), 465 (top).

The Manitoba Archives for pictures appearing on pages 43 (bottom), 65 (top), 368 (bottom).

The Notman Photographic Archives, McCord Museum, for the picture on page 75.

The Provincial Archives of Alberta for pictures from the Ernest Brown collection appearing on pages 61 (bottom left), 87, 94, 102, 129 (top right and bottom), 176 (bottom), 180-1, 186, 257, 314, 362-3, 472, 475, 476 (bottom), 477 (bottom); pictures from the Harry Pollard collection appearing on pages 216-17, 245 (bottom right), 479 (bottom); and for the picture on page 226.

The R.C.M.P. Museum, Regina, for pictures appearing on pages 10-11, 12, 37.

The following pictures are from the personal collection of the author: 91, 117 (top), 187, 191 (top right), 198 (bottom), 213, 214, 254 (top right), 356, 358 (top), 364 (bottom), 370 (top), 379, 394, 427.

Every reasonable effort has been made to identify and credit the owners of previously copyrighted material. The author and publishers sincerely apologize if any such persons have inadvertently been overlooked, and would appreciate information that would enable us to correct any omissions in future editions.